POWER

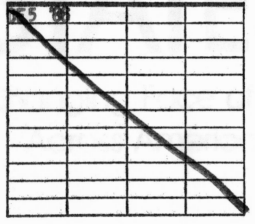
The   Politics

Congressional Quarterly Inc.
1414 22nd Street, N.W.
Washington, D.C. 20037

Congressional Quarterly Inc.

Congressional Quarterly Inc., an editorial research service and publishing company, serves clients in the fields of news, education, business and government. It combines Congressional Quarterly's coverage of Congress, government and politics with the more general subject range of an affiliated service, Editorial Research Reports.

Congressional Quarterly, founded in 1945 by Henrietta and Nelson Poynter, publishes the *Congressional Quarterly Weekly Report* and a variety of books, including college political science textbooks under the CQ Press imprint and public affairs paperbacks designed as timely reports to keep journalists, scholars and the public abreast of developing issues, events and trends. Recent public affairs titles include *Presidential Elections Since 1789, Third Edition, Employment in America, Defense Policy, Third Edition*, and *National Party Conventions, 1831-1980*. New CQ Press texts include *Interest Group Politics, Change and Continuity in the 1980 Elections, Revised Edition*, and *The Presidency and the Political System*.

CQ also publishes information directories and reference volumes on the federal government, national elections and politics. They include the *Guide to Congress*, the *Guide to the Supreme Court*, the *Guide to U.S. Elections* and *Politics in America*. The *CQ Almanac*, a compendium of legislation for one session of Congress, is published each year. *Congress and the Nation*, a record of government for a presidential term, is published every four years.

CQ publishes *The Congressional Monitor*, a daily report on current and future activities of congressional committees, and several newsletters, including *Congressional Insight*, a weekly analysis of congressional action, and *Campaign Practices Reports*, a semimonthly update on campaign laws.

CQ conducts seminars and conferences on Congress, the legislative process, the federal budget, national elections and politics, and other current issues. CQ Direct Research performs contract research and maintains a reference library and query desk for clients.

Editorial Research Reports covers subjects beyond the specialized scope of Congressional Quarterly. It publishes reference material on foreign affairs, business, education, cultural affairs, national security, science and other topics of news interest. Founded in 1923, the service merged with Congressional Quarterly in 1956.

Library of Congress Cataloging in Publication Data

Main entry under title:

Power in the states.

1. State governments. 2. United States — Economic conditions — 1981-
—Regional disparities. I. Congressional Quarterly, inc.
JK2408.P68 1984   973.927   83-20990
ISBN 0-87187-309-5

Editors: Harrison Donnelly, Alan Ehrenhalt, Andy Plattner

Principal Writers, Political Profiles: Rhodes Cook, Phil Duncan, Rob Gurwitt, Robert Rothman, Tom Watson

Other Writers, Political Profiles: Nadine Cohodas, Diane Granat

Writers, Economics Section: Mary L. McNeil, Tom Arrandale, Hoyt Gimlin, Richard Kipling, Marc Leepson, Sandra Stencel, William Sweet, William V. Thomas

Production Editor: William L. Bonn

Photo Editor: Lynnemarie Hofman

Statistical Coordinator: Nancy J. Rowe

Editorial Assistants: Eugene J. Gabler, Tatiana Goodman

Cover: Richard A. Pottern

Graphics: Robert O. Redding

Table of Contents

Introduction: Power Shifts in State Capitols   1

The Highest and the Lowest: How States Rank   4

Profiles of the 50 States

Economic Profiles of America's Regions   107

Editor's Note. A new breed of legislator is arriving in the nation's 50 state capitols. Younger, more activist, more partisan and more willing to work full time, they are replacing traditional older, part-time politicians.

In many states, the changes have caused a realignment of power. This shift, as well as the impact of redistricting following the 1980 Census, is examined in detail in *Power in the States*. The book is based on a special issue of the *Congressional Quarterly Weekly Report*, published Sept. 3, 1983.

The introduction, written by CQ political editor Alan Ehrenhalt, gives an overview of the changing politics of state legislatures. This is followed by individual reports on each of the states, together with statistical profiles, biographical data on the nation's governors and party breakdowns of the state legislatures. A separate section discusses the economic conditions of the nation's regions.

POWER
IN THE
STATES

INTRODUCTION

Power Shifts in State Capitols
As New Breed Takes Over Leadership

Power is changing hands in America's state capitols. The part-time citizen legislators who used to run them are yielding not only to a new generation but a new kind of leader. And the result is a growing realignment of political control that is certain to affect the course of state politics nearly everywhere in the years to come.

L. Marion Gressette is the symbol of legislators past. President pro tempore of the South Carolina Senate, he has served in it as a Democrat since 1937, but did not become its presiding officer until 1972, when he was more than 70 years old. A lifelong resident of rural Calhoun County, he goes home to practice law there between legislative sessions.

Thomas A. Loftus is the symbol of legislators to come. After taking a political science degree and studying public administration in graduate school, he went to work for the Democrats in the Wisconsin Assembly, and served as an aide to its Speaker. He became a member of the Assembly in 1977; six years later, at age 37, he became Speaker himself. Loftus is a full-time legislator — he has done nothing but political work since he left the University of Wisconsin.

The gulf between these two leaders is more than a question of youth and age, or of the differences between Wisconsin and South Carolina. Gressette is in the mold of the small-town lawyers, bankers and businessmen who have dominated state politics for a century. But in the past decade, as state government has become more complex and more time-consuming, it has increasingly become the province of specialists who devote most of their time to mastering it. The old-fashioned part-time legislators are not disappearing — most legislatures are still officially part-time bodies — but they are not the emerging leaders.

The changes in America's legislatures go far beyond the pace of legislative life. The people who enter legislatures these days are different from the people who entered in Gressette's generation, or even a generation ago.

In much of the country, the losers in this legislative realignment have been — or will be — conservative Democrats. Throughout the South, but also in other states as diverse as New Mexico and Oregon, a disproportionate amount of power traditionally has been held by a rural Democratic bloc whose conservative members remained in office for decades. They dominated legislative affairs on their own in some places, and with the help of a Republican faction in others. In the 1980s, however, this group was gradually losing out to a diverse new generation of Democrats. The one obvious reason for change was reapportionment. Until one person, one vote became a reality in the 1960s, most state Legislatures were even more severely malapportioned than the U.S. House; the universal beneficiaries were the rural counties and their representatives. In some states, each county was entitled to a state senator of its own, whether the county had 5,000 people or 500,000. In many cases, state senators possessed small fiefdoms that they dominated through control of government patronage and contracts.

Declining Rural Power

That sort of system has been against the law for more than two decades, since the Supreme Court handed down its one-person, one-vote decision in *Baker v. Carr* in 1962. The urban and suburban areas in every state now have the number of seats to which they are entitled by population; rural representation has shrunk. Still, rural power has been slow to dissipate, especially in the South and West. Although reapportionment has limited the number of seats from rural areas, many of the individual legislators have remained in office, and deference to tradition has guaranteed them continued influence. Through most of the 1960s and 1970s, Texas, Virginia and Florida, for example, continued to place rural conservative Democrats in key leadership positions.

But that was changing in the 1980s. The most striking turnabout in 1983 was in Alabama, where Democrat George C. Wallace returned to the governorship not as the voice of rural south Alabama — which he once was — but as the head of a new coalition headed by the state's black community, teachers and labor. The House Speaker pledged loyalty both to Wallace and to the coalition itself.

Equally important in the long run, the elements of the coalition now seem to control the nominating process in the Democratic Party, Alabama's overwhelming majority. The state held special legislative elections in the fall of 1983, but the Democrats did not have a primary. Nominees were chosen by party officials — most of them coalition loyalists. The result was that the traditionally dominant conservative bloc found itself on the outside not only in legislative affairs but in the crucial business of nominating and electing legislators. Two senior, conservative Democratic legislators, worried that they might not be renominated, decided to run for re-election as Republicans.

The changes in Alabama politics may be explained as a result of Wallace's personal appeal rather than any long-term trend. But it was not hard to find other Southern states where conservative rural Democrats were struggling against new legislative forces in the Democratic Party.

In South Carolina, where conservatives such as Gressette dominated the Senate, the House had become a tempestuous forum in which urban interests wielded at

1

least as much power as the rural bloc. Younger conservatives, aware of their diminishing influence, banded together in a caucus they themselves referred to as the "Fat and Uglies." Often they collaborated with the Republican minority to increase their strength — something conservatives did not need to do in South Carolina in the past.

In the late 1970s, several New Right organizations worked hard to promote the idea of coalition government in state legislatures — Republicans and conservative Democrats joining forces to keep power out of the hands of liberal Democrats. There were some notable successes. Between 1978 and 1981, such coalitions achieved governing status in at least one legislative chamber in Missouri, New Mexico and Alaska.

In close legislative situations, arrangements like those may continue to be the best way for traditional forces to maintain legislative power. In the long run, though, it seemed certain that conservative Democrats would make a shrinking contribution to coalition strength. Reapportionment was gradually wiping their rural districts off the map and, just as important, they were losing their role in the Democratic Party nominating process to the pressure groups willing to engage in politics on a full-time, professional basis — teachers in most states, labor in some, minorities in others.

Full-Time Legislators

In most of the Northern states, the changes of the 1980s were different. There, conservative Democrats never were the dominant influence. The balance of power used to fluctuate between rural Republicans and labor-oriented urban Democrats. That balance was being upset by a new political force — the full-time legislator.

Full-time legislating was far from a universal phenomenon, of course — it had been common in California and several other populous states for years. But some of the smallest states still held sessions only every other year, and for as little as three months at a time. In most places, though, the trend was in the other direction. And even in states whose schedules were light enough to allow legislators time for regular private work, the past few years saw the emergence of a corps of youthful legislative activists who liked the job enough to spend months campaigning for it and devoted most of their energy to it once they were in office. These people were rearranging political influence between the two parties and also within the Democratic Party.

In state capitols in the East and Midwest, power in the Democratic Party was passing from the urban labor allies to a bloc of legislators who were best identified by their youth, political independence and intellectual approach to the issues. They came out of backgrounds in academia, teaching and political staff work. They usually arrived before age 30, at a stage in life when the modest annual salaries — still under $20,000 a year in most states — were not considered an impossible burden. Nearly all of them won their seats through intense personal campaigning, not through the assistance of labor, party leaders or any traditional center of political strength. They tended to be liberal on social questions but skeptical of some of the Democratic Party's traditional bread-and-butter priorities. Ironically, their emergence was cutting into labor strength in the East and Midwest just as labor was emerging as a major governing force for the first time in some areas of the South and West.

Washington State's House of Representatives was rocked in 1983 by the arrival of a huge freshman class that occupied about half the seats held by the Democratic majority. The members of this group became an instant "third force" among Democratic legislators, siding neither with the pro-labor faction nor with the environmentalists who had been its main opposition during the past decade. The new group stressed economic development, promoting business-labor cooperation and the attraction of high-technology industry, whether that industry was likely to be unionized or not.

Meanwhile, in Wisconsin, a similar corps of youthful Democrats mortified labor leaders by accepting a proposal to freeze jobless benefits to keep the state's unemployment compensation system stable. Not too long ago, veterans of the state Assembly recalled, it was difficult to find Democrats willing to stand up against the labor position. Now, such votes are routine.

In dozens of states, the emergence of aggressive young Democratic talent has broadened the party's geographical base, allowing it to win numerous suburban and rural constituencies that used to be solidly Republican. But the independent operators who win these seats tend to remain independent operators once in office.

Democrats made massive gains in the Iowa Legislature in 1982, taking it out of Republican control even though the state was electing a GOP governor. But that change meant few important victories for the United Auto Workers or other pillars of Democratic politics in Iowa.

Generally, teachers were an exception to the pattern of declining labor power in Northern state legislatures. In addition to becoming a crucial source of volunteer help for Democratic campaigns, teachers were one of the few professional groups expanding their numerical presence in the chambers. As recently as the early 1970s lawyers were the dominant occupational category in most legislatures, as they continued to be in Congress. Now, however, teachers have replaced them in many states. Unlike lawyers and most other professionals, teachers can move from private life to a legislative career without a major sacrifice in salary, and many choose to do so.

Republican Problems

The Republican Party was another loser in the legislative power shifts taking place in many states. Even in favorable years, the GOP never seemed to come very close to parity with the Democrats. The 1980 election that installed Ronald Reagan in the White House gave Republicans just 39 percent of the seats in the nation's legislatures; that figure declined in 1982 to 37 percent. In 1983 the Republicans controlled both legislative chambers in just 11 states. Democrats controlled both chambers in 34 states.

This consistent pattern of Republican misfortune was not simply a protest against GOP policies at the state and national levels. It was the result of the changing nature of legislative affairs. The move toward full-time legislating had undercut Republicans' ability to recruit strong candidates.

In most states where they were strong in earlier years, Republicans drew most of their candidates from a pool of successful small-town lawyers, grain farmers, real estate and insurance agents. These people have always tended to be skeptical of government activism; that is one reason they are Republicans. But in past years they were willing to take a few months a year to do their part to prevent Democrats from carrying government activism too far.

Those same Republicans were far more reluctant to

spend eight or nine months of the year in legislative session and a sizable portion of each election year campaigning — all to participate as part of a minority in a state government process dominated by liberal Democrats they essentially distrusted — and for a small salary, in most states.

GOP leaders in many states were candid in admitting that they could not find strong candidates for many legislative seats, even in districts historically friendly to their party. In many states where Republicans used to be dominant, they were losing these crucial seats to youthful Democrats who considered politics their profession. In Wisconsin, the GOP was turning to retirees and the independently wealthy.

There was another solution to the party's problem, however — female candidates. Many of the more striking Republican legislative victories of the past few years have been won by women, some of them young professionals willing to make a career change and some of them housewives for whom the modest salary was an acceptable second income.

In June 1983, when Rhode Island was forced by court order to hold a special election for its Senate, Republicans came back from oblivion in state politics to increase their representation from 7 to 21 seats in the 50-member chamber. Half of the new Republican senators were women. Running on a platform that combined fiscal conservatism with a "good government" crusade against cronyism in the Democratic majority, these candidates ignited optimism about the GOP future in Rhode Island that had been nonexistent for years. ∎

Guide to Statistics in State Profiles

Each state profile contains a chart of statistics illustrating important aspects of life in that state. Following is an explanation of the sources for the figures used in the statistical profiles:

People, Major Cities. Statistics were obtained from the 1980 census. Figures for Spanish origin include persons of all races who identify themselves as being of Spanish origin. All city populations are for incorporated areas except in Hawaii, which has no corporate boundaries for cities. Census Bureau area figures were used for that state.

Land. Farm acreage was obtained from the Economic Research Service of the Agriculture Department, based on 1982 reports from the Agriculture and Commerce Departments, public land agencies and conservation agencies. Forest land information was obtained from the latest (1977) reports of the Agriculture Department's Forest Service. It includes national, state and privately owned forest land. Because some farm land, particularly in the Southern and Pacific coastal states, includes privately owned timberland, statistics for farm land and forest land may overlap. Information on federally owned land was obtained from the Office of Administration of the General Services Administration and is accurate as of the end of fiscal year 1982.

Work. Occupational categories were calculated from figures obtained from the 1980 census. State and local government employment statistics come from October 1981 figures of the Census Bureau, and pertain to both full- and part-time employees. Federal employment statistics were obtained from the Office of Personnel Management and pertain to non-military federal civilian employees as of Dec. 31, 1981.

The state unemployment rates were obtained from the Labor Department's Bureau of Labor Statistics, and are preliminary figures for June 1983.

Money. Median family income was obtained from the 1980 Census Bureau reports. The tax burden figures come from the Census Bureau report on state government tax collections in 1982.

Education. Education expenditures were obtained from the National Center for Education Statistics of the U.S. Department of Education. They reflect the average spending per pupil in public elementary and secondary schools for the school year 1980-81. The percentage of persons with college degrees is from the 1980 census, and represents those with four or more years of college.

Crime. Crime statistics were obtained from the FBI's Uniform Crime Reports for 1981. Violent crimes are defined as offenses of murder, forcible rape, robbery and aggravated assault.

Politics. Voter turnout figures for the 1980 presidential election and 1982 congressional elections were calculated by the Census Bureau.

The Highest and the Lowest: How States Rank

The following lists rank the top five and bottom five states in each category.

Unemployment Rate (June 1983 preliminary figures):

1. West Virginia	(17.5%)	46. Virginia	(5.8%)
2. Michigan	(14.6%)	47. Nebraska	(5.7%)
3. Mississippi	(13.6%)	48. South Dakota	(5.2%)
4. Pennsylvania	(12.9%)	49. New Hampshire	(4.7%)
5. Ohio	(12.8%)	North Dakota	(4.7%)
Louisiana	(12.8%)		

Median Family Income (1980):

1. Alaska	($28,395)	46. Alabama	($16,347)
2. Connecticut	($23,149)	47. Maine	($16,167)
3. Maryland	($23,112)	48. South Dakota	($15,993)
4. New Jersey	($22,906)	49. Arkansas	($14,641)
5. Hawaii	($22,750)	50. Mississippi	($14,591)

Tax Burden Per Capita (1982):

1. Alaska	($6,316)	46. Ohio	($539)
2. Wyoming	($1,622)	47. South Dakota	($476)
3. Hawaii	($1,105)	48. Missouri	($470)
4. Delaware	($1,001)	49. Tennessee	($467)
5. New Mexico	($942)	50. New Hampshire	($353)

Spending Per Pupil Through Grade 12:

1. Alaska	($5,369)	45. Alabama	($1,835)
2. New York	($3,769)	Kentucky	($1,835)
3. New Jersey	($3,285)	47. Tennessee	($1,831)
4. Oregon	($3,130)	48. Georgia	($1,721)
5. Delaware	($3,125)	49. Arkansas	($1,713)
		50. Mississippi	($1,685)

Persons With College Degrees (four or more years of college):

1. Colorado	(22.9%)	46. Mississippi	(12.3%)
2. Alaska	(21.1%)	47. Alabama	(12.2%)
3. Connecticut	(20.7%)	48. Kentucky	(11.1%)
4. Maryland	(20.4%)	49. Arkansas	(10.8%)
5. Hawaii	(20.4%)	50. West Virginia	(10.4%)

Violent Crime Rate (per 100,000):

1. New York	(1,070)	46. West Virginia	(175)
2. Florida	(965)	47. New Hampshire	(147)
3. Nevada	(896)	48. Vermont	(128)
4. Maryland	(887)	49. South Dakota	(105)
5. California	(863)	50. North Dakota	(68)

Federally Owned Land:

1. Alaska	(89.5%)	46. Rhode Island	(0.9%)
2. Nevada	(81.6%)	47. New York	(0.8%)
3. Idaho	(64.9%)	48. Maine	(0.7%)
4. Utah	(61.2%)	49. Iowa	(0.6%)
5. Wyoming	(49.3%)	50. Connecticut	(0.3%)

ALABAMA:

Wallace Governs With Help Of Teachers, Blacks, Labor

George C. Wallace's fourth term as governor of Alabama represents a return to the sort of politics Wallace practiced a generation ago, before race became the focus of his political career.

Physically incapacitated and scarcely visible in Montgomery for much of the year, the 64-year-old governor has nevertheless set in motion a significant turnabout in Alabama government, presiding over a populist-style administration in which business is on the outside and labor, teachers and the black community on the inside. In some ways, it is a throwback to the pre-civil rights days in which Wallace himself served on the board of trustees of all-black Tuskegee Institute.

Wallace's personal wishes are not always easy to determine; his few public appearances tend to be carefully planned, with a minimum of informal contact, and he does not see many state legislators. But the governor's popularity is so high that his close-knit and effective corps of top advisers — occasionally referred to as Wallace Inc. — can exercise great power on his authority.

The four crucial members of the team, all longtime Wallace associates, are Executive Secretary Elvin Stanton; press secretary Billy Joe Camp; Industrial Relations Director Bill Rushton; and Henry Steagall II, director of economic and community affairs. On day-to-day matters, it is generally conceded, they run the state.

They work in concert with an unusual political coalition that formed for the 1982 election and has, if anything, gained strength since then. The coalition is composed of the Alabama Education Association (AEA), the state labor council, the all-black Alabama Democratic Conference (ADC) and, in a somewhat lesser role, the Trial Lawyers Association.

These groups were less influential from 1979 to 1983, during the administration of Gov. Fob James, a business-oriented conservative who ran as a Democrat but used the party only as a convenience. James had been on the executive committee of the state Republican Party shortly before he filed for the Democratic nomination.

In 1982, with James planning to retire, Wallace and the coalition found each other, and each gained something important by joining forces. Wallace acquired support and active campaign help from Democratic Party factions that had been alienated by his 1960s civil rights record, and the coalition picked up access to rural white Democrats.

New Legislative Elections

The 1983 session of the Legislature showed that the coalition is far from an automatic winner on many legislative matters. Labor made little progress on its legislative agenda, and the trial lawyers were rebuffed sharply on a move to change the means of handling damage suits. But in the political decisions of the dominant Democratic Party, the coalition clearly seems to be in control.

Earlier in 1983, when a federal court redrew state House and Senate districts and ordered a new election to fill them, Wallace ordered that it be a general election only — the Democratic nominees would be chosen by party officials, rather than by open primary. This was a grant of unusual power to the party leadership, most of which is currently composed of coalition loyalists.

Alabama politicians differ on the effect this procedure and the Sept. 27, 1983, election will have on the Legislature. The absence of primaries indicates an easy road for most incumbents in both chambers. But the party hierar-

---

STATE LEADERSHIP

Gov. George C. Wallace (D)

Born: Aug. 25, 1919, Clio, Ala.
Home: Montgomery, Ala.
Education: U. of Ala., LL.B. 1942.
Military Career: Army Air Corps 1942-45.
Occupation: Lawyer.
Family: Wife, Lisa Taylor; four children.
Religion: Methodist.
Political Career: Ala. House, 1947-53; Judge, Third Judicial Circuit, 1953-58; sought Democratic presidential nomination, 1964, 1972, 1976; American Independent candidate for president, 1968; elected governor 1962, 1970, 1978, 1982; term expires Jan. 1987.

LEGISLATURE

SENATE

32D, 3R

John A. Teague (D)
President pro tem

HOUSE

97D, 8R

Tom Drake (D)
Speaker

A PROFILE OF
Alabama

PEOPLE

Total Population: 3,893,888 (22nd).
White 74%, Black 26%. Spanish
origin 1%.

Urban:	60%
Rural:	40%
Born in state:	79%
Foreign-born:	1%

MAJOR CITIES

Birmingham (284,413), Mobile (200,452),
Montgomery (177,857), Huntsville
(142,513), Tuscaloosa (75,211)

LAND

Farm	38%
Forest	66%
Federally owned	4%

WORK

Occupations: 47% white-collar; 39% blue-
collar; 12% service workers

Government workers:	49,937	federal
	71,689	state
	143,389	local

Unemployment rate: 13%

MONEY

Median family income (1980)	$16,347	(46th)
Tax burden per capita (1982)	$564	(42nd)

EDUCATION

Spending per pupil through grade 12	$1,835	(45th)
Persons with college degrees	12%	(47th)

CRIME

Violent crime rate: 471 per 100,000 (21st)

POLITICS

1980 Presidential Vote: Reagan 49%,
Carter 48%, Anderson 1%

Turnout rate in 1980:	56%
Turnout rate in 1982:	49%

U.S. House Delegation: 5D, 2R

chy may choose not to renominate some conservative Democrats; two House members, fearing that this will happen, have announced plans to run for re-election as Republicans. If this turns out to be more than an isolated incident, the result could be a mini-realignment in Alabama politics, with the Democratic Party moving further left and the still-weak GOP absorbing conservative Democrats.

Whatever happens in the election, the state House is likely to remain Wallace territory for some time to come. Its Speaker, Tom Drake of Cullman, is a gushing admirer of the governor who refers to state government in military terms, with Wallace as the general and himself as a lieutenant. Drake also is backed by the coalition.

The coalition opponents in the House tend to be members from rural south Alabama with close ties to business or to Joe McCorquodale, the conservative former Speaker who challenged Wallace in the 1982 gubernatorial primary. But their numbers are limited — some south Alabamans who would otherwise keep their distance from teachers, blacks and labor are accepting the coalition out of deference to Wallace.

In the 1983 session, the House speedily passed the administration's main initiative, a bill to raise new state revenue through

Speaker Tom Drake

a variety of indirect tax increases, including higher license fees and rescheduling of corporate tax payments. But that legislation had some problems in the Senate, where Lt. Gov. Bill Baxley, the presiding officer, held it hostage to obtain passage of his personal priority, a package of amendments to the state constitution. The amendments provide a significant amount of new home rule authority to local communities. Eventually the House accepted the constitutional changes, and the Senate passed the tax bill.

Baxley identifies himself as a supporter of Wallace, who endorsed him as his successor in a runoff against James in 1978. But as the dominant figure in the Senate, Baxley has been determined to stake out a role of independence, and he is in a position to do it, since he appoints all the chamber's committees and controls the schedule. At Baxley's insistence, the Senate essentially did no work for three months while demanding House action on the constitutional changes.

The two chambers agreed on several bills whose passage reflected the power of the AEA. One bill increased the state contribution to health insurance funding for teachers, and another made it more difficult for school systems to dismiss support employees such as maintenance and cafeteria workers. Both were AEA priorities, and both had Wallace backing.

The historic split between legislators from north and south Alabama is fading in the 1980s. These days, divisions are more likely to come along urban and rural lines, and reapportionment has given the cities increased strength. But several of the metropolitan delegations suffer from internal differences that pit labor-oriented inner-city members, an increasing number of them black, against conservative suburbanites. The result has been a longer lease on power for the rural Democrats.

ALASKA:

Parties Wield Little Power In Coalition-Run Legislature

First-term Democratic Gov. Bill Sheffield got off to a rocky start with Alaska's 13th Legislature in 1983. Unable to gain conservative House members' cooperation even on routine matters, he won confirmation of his Cabinet nominees only after calling out state troopers to force attendance at a special joint session.

That battle, along with budget skirmishes, dominated the 1983 session, which was widely considered to be the most bizarre in the 24 years of statehood.

But then Alaska politics has always been rather chaotic by national standards. Many legislators are recent arrivals from outside the state, and they bring with them disparate notions about the role government ought to play in charting Alaska's social and economic future. Elected officials regularly turn major issues over to the voters to be decided via ballot initiatives — a symbol of the political culture in a state whose individualism is as rugged as its terrain.

Political parties here are weaker than anywhere else in the country. Although Republicans won nominal control of the Legislature in 1982 — picking up one seat to break a tie in the Senate and gaining five to take the House out of Democratic hands — the changes have had little practical political effect. Both chambers are run by bipartisan coalitions in which informal legislative alliances are far more important than party affiliation.

The Senate coalition, under the leadership of Senate President Jalmar M. Kerttula of Palmer, bears the marks of a traditional "old boy" network. Kerttula enjoys the support of six fellow Democrats and five Republicans — most of whom are veteran members who share a predilection for conducting business behind closed doors.

Kerttula is credited with being an astute political strategist, capable of accommodating demands from his coalition while concealing his legislative priorities from the six Republicans and two Democrats outside his group. Frustrated members of the minority complain that Kerttula's skill makes it difficult for them to develop effective countermeasures. The minority would like to see more attention paid to energy development and contracts for oil royalties.

House Autocracy

The House is a less seasoned body than the Senate; 23 of its 40 members were elected as freshmen in 1982, and several of the newcomers already hold committee chairmanships. The majority coalition is headed by Speaker Joe L. Hayes, an Anchorage Republican who sometimes wields his power with autocratic zeal.

Hayes' supporters say that presiding over so many freshmen requires a certain rigidity. But his detractors claim the Speaker exercises "rule by fear," requiring members to swear allegiance to him or lose out on committee chairmanships, staff and office space.

Hayes' current coalition developed as the result of an unusual coup in the summer of 1981. Three Democrats and two Libertarians teamed with the chamber's 16 Republicans to oust the Democratic leadership. The Hayes group, largely pro-development, wanted to see more of Alaska's oil revenue spent on capital projects. The former leadership was more inclined to use it for a variety of social programs.

Hayes' majority coalition has remained largely intact, but it is smaller these days — three Republicans were effectively kicked out after the controversy over Sheffield's Cabinet nominees. The three have not been absorbed by the Democratic minority, and thus constitute a third, minor faction in the House.

Legislators from Alaska's remote "bush" country often provide the balance of power for the majority coalitions in both chambers. Although they are outnumbered by their colleagues from Anchorage and south central Alaska, bush representatives are generally more unified in their legislative agenda. Their favorite programs include hunting and fishing laws giving priorities to native Alaskans, liberal welfare spending, and capital projects to improve transportation and communication in their areas.

STATE LEADERSHIP

Gov. Bill Sheffield (D)

Born: June 26, 1928, Spokane, Wash.
Home: Anchorage, Alaska.
Education: Attended DeForest Training School, 1949-51.
Military Career: Army Air Corps, 1946-49.
Occupation: Hotel owner.
Family: Widowed.
Religion: Presbyterian.
Political Career: Elected governor 1982; term expires Dec. 1986.

LEGISLATURE

SENATE
9D, 11R
Jalmar M. Kerttula (D)
President

HOUSE
19D, 21R
Joe L. Hayes (R)
Speaker

A PROFILE OF
Alaska

PEOPLE

Total Population: 401,851 (50th).
White 77%, Black 3%, American
Indian, Eskimo and Aleut 16%, Asian
and Pacific Islander 2%. Spanish
origin 2%.

Urban:	64%
Rural:	36%
Born in state:	32%
Foreign-born:	4%

MAJOR CITIES

Anchorage (174,431), Fairbanks (22,645),
Juneau (19,528), Sitka (7,802), Ketchikan
(7,198)

LAND

Farm	1%
Forest	33%
Federally owned	90%

WORK

Occupations: 60% white-collar; 24% blue-
collar; 14% service workers

Government workers:	15,150 federal
	19,349 state
	17,432 local

Unemployment rate: 10%

MONEY

Median family income (1980)	$28,395	(1st)
Tax burden per capita (1982)	$6,316	(1st)

EDUCATION

Spending per pupil through grade 12	$5,369	(1st)
Persons with college degrees	21%	(2nd)

CRIME

Violent crime rate: 616 per 100,000   (12th)

POLITICS

1980 Presidential Vote: Reagan 54%,
Carter 26%, Clark 12%, Anderson 7%

Turnout rate in 1980:	57%
Turnout rate in 1982:	59%

U.S. House Delegation: 1R

Some of the most influential bush country delegates are native Alaskans. Republican John C. Sackett of Galena, an Athapascan Indian, and Democrat Frank Ferguson of Kotzebue, an Eskimo, are powerful in the Senate. Al Adams, also an Eskimo, chairs the House Finance Committee.

'Boomers' vs. 'Greenies'

The Anchorage-area delegation is rife with ideological differences, and has been plagued by high turnover. But Anchorage remains the crucible of financial and political power in Alaska. The region around Anchorage is the fastest-growing part of the state, so it will retain its strength in future Legislatures.

Throughout the 1970s, the most crucial line of political division in Alaska was between pro-development "boomers" and enviromentalist "greenies." Former Republican Gov. Jay S. Hammond, who dominated state government during his two terms (1974-82), joined Alaska's congressional delegation in arguing against federal control of state lands. But he was known at home as a man with environmentalist sympathies. Sheffield has given mixed signals on the land issue, which has paled somewhat in importance since the 1980 Alaska lands compromise became law.

A millionaire hotel owner from Anchorage, Sheffield was a political neophyte when he won election to the governorship in 1982. Critics say his lack of experience is largely responsible for the rocky legislative session. Others point out that Alaska's once-booming oil revenues have been declining, and claim that the task of governing has been made more difficult by legislators who are accustomed to spending money freely and have yet to adjust to new fiscal realities.

Oil still drives the state's economy, although the industry's political influence has been hampered somewhat by the lack of a well-organized lobbying organization. But petroleum interests in the Prudhoe Bay area benefit from the political clout of the North Slope Borough, geographically the world's largest municipality and one whose government is an effective pressure group on a range of issues. Other important interest groups include the Alaska Public Employees Association, the Teamsters union and the state affiliate of the National Education Association. ∎

ARIZONA:

New Era of GOP Dominance Based in Fast-Growing Cities

Arizona politics has undergone a remarkable transformation in the last three decades. Once the domain of rural, conservative "pinto" Democrats, the state today is dominated by urban dwellers who display a marked preference for the Republican Party.

The old pinto Democrats carved out their base in the malapportioned Arizona Legislature. With state law allowing two senators from every county, they marshaled sufficient numbers to command veto power over legislation not tailored to their interests. But the growing influence of populous, Republican-minded Phoenix, coupled with the U. S. Supreme Court's "one man, one vote" decision, conspired to end their heyday. Republicans have held both chambers of the Legislature for 13 of the last 17 years.

Still, the GOP-controlled Legislature today hardly writes its own ticket. Its members must deal with Democratic Gov. Bruce Babbitt, the strongest activist to occupy Arizona's Statehouse in recent history.

A civil rights lawyer in the Johnson administration, Babbitt served as an aggressive attorney general before succeeding to the governorship in 1978. He holds the state record for vetoing bills as chief executive, and has combined his veto power with compromise to establish his influence with Republican legislative leaders.

Babbitt frequently exchanges political intelligence with Republican House Majority Leader Burton S. Barr of Phoenix, widely considered the most powerful figure in the Legislature. After 16 years in his job, Barr is the senior majority leader in the country. House Speaker Frank Kelley is regarded as more of an administrator than a political leader, and operates in Barr's shadow.

Barr's influence stems largely from his skill in the art of compromise. Calling representatives into his office one at a time, he bargains for votes, often building bipartisan coalitions with the 21-member Democratic minority. Although he considers himself a conservative, Barr's politics are difficult to pin down. He judges a bill not by its ideological bent, but by its ability to attract enough votes for passage.

Republican Split

Political power in Arizona's 30-member Senate is more diffuse. Smaller GOP margins there have made party control more tenuous, and internal politics have been more divisive. The split between moderate and hard-right Republicans is one of the most significant factors in the Senate. Tensions between the two factions peaked during budget battles in the 1983 session.

Bolstered by the election in 1982 of several like-minded colleagues who came over from the House, the conservative GOP bloc fought with the more moderate Republicans in the Senate over a proposal to hike the state sales tax by one cent. The conservatives preferred further cuts in government spending as a means of assuring a balanced budget, which is required by state law. When protracted negotiations failed to produce a compromise, Senate President Stan Turley broke with caucus precedent in taking the issue to the floor without sufficient Republican support. Turley, who favored the tax increase, enlisted enough Democratic votes to pass the revenue measure.

Turley, in his first term as Senate President, is viewed by both moderates and conservatives as a fair leader whose primary concern is enacting the will of the majority. But he faces a difficult task in trying to unify the Republican ranks. Battle scars from the budget battle have been slow

STATE LEADERSHIP

Gov. Bruce Babbitt (D)

Born: June 27, 1938, Los Angeles, Calif.
Home: Phoenix, Ariz.
Education: U. of Notre Dame, B.S. 1960; U. of Newcastle, England, M.A. 1962; Harvard Law School, LL.B. 1965.
Occupation: Lawyer.
Family: Wife, Hattie Coons; two children.
Religion: Roman Catholic.
Political Career: Ariz. attorney general, 1975-78; assumed governorship March 1978 upon death of Gov. Wesley H. Bolin; elected governor 1978, 1982; term expires Jan. 1987.

LEGISLATURE

SENATE

12D, 18R

Stan Turley (R)
President

HOUSE

21D, 39R

Frank Kelley (R)
Speaker

A PROFILE OF
Arizona

PEOPLE

Total Population: 2,718,215 (29th).
White 82%, Black 3%, American
Indian, Eskimo and Aleut 6%, Asian and
Pacific Islander 1%. Spanish
origin 16%.

Urban:	84%
Rural:	16%
Born in state:	33%
Foreign-born:	6%

MAJOR CITIES

Phoenix (789,704), Tucson (330,537), Mesa
(152,453), Tempe (106,743), Glendale
(97,172)

LAND

Farm	55%
Forest	26%
Federally owned	40%

WORK

Occupations: 56% white-collar; 28% blue-
collar; 14% service workers

Government workers:	36,263	federal
	46,093	state
	117,152	local

Unemployment rate: 10%

MONEY

Median family income (1980)	$19,017	(30th)
Tax burden per capita (1982)	$683	(23rd)

EDUCATION

Spending per pupil through grade 12	$2,305	(25th)
Persons with college degrees	17%	(19th)

CRIME

Violent crime rate: 576 per 100,000 (13th)

POLITICS

1980 Presidential Vote: Reagan 61%,
Carter 28%, Anderson 9%

Turnout rate in 1980:	54%
Turnout rate in 1982:	43%

U.S. House Delegation: 2D, 3R

to heal. Some moderates are pushing to have Tucson Sen. Jeffrey J. Hill, a key figure in the conservative GOP faction, stripped of his Finance Committee chairmanship.

Despite their infighting, Republicans in Arizona are in little danger of losing their strength in the near future. The state's climate and pro-development attitude helped boost its population by over 53 percent during the 1970s, and many of the newcomers have brought GOP habits with them. One of the state's most powerful Republican blocs lies in Sun City, a well-organized, politically active community of affluent retirees. Since 1975, however, the influx of retirees has slowed. An increasing number of the newer arrivals have been engineers and other professionals drawn to jobs in high-technology industry.

Hispanic Power

Over the course of the last decade, Hispanics have developed into an important force in Arizona politics, especially in the Democratic Party. Comprising 16 percent of the state's population, they currently occupy six of the 12 Democratic seats in the Senate.

Former Democratic Gov. Raul Castro, 1975-77, helped to open the door for Hispanics in Arizona. A lawyer and international diplomat, Castro won election as Arizona's first Hispanic governor in 1974 by building a coalition of Spanish-speaking groups, labor union members, liberals and American Indians. Among the most prominent Hispanic officeholders today is Democratic Sen. Alfredo Gutierrez of Phoenix, a former majority leader in the Senate. Democrat Jaime Gutierrez of Tucson (no relation) currently serves as the Senate's minority whip.

Arizona's Hispanic legislators thus far have placed more emphasis on building recognition for members of their minority than on hammering out a distinctive legislative agenda. Tucson-area Hispanics have formed a group called Acción 80s to develop community leadership.

While most of Arizona's Hispanics live in either Phoenix or Tucson, the state's American Indian population remains largely rural. Although the Indians' political efficacy has been hampered by low voter turnout and intertribal animosity, they have a voice in the Legislature. Arizona's northernmost district, dominated by the Navaho tribe, has elected two Indians to the House — a Democrat and a Republican — giving them a say in both party caucuses.

Prior to World War II, Arizona's economic landscape was dominated by the copper industry in general, and the Phelps Dodge company in particular. Copper is still an important interest group. But the state's postwar economic diversification, combined with the industry's sagging fortunes, have greatly reduced its clout.

Agricultural interests have remained strong despite the state's rapid urbanization. Agribusiness groups fight hardest over water projects. Striving to protect their majority share of the state's water supply, they are pitted against mining interests and urban spokesmen. Babbitt helped push through legislation in 1980 establishing a major statewide water management program — the product of years of negotiations between the three water-user factions.

Business has long been dominant over organized labor in Arizona, one of the first states in the country to pass a right-to-work law. Utilities such as the Arizona Public Service Company are particularly influential. Members of Phoenix's downtown business community — including the Phoenix 40, a quiet but effective group of corporate executives — have close ties to Republican officeholders. ∎

ARKANSAS:

Clinton Confronts Legislature Controlled by Business Allies

Arkansas politics has been characterized for much of the last two decades by relatively liberal governors and a conservative Legislature.

The first such governor was Republican Winthrop Rockefeller (1967-71). He lifted the state from the politics

of segregation that dominated during the reign of his Democratic predecessor, Orval E. Faubus (1955-67). Since then, Arkansas voters have chosen moderate Democrats Dale Bumpers, David Pryor and the current incumbent, Bill Clinton, who is back in office after avenging his 1980 loss to Republican Frank White, the one

conservative governor of recent times.

The Arkansas Legislature, however, has seen no such dramatic break with the "old" pre-Rockefeller politics. Though the Legislature is not quite a hidebound relic from the Faubus era, it is still the center of power for politicians sympathetic to business, skeptical of new government initiatives and unreceptive to higher taxes.

The Senate in particular is a model of the old-style Southern legislative body. It is almost exclusively Democratic, and power is closely held by a small number of white conservatives with long years of seniority. Two senators are widely regarded as the chamber's kingpins — Knox Nelson of Pine Bluff and Max Howell of Little Rock. Between them they have 62 years of legislative experience, and through committee positions and personal alliances they exercise tremendous influence on the fate of legislation and the distribution of power within the Senate.

Powerful Utilities

A cozy relationship between state legislators and the business establishment is an Arkansas tradition still thriving. Especially powerful are the utility companies — among them Arkla Gas, Arkansas Western Power and Arkansas Power and Light, whose lobbyist is former state House Speaker Cecil Alexander. The utilities' clout was demonstrated clearly in the 1983 legislative session.

Clinton had made attacks on the influence of the utility companies a major element of his 1982 campaign. He proposed shifting the state public service commission, which regulates the utilities, from an appointive body to a publicly elected one. But the idea, which was fiercely opposed by the utilities, died in the Legislature. Also rejected was a Clinton proposal to increase the severance tax on natural gas.

For years a key behind-the-scenes power in Arkansas business and politics has been Stephens, Inc. The company, based in Little Rock, is the nation's 12th-largest investment banker, and the biggest outside Wall Street. It is little-known outside Arkansas, however, because the two brothers who run it — Witt and Jack Stephens — are not spotlight-seekers. The Stephens brothers were very close to Faubus, and their influence peaked during his tenure, but even today their opinion of a candidate often influences his ability to raise money from the business community. In the close 1982 gubernatorial contest, the brothers played both sides, with Witt supporting Clinton and Jack backing White.

Another force worth noting is the state Highway Department, sometimes referred to as a "fourth branch" of the Arkansas government. Its quasi-independence stems from the fact that it receives its money directly from gasoline tax revenues, not from the Legislature. For a legislator wanting road work done in his district, the director of the Highway Department, whose term is 10 years, is more important to court than the governor.

The Legislature in the past few years has been touched by some winds of change, most of them generated by newly elected Democrats who want the older members to begin passing down the mantle of power. This struggle is seen not

---

STATE LEADERSHIP

Gov. Bill Clinton (D)

Born: Aug. 19, 1946, Hope, Ark.
Home: Little Rock, Ark.
Education: Georgetown U., B.A. 1968; Yale Law School, LL.B. 1972.
Profession: Lawyer; law professor.
Family: Wife, Hillary Rodham; one child.
Religion: Baptist.
Political Career: Democratic nominee for U.S. House, 1974; Arkansas attorney general, 1977-79; elected governor, 1978; defeated for re-election, 1980; elected governor, 1982; term expires Jan. 1985.

GENERAL ASSEMBLY

SENATE
32D, 3R

William D. Moore Jr. (D)
President pro tem

HOUSE
93D, 7R

John Paul Capps (D)
Speaker

Sen. William D. Moore Jr.   **Rep. John Paul Capps**

A PROFILE OF
Arkansas

PEOPLE

Total Population: 2,286,435 (33rd).
   White 83%, Black 16%. Spanish
   origin 1%.

Urban:	52%
Rural:	48%
Born in state:	69%
Foreign-born:	1%

MAJOR CITIES

Little Rock (158,461), Fort Smith (71,626),
   North Little Rock (64,288), Pine Bluff
   (56,636), Fayetteville (36,608)

LAND

Farm	49%
Forest	55%
Federally owned	10%

WORK

Occupations: 44% white-collar; 38% blue-
                  collar; 12% service workers

Government workers:	19,011	federal
	42,812	state
	79,605	local

Unemployment rate: 9%

MONEY

Median family income (1980)	$14,641	(49th)
Tax burden per capita (1982)	$553	(44th)

EDUCATION

Spending per pupil through grade 12	$1,713	(49th)
Persons with college degrees	11%	(49th)

CRIME

Violent crime rate: 310 per 100,000   (34th)

POLITICS

1980 Presidential Vote: Reagan 48%,
      Carter 48%, Anderson 3%

Turnout rate in 1980:	57%
Turnout rate in 1982:	53%

U.S. House Delegation: 2D, 2R

so much in battles over issues — many of the young legislators are just as conservative as their elders — but rather in disputes over power within the Legislature itself.

In 1981, then-freshman state Sen. John Lisle of Springdale successfully mobilized a group of junior senators and won approval of his proposal to open up the membership of the powerful Joint Budget Committee, which had been ruled by a clique of senior members from a few Mississippi River counties in the southeastern part of the state. The junior senators also gained strength by winning changes in the membership criteria for committees governing internal Senate affairs.

The same inter-generational conflict is occurring in the state House, where there is a large contingent of members who have been elected since 1978. The obstacles for younger members are not so great in the House; the speakership of the chamber is rotated regularly, so power has never been as concentrated as in the Senate.

Cautious Clinton

Governor Clinton today is a more cautious politician than the brash young reformer who won the governorship in 1978 and lost it two years later because Arkansans found his style too saucy. Liberals say he governs too timidly, but Clinton maintains he is fulfilling his 1982 campaign promise not to "lead without listening."

The governor's critics are particularly frustrated that he is not putting Arkansas at the cutting edge of the drive to improve education, a cause now being promoted heavily by governors in several other Southern states. Clinton has appointed a commission to study education standards, but has been slow to endorse an increase in the state sales tax that would pay for improvements.

Arkansas Republicans are not a major factor in state politics, despite the election of White over Clinton in 1980. During the past decade, the moderates and liberals who dominated the Arkansas GOP in Rockefeller's era were eclipsed by conservatives, who now completely control the state party. The conservatives predicted that the Reagan-White 1980 sweep was the start of greater things, but with White out of office, good news for the GOP is hard to find.

One positive trend for the GOP, however, is the influx of retirees into the scenic mountains in the northwestern part of the state. Arkansas now has a larger retiree population than any other state except Florida. Many of these people come from Northern states such as Indiana, Illinois and Iowa, where Republicans are traditionally strong, and many of them retain their allegiance to the GOP when replanted in Arkansas.   ∎

CALIFORNIA:

Deukmejian and Legislature Polarized By Budget Debate

For the first time since 1974, Ronald Reagan's last year in office, California has a Republican governor and a Democratic Legislature. The competition between them for power has left state government more polarized than at any time since the early years of Reagan's first term, in the mid-1960s.

For three weeks in July 1983 the state was without a budget as Republican Gov. George Deukmejian fought with the Democratic legislators. At issue was state funding for a range of programs Democrats wanted to protect and Deukmejian wanted to cut, and a GOP-sponsored re-districting initiative that is certain to hurt Democrats in the Legislature and in Congress if passed. Hoping to pressure Deukmejian not to call a special election for the initiative, Democrats held the budget hostage, refusing to send it to him for 19 days past the start of the new fiscal year.

It made no difference. Bending to considerable pressure from Republicans statewide, the governor eventually called a special remap election for two weeks before Christmas. That battle lost, Democrats passed the budget, then watched helplessly as Deukmejian slashed $1.1 billion from social service and education programs, the Agricultural Labor Relations Board and the state's Coastal Commission, which regulates development along the Pacific shoreline. Fuming, they left Sacramento for a month's recess.

Deukmejian and his aides have played down the seriousness of the breach, but Democrats seem in no mood to smooth things over. The redistricting issue alone is enough to explain their anger. They contend, with good cause, that it is a direct attack on their hard-won political power in California.

But Democrats are not just angry at Deukmejian — they are frustrated at their inability to sway him from his anti-tax, budget-cutting stance, despite their majority.

In his last years in office, Democratic Gov. Edmund G. Brown Jr. basically left the budget process up to the Legislature, giving individual Democrats there considerable influence over state spending. Deukmejian has not been so accommodating, and Democratic efforts to force him to come to terms on the budget and on redistricting — by holding the budget hostage, threatening his appointments, even stripping his aides of their Capitol parking places — have not worked. The new governor has used his veto power and a Republican minority large enough to prevent veto overrides to win the major battles while losing the skirmishes.

Deukmejian's allies defend him against charges of overly rigid conservatism. They point to his willingness earlier in 1983 to agree to a standby sales tax in case his efforts to balance the budget did not work, and his agreement, under pressure from legislators of both parties, to accept more state spending on elementary and secondary education. But they also applaud his overall firmness in dealing with the Legislature.

Critics counter that at some point Deukmejian may find the political price of his position too high. Democrats still can hold hostage any initiatives he may want from them, as well as block his appointments to administrative posts. And although the leaders of the GOP caucuses have promised to back Deukmejian's line-item vetoes, Democrats may still be able to woo over enough moderate Republicans to re-appropriate some of the lost funds; public demonstrations against particular cuts have become an almost daily occurrence in Sacramento.

Legislative Bazaar

What has been easy to forget during the face-off between governor and Legislature is that, in the words of the *California Journal*, "it's incorrect to speak of the Legisla-

---

STATE LEADERSHIP

Gov. George Deukmejian (R)

Born: June 6, 1928, Menands, N.Y.
Home: Long Beach, Calif.
Education: Siena College, B.S. 1949; St. John's U., J.D. 1952.
Military Career: Army, 1953-55.
Occupation: Lawyer.
Family: Wife, Gloria Saatjian; three children.
Religion: Episcopalian.
Political Career: Calif. Assembly, 1963-67; Calif. Senate, 1967-79, Republican leader, 1969-71, 1975-79; Calif. attorney general, 1979-83; elected governor 1982; term expires Jan. 1987.

LEGISLATURE

SENATE

25D, 14R, 1 Ind.

David A. Roberti (D)
President pro tem

ASSEMBLY

48D, 32R

Willie L. Brown Jr. (D)
Speaker

A PROFILE OF

California

PEOPLE

Total Population: 23,667,902 (1st).
White 76%, Black 8%, American
Indian, Eskimo and Aleut 1%, Asian and
Pacific Islander 5%. Spanish
origin 19%.

Urban:	91%
Rural:	9%
Born in state:	45%
Foreign-born:	15%

MAJOR CITIES

Los Angeles (2,966,850), San Diego
(875,538), San Francisco (678,974), San
Jose (629,442), Long Beach (361,334)

LAND

Farm	34%
Forest	40%
Federally owned	48%

WORK

Occupations: 58% white-collar; 27% blue-
collar; 13% service workers

Government workers:	302,429 federal
	309,461 state
	1,120,277 local

Unemployment rate: 10%

MONEY

Median family income (1980)	$21,537	(10th)
Tax burden per capita (1982)	$922	(8th)

EDUCATION

Spending per pupil through grade 12	$2,427	(21st)
Persons with college degrees	20%	(8th)

CRIME

Violent crime rate: 863 per 100,000 (5th)

POLITICS

1980 Presidential Vote: Reagan 53%,
Carter 36%, Anderson 9%

Turnout rate in 1980:	54%
Turnout rate in 1982:	49%

U.S. House Delegation: 28D, 17R

ture as a single entity. It's more like an Oriental bazaar with 120 rug merchants (80 in the Assembly and 40 in the Senate) peddling their wares to colleagues, lobbyists, the governor and whoever else may come along." The give-and-take of legislative maneuvering can assume a life of its own, over which Deukmejian has only limited say.

And despite the new governor's ability to keep Republicans in line during the July budget battle, the GOP caucus is not unified in either chamber. In the Senate, the ideological range extends from liberal Milton Marks of San Francisco to the leader of the GOP's New Right bloc in Sacramento, H. L. "Bill" Richardson. Longtime Senate GOP leader William Campbell was overthrown early in July by a Richardson-led coalition of conservatives bothered by Campbell's tendency to cooperate with the majority and moderates angered by his lack of attention to caucus matters.

In the Assembly, where Republicans are more consistently conservative, GOP leader Robert W. Naylor just missed losing his position that same month in a right-wing coup attempt. The move was engineered by members of a group of about 10 assemblymen dubbed "the Cavemen" by the press for their rigidly conservative views.

Registered Republicans form a distinct minority in California, but conservative Democrats who owe no particular allegiance to their party have given the GOP strength that belies the numbers. Nowhere is that more true than in Orange County, whose middle- and upper-class voters have come to symbolize conservative values nationwide. Signs of moderation began to appear in Orange County during the 1970s, with the election of several Democrats to the Legislature, but now they have begun to disappear; after the 1982 elections, only two of Orange County's nine legislators in Sacramento were Democrats.

The wellsprings of Democratic strength in California are the San Francisco Bay Area and Los Angeles County. Well over half of the Democrats in the Legislature come from those two parts of the state.

San Francisco's urban voters, together with their counterparts in Oakland, Berkeley and San Jose, give the Bay Area delegation a basically liberal complexion that is tempered by the more moderate vote coming from blue-collar suburbs and wealthier communities in the Silicon Valley and Marin County. The Democratic

Speaker Willie L. Brown Jr.

vote in the Los Angeles area is even more varied. The wealthy residents of West Los Angeles and Beverly Hills, whose money goes to support Democratic candidates statewide, join with fixed-income Santa Monicans, Hispanics in East Los Angeles and blacks in the southern neighborhoods of the city to anchor the liberal Democratic vote. Voters living north of Beverly Hills in the middle-class neighborhoods of the San Fernando Valley, and those in the suburbs stretching south and east of the city, elect more conservative Democrats or Republicans.

There are a few other pockets of liberal Democratic strength in California, but most legislators from outside Los Angeles and the Bay Area, whatever their party label, are moderate or conservative in outlook.

The second most powerful political figure in the state after Deukmejian is Assembly Speaker Willie L. Brown Jr., a Democrat from San Francisco. A flamboyant and wily politician, Brown is the dominant force in the Assembly. He has the authority to appoint committee members and chairmen, and decides which committees will consider specific bills. This gives him considerable control over legislation and enormous influence with his colleagues.

Although Brown often sides with Assembly liberals, he takes a less predictable ideological line than Senate President David A. Roberti, a liberal partisan. Brown's inner circle of allies is made up largely of centrist Democrats. He took an accommodating attitude toward Deukmejian early in 1983, shepherding the governor's first budget-balancing plans through to enactment. Having ended up with nothing in return during the later budget battles, however, Brown is now the object of some sniping among Assembly liberals who contend that he went too far.

Roberti, on the other hand, has taken a strident tone in his dealings with the governor, although he has compromised when necessary. In part, his rhetoric is ideological. But it may also be a way to keep Senate Democrats in line. The institutional functions that give Brown influence in the Assembly are performed by the Rules Committee in the Senate, making power there more dependent on active leadership.

$100,000 Assembly Seats

One means Roberti has found to expand his influence has been fund raising. Both he and Brown have become masters at raising enormous amounts of money to help fellow Democrats win election or re-election, cementing their own power in the process. Legislative elections in California have grown very expensive; in 1982, 19 of the 80 contests for the Assembly saw candidates on both sides spend more than $100,000 each. With the state's political parties traditionally weak, legislators have come to rely on their own political organizations, on outside contributors and on their leadership for campaign help.

Hundreds of interest groups and some 700 lobbyists are registered in Sacramento, and they use campaign contributions to advance their causes. Public interest groups and environmentalists have noted with alarm the proliferation of so-called "juice bills" aimed at helping out a particular industry or individual — giving the movie industry tax loopholes, for example, or helping a land developer bypass local regulations on land use.

Because of California's size and diversity, and the multitude of attitudes represented in the Legislature, no one interest is pre-eminent. But on issues directly affecting them, many have considerable influence. When Deukmejian proposed financing an education package by withdrawing sales tax exemptions from liquor, beer and cigarettes, the lobbies for each quickly killed the proposal.

The change in administrations has put minorities and groups representing the poor, organized labor, farm workers and environmentalists on the defensive. Unable to compete with wealthier interests in making campaign donations, they relied during the 1970s on Brown and on ideologically sympathetic legislators. The results included creation of such agencies as the Agricultural Labor Relations Board and the coastal commission, and passage of the state's strong water and air quality laws.

In recent years, however, those gains have come under attack. Now, conservatives are not intimidated by the prospect of a gubernatorial veto, and are more inclined to invest their efforts in rolling back past liberal initiatives. This in turn has given heart to business people and others whose influence has been strengthened by Deukmejian's support.∎

COLORADO:

Lamm Enjoys 'Bully Pulpit' But Republicans Hold Power

Although Colorado has a Democratic governor and a Republican Legislature, control of state government is not evenly divided.

Gov. Richard D. Lamm enjoys the "bully pulpit" that his forceful personality, favorable media attention and

1982 landslide re-election victory have provided. But the Legislature controls the purse strings, and as Colorado has grappled throughout 1983 for ways to erase a budget deficit, the power of the legislative branch has been evident.

Its dominant figures are members of the Republican leadership. In the lower chamber, that is clearly one person — House Speaker Carl "Bev" Bledsoe, a tight-lipped, politically astute rancher from Colorado's eastern plains. In the upper chamber, power is changing hands. The majority leader traditionally has been the key decision maker, but the Senate president, long a ceremonial figure, is becoming a rival for influence. At the moment, the Senate president is Ted Strickland, a business executive from the Denver suburbs who unsuccessfully challenged Lamm for the governorship in 1978. Strickland shares authority in the Senate with Majority Leader Dan Noble, who comes from the sparsely populated Western Slope.

In both chambers the Republican leadership oversees committee assignments, including seats on the most important panel, the Joint Budget Committee. The committee has six members, three from each chamber, who annually prepare the state budget. But with the membership on the committee often changing, much of the actual power resides with the committee's GOP-appointed staff director.

Pragmatic, moderate Republicans dominate their party's caucuses in both chambers. But the militant right, allied with politically active brewing magnate Joseph Coors, has enough votes to exert leverage on most issues. That was evident early in 1983 when the Legislature was wrestling with ways to close a budget deficit of more than $100 million. The GOP leadership preferred a mix of tax increases and spending cuts, while the Republican right wanted to focus on cuts. The conservative group was able to use its strength in the GOP House caucus to force deeper cuts in several areas, including public education, than the leaders had initially wanted to make.

Still, far-right elements in the Legislature are not as obstreperous as they were in the late 1970s, when the zealous band of budget-cutting conservatives was dubbed the House "crazies." Some members of that group, such as former state Reps. Anne M. Gorsuch and her future husband, Robert Burford, left to join the Reagan administration. Interior Secretary James G. Watt was a familiar figure to conservative legislators in those days as head of the Mountain States Legal Foundation, a pro-development pressure group.

Lamm Seeks Accommodation

Although many allies of the Watt-Gorsuch-Burford group remain, Lamm has helped ease the once-frenzied opposition of the Legislature by adopting a less contentious style of relating to it. In 1982 he vetoed nearly 40 bills; in 1983, he was using his veto power far fewer times.

Some Democrats complain that the governor has submerged his policy differences with the Legislature in an effort to create an artificial era of good feeling. But his less strident manner has increased his effectiveness. He has developed a working relationship with House Speaker Bledsoe. His dealings with Senate President Strickland remain somewhat strained. But the more moderate complexion of the upper chamber has created some maneuvering room. In the end, the budget adopted by the Legislature in 1983 was not much different from the one Lamm had proposed, with an increase in the gasoline and sales taxes coupled with about $50 million in program cuts.

The days are long past when the financial and banking interests of downtown Denver could count on getting virtu-

---

STATE LEADERSHIP

Gov. Richard D. Lamm (D)

Born: Aug. 3, 1935, Madison, Wis.
Home: Denver, Colo.
Education: U. of Wis., B.B.A. 1957; U. of Calif. (Berkeley), LL.B. 1961.
Military Career: Army, 1957-58.
Occupation: Lawyer; accountant.
Family: Wife, Dorothy Vennard; two children.
Religion: Unitarian.
Political Career: Colo. House, 1967-75; elected governor 1974, 1978, 1982; term expires Jan. 1987.

GENERAL ASSEMBLY

SENATE
14D, 21R
Ted L. Strickland (R)
President

HOUSE
25D, 40R
Carl B. Bledsoe (R)
Speaker

ally all they wanted from the Legislature. But business and agricultural lobbyists still have the ear of the Republican leadership. In 1982, when the House appointed a citizens' commission to study changes in the property tax, the group conspicuously included lobbyists for ranching interests and for the telephone company.

Although the last two House Speakers and Strickland's predecessor as Senate president were farmers or ranchers, rural Colorado's legislative influence is likely to fade in the coming years. The state's recent population boom has been concentrated in the budding megalopolis along the Front Range, which stretches from Fort Collins in the north to Colorado Springs in the south.

That demographic trend is not particularly good news for the Democrats, since the growth has been in the Republican suburbs rather than the Democratic bastions of Denver and Pueblo. Barring a major political blunder by the Republicans, it seems unlikely that the Democrats will capture the Legislature any time this decade.

GOP party officials are working hard to make sure that Republicans maintain their dominance in the Legislature. From their state headquarters a stone's throw from the Capitol, party officials act as a conduit of information between GOP legislators and their constituents. It is a sophisticated operation: they regularly do polls to gauge voter reaction on key issues and develop mailings that legislators can send to their constituents.

Meanwhile, there are increasing numbers of young people and women in the Legislature. Following the 1982 election, nearly half the members of the House were newcomers, and one-quarter of the members of both chambers were women.

Several of the women hold key positions. GOP Sen. Ruth Stockton, a 22-year legislative veteran, is chairman of the Joint Budget Committee (the position alternates between members of the House and Senate); Martha Ezzard is chairman of the Republican caucus in the Senate. Women have not yet formed their own bipartisan caucus in the Legislature, but they are considering it, and may do so in the near future.

A former Colorado House member, Democrat Lt. Gov. Nancy Dick does not have a formal role in the Legislature. But the Aspen resident regularly lobbies the House and Senate on rural issues. Elected twice on the gubernatorial ticket headed by Lamm, she has been widely mentioned as a possible challenger to Republican U.S. Sen. William L. Armstrong next year.

■

A PROFILE OF
Colorado

PEOPLE

Total Population: 2,889,964 (28th).
White 89%, Black 4%, American Indian, Eskimo and Aleut 1%, Asian and Pacific Islander 1%. Spanish origin 12%.

Urban:	81%
Rural:	19%
Born in state:	42%
Foreign-born:	4%

MAJOR CITIES

Denver (492,365), Colorado Springs (215,150), Aurora (158,588), Lakewood (112,860), Pueblo (101,686)

LAND

Farm	56%
Forest	34%
Federally owned	36%

WORK

Occupations: 58% white-collar; 27% blue-collar; 13% service workers

Government workers:	49,471	federal
	59,221	state
	130,356	local

Unemployment rate: 7%

MONEY

Median family income (1980)	$21,279	(12th)
Tax burden per capita (1982)	$585	(39th)

EDUCATION

Spending per pupil through grade 12	$2,708	(14th)
Persons with college degrees	23%	(1st)

CRIME

Violent crime rate: 532 per 100,000 (17th)

POLITICS

1980 Presidential Vote: Reagan 55%, Carter 31%, Anderson 11%

Turnout rate in 1980:	63%
Turnout rate in 1982:	52%

U.S. House Delegation: 3D, 3R

CONNECTICUT:

Democrats Split by Conflicts Over Factory Moves, Taxes

Not so long ago, the course of the Connecticut Legislature was determined by Democratic boss John M. Bailey and a few key lawmakers he chose to consult. Competing factions were kept at bay by Bailey's great influence — he was state party chairman for three decades and national

Democratic chairman during the Kennedy and Johnson administrations. If a particular Democratic legislator proved consistently uncooperative with Bailey, there was a good chance he would not be renominated.

Because of Bailey, party discipline remained intact in Connecticut long after it had declined in nearly all the other states. Since the chairman's death in 1975, however, factionalism between liberal and conservative Democrats has grown intense, and discipline has unraveled. Connecticut is no less a Democratic state than it was in Bailey's day, but contention is now the essence of Democratic politics.

The state House is the forum for the Democrats' intra-party disputes. The margin of Democratic control in the House — only 23 votes — means that conservative Democrats, though they are a minority in their party caucus, can quash liberal initiatives by threatening to team with the Republicans.

Labor-Business Battle

In the Legislature's 1983 session, a classic labor vs. business dispute pointed out the ideological rivalries within the Democratic Party. Labor pushed for a bill that would require a company to notify employees a year in advance if it planned to relocate or make layoffs. The notification bill was strongly supported by liberals in the House, including House Speaker Irving J. Stolberg, a geography professor who represents a district in New Haven, the state's third-largest city.

Pitted against Stolberg and the liberals was House Majority Leader John G. Groppo, a building contractor from a largely rural district in northwestern Connecticut. He and other fiscally conservative Democrats argued that passage of the notification bill would send an anti-business signal that might discourage companies from coming to Connecticut, thereby limiting future job opportunities.

That view was shared by one of the state's most influential lobby groups, the Connecticut Business and Industry Association (CBIA), which speaks for chambers of commerce, retailers and manufacturers such as United Technologies, Xerox, Union Carbide and others with headquarters or branch operations in Connecticut. (The state's powerful insurance industry has its own lobbying association.)

Groppo and his allies managed to get the bill referred to a committee where they knew it faced stiff opposition, and the measure died there. At that point, Democratic Gov. William A. O'Neill, who opposed the labor position, offered a watered-down alternative that unions grudgingly accepted even though it contained only a small part of what they wanted.

O'Neill's behavior in the notification issue is a fairly typical example of the way he governs. Not a bold innovator, he often lets competing interests flail at each other over controversial matters before he steps in to propose a compromise. That approach stems partly from his cautious nature and partly from his belief that legislators should have a chance to haggle over issues without premature meddling by the governor. His outlook reflects the 12 years he spent in the state House (four as majority leader) before becoming lieutenant governor in 1979.

When O'Neill does take a firm stand, his kinship with

STATE LEADERSHIP

Gov. William A. O'Neill (D)

Born: Aug. 11, 1930, Hartford, Conn.
Home: East Hampton, Conn.
Education: Attended New Britain
    Teachers College; U. of Hartford.
Military Career: Air Force, 1950-53.
Occupation: Restaurateur.
Family: Wife, Natalie Damon.
Religion: Roman Catholic.
Political Career: Conn. House, 1967-
    79, majority leader, 1975-79;
    lieutenant governor, 1979-80;
    became governor Dec. 31, 1980 when
    Gov. Ella T. Grasso resigned due to
    ill health; elected governor 1982;
    term expires January 1987.

GENERAL ASSEMBLY

SENATE
23D, 13R

James J. Murphy Jr. (D)
President pro tem

HOUSE
87D, 64R

Irving J. Stolberg (D)
Speaker

the more conservative element of the Democratic Party is usually evident. That is clearly the case in the issue that has been the centerpiece of Connecticut politics for years: the state income tax. Connecticut does not have one, and one of O'Neill's most important 1982 campaign themes was his pledge to oppose any effort to impose one.

His stand would not have been unusual in past years, because both parties, fearing the wrath of voters, traditionally have shunned the income tax. But a growing number of Democrats and some Republicans argued during the 1983 legislative session that the current patchwork of taxes on a wide range of commodities and transactions — sales, property, gasoline, cigarettes and professional services, to name a few — will not pay for basic needs such as education and highway and bridge maintenance.

A majority of Democrats in both the House and the Senate endorsed an income tax, and a March 1983 survey by the University of Connecticut's Institute for Social Inquiry found about two-thirds of those polled favoring an income tax if other taxes were reduced.

But there are strong constituencies that remain opposed to an income tax. Those include affluent residents of Fairfield County, many of them corporate executives who fled New York because of its income tax, and a sizable bloc of middle-class people in rural areas, factory towns and city neighborhoods who fear that imposition of an income tax will touch off a binge of government spending. O'Neill has not budged from his opposition to an income tax, and he has been backed up by conservatives in both parties.

Poor Cities, Wealthy Suburbs

The urban-suburban conflict in Connecticut is sharper than in many states, partly because there is a wide disparity of wealth between some of the state's cities and the residential areas surrounding them. In the capital city of Hartford, for example, about one-fourth of the population is below the official poverty level.

One of the current urban struggles against the suburbs is the dispute over the amount of aid the state sends to local schools under the Guaranteed Tax Base (GTB) program. Cities rely heavily on GTB funds because their low-income populations cannot afford a property tax high enough to meet education costs. In the suburbs, property taxes bring in so much revenue that there is comparatively little need for GTB money.

As a cost-cutting move, O'Neill in early 1983 proposed committing less money to the GTB program than had been pledged when the program was established five years ago. Urban representatives fumed that children in their districts were being condemned to receive inferior schooling. But their demands for full funding went unheeded.

Though the Democrats are riven with internal bickering, the grip on state government they have enjoyed for most of the past 30 years has slipped very little. Since 1970, the only Republican to win election to a statewide office has been U.S. Sen. Lowell P. Weicker Jr. He has quarreled with the party leadership, which has been dominated by conservatives. But there are signs that the GOP is now interested in projecting a more moderate image in hopes of improving its electoral fortunes.

In the Legislature, the Republican leaders in both chambers — Rep. R. E. Van Norstrand and Sen. Philip S. Robertson — have gone out of their way to court labor, telling union lobbyists that the GOP cannot hope to become the majority party without more working-class support.

A PROFILE OF

Connecticut

PEOPLE

Total Population: 3,107,576 (25th).
  White 90%, Black 7%, Asian and
  Pacific Islander 1%. Spanish origin 4%.

Urban:	79%
Rural:	21%
Born in state:	58%
Foreign-born:	9%

MAJOR CITIES

Bridgeport (142,546), Hartford (136,392),
  New Haven (126,109), Waterbury
  (103,266), Stamford (102,453)

LAND

Farm	16%
Forest	60%
Federally owned	1%

WORK

Occupations: 58% white-collar; 30% blue-collar; 11% service workers

Government workers:	20,100 federal
	57,527 state
	107,700 local

Unemployment rate: 6%

MONEY

Median family income (1980)	$23,149	(2nd)
Tax burden per capita (1982)	$753	(18th)

EDUCATION

Spending per pupil through grade 12	$2,683	(16th)
Persons with college degrees	21%	(3rd)

CRIME

Violent crime rate: 448 per 100,000 (22nd)

POLITICS

1980 Presidential Vote: Reagan 48%,
  Carter 39%, Anderson 12%

Turnout rate in 1980:	68%
Turnout rate in 1982:	54%

U.S. House Delegation: 4D, 2R

DELAWARE:

Business Interests Dominant In Democratic Legislature

The Delaware Legislature has a reputation as a place where business interests nearly always win. It is, after all, the body that enacted the liberal incorporation laws under which half the "*Fortune* 500" corporations chose to make the state their official headquarters. The bills it passes go

on to the desk of popular Republican Gov. Pierre S. "Pete" du Pont IV, whose family business has dominated Delaware's economy for much of this century.

But business interests are not monolithic in Delaware, and they do not always have a single set of legislative goals. In 1983, that point was reinforced when the governor strongly supported a measure that would have allowed banks to sell insurance. On that he had the active help of Irving S. Shapiro, former chairman of the board of Du Pont. But the bill created a split between the banking industry and insurance companies, and the insurance faction turned out to be stronger. The bill was withdrawn.

In recent years, business has won some notable victories in Delaware politics. Among them have been a 1981 law lifting usury ceilings on loan interest rates and another providing tax incentives for large banking operations. These initiatives prompted several large banks to locate in the state. On the other hand, Delaware has some of the strictest coastal zoning laws in the country, despite complaints by some industries that they hinder development.

The Legislature is firmly Democratic, despite its business ties, and labor support is crucial to the Democratic Party. John Campanelli, the former head of the state AFL-CIO who was elected to the state House, kept his union presidency for two years after his 1980 election. Perhaps

the strongest supporter of organized labor in the Legislature is Senate Majority Leader Thomas Sharp, a former sheet metal worker.

But organized labor's victories are usually defensive. Union backers in the Legislature have succeeded in blocking repeated attempts to impose a "right-to-work" law, as well as a concerted effort to weaken the state's workmen's compensation law. Labor's allies succeeded in boosting the state's unemployment compensation.

Many of the anti-labor initiatives have come from the southern part of the state, which, though Democratic, more closely resembles Maryland's conservative Eastern Shore than it does the Wilmington area. Its customs and political habits are similar in many ways to those of the South, and it did not undertake the integration of its elementary schools until the late 1950s. George Wallace won nearly 20 percent of the vote there in 1968.

Members from the southern part of the state tend to have long careers in the Legislature, learn the levers of power and stick together for advantage. But the Democratic leadership also includes people such as Sharp from the northern part of the state.

Du Pont Budget Victory

At the start of the 1983 session, du Pont's effectiveness seemed to be in question. Constitutionally unable to run for a third term in 1984, he was a lame duck, which threatened his influence over the Legislature. Moreover, the 1982 elections turned a nine-vote Republican majority in the House into a nine-vote Democratic majority, so that Republican du Pont faced a Legislature in which both chambers were controlled by Democrats.

He proposed a bare-bones budget, recommending no pay increase for public employees and no tax increases. Labor backers and liberals seeking increases for social programs vowed to fight him. But at the end of the session, he saw his budget pass almost intact. The Legislature approved the pay freeze, and passed no tax increase.

Du Pont's success in 1983 and throughout his six years in office can be attributed to several factors, both institutional and political. Traditionally, the Delaware Legislature plays an "advise and consent" role on state budget matters, waiting to act until after the governor submits his proposal. Then, the 10-member Joint Finance Committee

---

STATE LEADERSHIP

Gov. Pierre S. "Pete" du Pont IV (R)

Born: Jan. 22, 1935, Wilmington, Del.
Home: Rockdale, Del.
Education: Princeton U., B.S.E. 1956;
    Harvard Law School, LL.B. 1963.
Military Career: Navy, 1957-60.
Occupation: Lawyer.
Family: Wife, Elise Wood; four children.
Religion: Episcopalian.
Political Career: Del. House, 1969-71;
    U.S. House, 1971-77; elected
    governor 1976, 1980; term expires
    Jan. 1985.

GENERAL ASSEMBLY

SENATE
13D, 8R

Richard S. Cordrey (D)
President pro tem

HOUSE
24D, 17R

Orlando J. George Jr. (D)
Speaker

Sen. Richard S. Cordrey   Rep. Orlando J. George Jr.

amends the governor's proposal, rather than writing its own. The joint committee's product rarely is amended on the floor.

It would have been difficult in 1983 for the Legislature to approve a budget substantially different from that which du Pont had recommended. A three-fifths majority is required to pass a tax increase, so Democrats would have had to hold all their members in both chambers or attract one Republican for each Democratic defector in order to defy the governor.

Similarly, it takes a three-fifths vote to override a veto. The last time the Legislature overrode a gubernatorial veto was in 1977, du Pont's first year in office, when the Legislature passed a budget over du Pont's objections.

Besides the institutional factors in du Pont's favor, he also has several political advantages. A winner in statewide political contests since 1970, du Pont is perhaps the state's most popular politician. After some initial skirmishes in his first term, du Pont seems to have attracted a high degree of support from legislators of both parties. No governor in recent times has been able to match his influence over the Legislature on budget matters.

Cohesive Legislative Leadership

On issues other than the budget, however, du Pont has more problems. Non-budget legislation can be moved by simple majority, and because bills are considered on the floor without being referred to committee, power is centralized in the Democratic leadership in both houses.

The current leadership — Sharp and President Pro Tem Richard S. Cordrey in the Senate and Speaker Orlando J. George Jr. and Majority Leader Robert F. Gilligan in the House — has worked together in the Legislature for a long time and bring an unusual cohesion to the Capitol.

Early in his first term, du Pont recognized that he needed to work with the Democrats, and the Democrats recognized that they needed to work with him. Democratic opposition has been muted. The governor's most persistent liberal critic, Sen. Harris B. McDowell III, has argued for years that the Democrats should present an alternative program. But McDowell's has been a lonely voice.

Nevertheless, the Democratic leadership has succeeded in blocking several of the governor's non-budget initiatives. Several key appointments await action in the Senate. The head of the Department of Elections, for example, is still a Democrat; the governor has been unable to put his own person in that post in six years in office. ∎

A PROFILE OF

Delaware

PEOPLE

Total Population: 594,338 (47th).
  White 82%, Black 16%, Asian and
  Pacific Islander 1%. Spanish origin 2%.

Urban:	71%
Rural:	29%
Born in state:	52%
Foreign-born:	3%

MAJOR CITIES

Wilmington (70,195), Newark (25,247), Dover (23,512), Elsmere (6,493), Milford (5,356)

LAND

Farm	53%
Forest	32%
Federally owned	3%

WORK

Occupations: 55% white-collar; 29% blue-collar; 13% service workers

Government workers:	4,800 federal
	18,354 state
	17,177 local
Unemployment rate:	8%

MONEY

Median family income (1980)	$20,817	(17th)
Tax burden per capita (1982)	$1,001	(4th)

EDUCATION

Spending per pupil through grade 12	$3,125	(5th)
Persons with college degrees	18%	(17th)

CRIME

Violent crime rate: 509 per 100,000 (18th)

POLITICS

1980 Presidential Vote: Reagan 47%, Carter 45%, Anderson 7%

Turnout rate in 1980:	60%
Turnout rate in 1982:	51%

U.S. House Delegation: 1D

FLORIDA:

Myriad of Interests Compete For Power in New Megastate

Florida's skill at promoting itself as paradise is unsurpassed — the state's booming growth rate testifies to that. But the rapid influx of people and businesses has created new demands so pressing that state leaders have been compelled to launch a different sort of public relations crusade — persuading people that their paradise has problems that demand higher taxes and more state spending.

Generating and dispensing revenue breeds controversy in any state. But the conflict is especially complicated in fast-growing Florida, where the political landscape has changed dramatically in the past generation and myriad interest groups clamor with roughly equal voices.

It is true that business has enjoyed a special status in Florida in the past; one of the cornerstones of the state's growth has been its success at luring employers south by dangling the enticements of a right-to-work law, low labor costs and modest tax rates. But in the 1983 legislative session, lawmakers imposed a tax (called a "unitary tax") on profits earned by Florida companies on overseas operations. Passage of that tax, which in 1984 was expected to bring in nearly $100 million from multinationals operating in Florida, was a clear sign that business does not enjoy a sacrosanct position. Democratic Gov. Robert Graham supported the measure.

Debates over whether and how taxes should be raised and who should get state money feature a wide array of competing voices — retirees, high-tech manufacturers, the phosphate mining industry, Hispanics, citrus agribusinesses, the tourism industry, boosters of Florida's cities and defenders of the rural Panhandle.

Sunshine and Pork Chops

Added into this maelstrom of competing influences is the assertive and unusual Florida Legislature. It is a strange blend of innovation and tradition, a reflection of the fact that although Florida is a megastate — one of the 10 most populous states — moving toward national prominence, it retains remnants of its era as a sleepy Southern state ruled by a clique of rural legislators.

On the innovation side of the ledger, the Legislature's 1967 "sunshine" law was a pioneer in the field of open government legislation. Its 1976 "sunset" law helped spur a national movement to require government to assess the effectiveness of agencies and programs. The leadership structure is more fluid than in many states — both the House and Senate install new leaders every two years.

The press in Florida plays a more influential role in state politics than is the case in many other states, and its orientation is to the "reform" position. The state has a number of prosperous and widely scattered cities that have spawned aggressive newspapers such as *The Miami Herald*, the *St. Petersburg Times* and the *Orlando Sentinel Star*, which compete vigorously for pre-eminence in reporting government affairs. With so many reporters' ears listening in, legislators' backroom deals that go unreported in some other states become public knowledge in Florida.

Yet coexisting with these progressive influences are characteristics that call to mind the heyday of the "Pork Chop Gang," the rural legislative clique that malapportioned the Legislature to favor its own interests at the expense of the fast-growing cities. The embodiment of that era in today's Legislature is Sen. Dempsey Barron, a conservative Democrat from the Panhandle who has served in the Legislature for 27 years, longer than any other member.

Barron was president of the Senate in 1975-76, and in subsequent years he has continued as the key tactician for the conservative Democrats and Republicans who sometimes combine to exert their will. When state and national advocates of the Equal Rights Amendment poured into Tallahassee to press their cause in 1982, they ran into Barron; his opposition to the ERA was instrumental in the Senate's rejection of the measure.

Liberals have groused for years about how the Senate defeats or bottles up bills that pass the House, but the ideological tilt of the upper chamber may be shifting. Re-

---

STATE LEADERSHIP

Gov. Robert Graham (D)

Born: Nov. 9, 1936, Coral Gables, Fla.
Home: Miami Lakes, Fla.
Education: U. of Fla., B.A. 1959;
    Harvard Law School, LL.B. 1962.
Occupation: Developer.
Family: Wife, Adele Khoury; four
    children.
Religion: United Church of Christ.
Political Career: Fla. House, 1967-71;
    Fla. Senate, 1971-78; elected
    governor 1978, 1982; term expires
    Jan. 1987.

LEGISLATURE

SENATE

32D, 8R

Curtis Peterson (D)
President

HOUSE

84D, 36R

H. Lee Moffitt (D)
Speaker

apportionment following the 1980 census established single-member legislative districts for the first time in Florida. Combined with the anti-Republican mood in the 1982 election, that step brought significant changes in the membership of the Senate. Two blacks won seats; before 1982, no black had served in the Senate since Reconstruction. Republicans lost five seats, reducing the strength of the bipartisan conservative coalition. In all, one-third of the current senators are freshmen.

The Senate's 1985 leadership — already chosen under the chamber's traditional practice of anointing leaders in advance of the term in which they serve — will be considerably more liberal than the 1983 group. Several of the incoming leaders were instrumental in passage of the unitary tax.

Early in his first gubernatorial term, which began in 1979, Graham at times seemed befuddled by the task of refereeing fights among the various interest groups and selling his ideas to the strong-minded Legislature. On one occasion he proposed a gasoline tax increase, then withdrew it when powerful lawmakers complained. The move prompted some critics to call him "Governor Jell-O."

But Graham has become more forceful in dealing with the Legislature. Many trace the governor's maturation to the influence of his chief legislative lobbyist, Charlie Reed, who has a direct, no-nonsense style. Graham pushed through a package of criminal justice laws in 1982, and his decisive re-election victory later that year emboldened him to propose sweeping tax increases in 1983.

Education Funding Fight

In 1983, there was a protracted struggle over Graham's foremost priority — raising more tax money to boost Florida's low-ranking education system. That fight demonstrated that even though modern-day Florida cherishes the concept of open government, the task of finding revenue to deal with the state's problems demands some old-fashioned political horse-trading.

The central element of Graham's education package was a generous pay raise for all teachers, a group that has strongly supported him at the polls. House Speaker H. Lee Moffitt of Tampa wanted merit pay for teachers and higher corporate taxes to finance the entire education package, two very controversial ideas. Republicans and conservative House Democrats balked at Moffitt's proposal.

The Legislature's regular session failed to reach a compromise suitable to Graham, so he called a special session and proposed raising a large chunk of the money for education from the unitary tax on corporations. That plan raised a howl from the Associated Industries of Florida (AIF), business' premier lobby group in the state. Influential AIF lobbyist Jon L. Shebel flew in representatives from several multinational corporations to argue against the tax.

But Graham unabashedly used the clout of his office, promising money for legislators' pet projects to garner support and warning opponents that he would cut off funds for projects they wanted. Graham was so aggressive in his deal-making that some called him "the Monty Hall of Tallahassee."

The deal that secured Graham's victory came in a 2 a.m. session at a Howard Johnson's restaurant on the day the special session opened. Meeting there with representatives of the Dade County (Miami) House delegation, Graham agreed to give Dade greater flexbility in allocating its education money, and they agreed to support the unitary tax. ∎

A PROFILE OF

Florida

PEOPLE

Total Population: 9,746,324 (7th).
  White 84%, Black 14%, Asian and
  Pacific Islander 1%. Spanish origin 9%.

Urban:	84%
Rural:	16%
Born in state:	31%
Foreign-born:	11%

MAJOR CITIES

Jacksonville (540,920), Miami (346,865), Tampa (271,523), St. Petersburg (238,647), Fort Lauderdale (153,279)

LAND

Farm	38%
Forest	49%
Federally owned	11%

WORK

Occupations: 55% white-collar; 27% blue-collar; 15% service workers

Government workers: 83,888 federal
  122,070 state
  399,225 local

Unemployment rate: 9%

MONEY

Median family income (1980)	$17,280	(39th)
Tax burden per capita (1982)	$570	(41st)

EDUCATION

Spending per pupil through grade 12	$2,276	(26th)
Persons with college degrees	15%	(29th)

CRIME

Violent crime rate: 965 per 100,000 (2nd)

POLITICS

1980 Presidential Vote: Reagan 56%, Carter 39%, Anderson 5%

Turnout rate in 1980:	56%
Turnout rate in 1982:	41%

U.S. House Delegation: 13D, 6R

GEORGIA:

Urban Forces Gain Share Of Traditional Rural Power

There is a balance to Georgia politics today that would have been unthinkable a generation ago. In the 1950s, governors such as Herman E. Talmadge and Marvin Griffin exercised freewheeling power over a Legislature totally dominated by rural interests. Georgia's current governor rules in concert with a Legislature whose rural, urban and suburban voting blocs have to pay close attention to each other's needs.

There are still a few vestiges of the old days. Both Gov. Joe Frank Harris and House Speaker Thomas B. Murphy are veterans of legislative politicking with roots in the traditions of rural white Georgia.

But both of these Democrats have been willing to move beyond their original constituencies. A non-drinker who allows nothing stronger than cooking sherry to be used in the governor's mansion, Harris pushed forcefully in 1983 for stiff legislation to curb drunken driving, an issue that has been promoted mainly by suburban and urban dwellers. Murphy, who resisted Harris' drunken driving bill, has given important backing to the Metropolitan Atlanta Rapid Transit Authority (MARTA) in its struggles to ensure itself adequate funding for expansion.

Murphy has been the dominant presence in the Legislature since 1974, when he succeeded the legendary George L. Smith, who was credited with being the architect of Georgia's independent Legislature. With the ability to appoint members and chairmen of House committees and to decide whether legislation will reach the floor, Murphy has influence over the House that his counterpart in the Senate, Lt. Gov. Zell Miller, is unable to match. A blunt and emotional man, Murphy has built a reputation for vindictiveness when he is crossed, but he has won praise as an effective and generally fair mediator of the competing factions in the Legislature.

Harmonious Austerity

Harris, who was a Murphy protégé during his own career in the House, kept his relations with the Legislature remarkably smooth during his first months in office in 1983. Part of the reason lay in his familiarity with the budget process, which he dealt with during eight years as chairman of the House Appropriations Committee. Having pledged during his campaign to avoid any tax increases, Harris made the austere budget that he submitted in January the centerpiece of the three-month legislative session. With the help of former colleagues anxious to be accommodating, he steered through relatively intact a budget allowing only 5 percent growth in spending. He even won the reluctant support of urban liberals anxious to make up for cuts in federal spending on social programs.

But critics complain that the Legislature is harmonious these days mainly because Harris — unlike predecessors such as Jimmy Carter, who launched a massive reorganization of state government during his one term (1971-75) — has avoided meaningful legislative initiatives. They say the House leadership is running the state. Although strong public pressure for drunken driving legislation prevented Murphy from killing Harris' bill, for example, the Speaker was able to water it down. Later, when Harris tried to move a bill to give state prosecutors more leeway in rejecting prospective jurors, Murphy, a defense lawyer, refused to allow the bill through.

One of the more important legislative actions of Harris' first year has come from the House leadership by way of the Ways and Means Committee. Under the control of Democrat Marcus E. Collins, a rural legislator of the old school, the committee pushed through a resolution amending the state constitution to shift financing for education from the state property tax to the state sales tax. The measure also raised the sales tax to 4 percent from 3 percent, while rolling back the property tax.

Metropolitan area legislators, who contend that their constituents will bear an unfair portion of the tax burden if

STATE LEADERSHIP

Gov. Joe Frank Harris (D)

Born: Feb. 16, 1936, Atco, Ga.
Home: Cartersville, Ga.
Education: U. of Ga., B.B.A. 1958.
Military Career: Army.
Occupation: Industrial development executive.
Family: Wife, Elizabeth Carlock; one child.
Religion: Methodist.
Political Career: Ga. House, 1965-83; elected governor, 1982; term expires Jan. 1987.

GENERAL ASSEMBLY

SENATE

49D, 7R

Joe Kennedy (D)
President pro tem

HOUSE

156D, 24R

Thomas B. Murphy (D)
Speaker

the legislation passes, had in the past successfully blocked it. But they worried that opposition to Collins and his rural allies would doom their efforts to increase the state's hotel/motel tax and to pass legislation refinancing MARTA. So they held back in committee, and then split on the House floor, allowing the bill to pass by five votes more than the two-thirds necessary. Whether the legislation will survive the Senate intact in the 1984 legislative session is unclear.

Atlanta's Clout

Such maneuvering among rural, urban and suburban factions is relatively new in the Georgia Legislature. The iron grip in which rural legislators held it began to loosen only after federal courts forced the state to reapportion itself in the 1960s, allowing metropolitan Atlanta and other cities to acquire legislative seats in accordance with their proportion of the state's population.

As the Atlanta metro area has grown to hold close to 40 percent of the state's voters, its clout in the state House in particular has grown accordingly. A sign of the change came when the "urban caucus," the formal means by which urban and suburban legislators agitated against rural control, broke down as its members moved from being outside critics of the leadership into positions of power in their own right. Meanwhile, as suburbanites have come to see their interests as distinct from those of the cities, the once solid "metropolitan" bloc has split on issues such as property taxes and social spending.

Another byproduct of the rise in metropolitan strength has been a slow growth in the influence of blacks in the Legislature. The first black legislator of the century took office in 1963; and the House now includes 21 blacks, and the Senate four. Their chief means of attempting to influence legislation is the Black Caucus, organized in the late 1960s by Rep. Julian Bond, now a state senator. Under the more recent leadership of state Sen. Al Scott, D-Savannah, the caucus has begun to use a whip system in the House to influence white legislators representing districts with large black populations. In 1980, caucus members succeeded in organizing the electoral defeat of a hostile white colleague, although the caucus has been slow in adopting that tactic with others.

Several members of the Black Caucus were close to Harris during his time in the House. Some two-thirds of them supported his gubernatorial bid, and blacks are hoping to parlay those ties into increased legislative clout on issues such as funding for education and social welfare programs. ∎

A PROFILE OF

Georgia

PEOPLE

Total Population: 5,463,105 (13th).
White 72%, Black 27%. Spanish origin 1%.

Urban:	62%
Rural:	38%
Born in state:	71%
Foreign-born:	2%

MAJOR CITIES

Atlanta (425,022), Columbus (169,441), Savannah (141,390), Macon (116,896), Albany (74,059)

LAND

Farm	42%
Forest	68%
Federally owned	6%

WORK

Occupations: 50% white-collar; 35% blue-collar; 12% service workers

Government workers: 77,882 federal
85,823 state
240,429 local

Unemployment rate: 7%

MONEY

Median family income (1980)	$17,414	(37th)
Tax burden per capita (1982)	$601	(37th)

EDUCATION

Spending per pupil through grade 12	$1,721	(48th)
Persons with college degrees	15%	(32nd)

CRIME

Violent crime rate: 548 per 100,000 (14th)

POLITICS

1980 Presidential Vote: Carter 56%, Reagan 41%, Anderson 2%

Turnout rate in 1980:	54%
Turnout rate in 1982:	39%

U.S. House Delegation: 9D, 1R

HAWAII:

Ethnically Diverse Electorate Creates Democratic Bastion

The same factor that made Hawaii a Republican state in its territorial days — GOP kinship to the Caucasian business community — has made it a Democratic state ever since. Burdened by their image as the party of the state's pineapple and sugar growers, Republicans have never been able to reach out to the Japanese, Chinese, Filipino and native Hawaiian voters who now hold the balance of power in state politics. As a result, Democrats reign virtually unchallenged.

The Democratic Party has held both houses of the Legislature continuously since 1963; Hawaii has not elected a Republican governor since statehood. Over the last two decades, only Rhode Island has rivaled Hawaii's loyalty to the Democratic Party.

The father of modern Democratic dominance in Hawaii was Gov. John A. Burns (1962-73). He pushed hard to engender an ethnic balance in state politics, and built the foundations of an influential party organization. The heir to the Burns organization is Gov. George Ariyoshi, the first Japanese-American elected governor of any state. His continuous service since 1973 (when he became acting governor upon Burns' disability) makes Ariyoshi the nation's senior chief executive.

Despite his lengthy tenure, Ariyoshi is not a particularly powerful leader. Soft-spoken and sometimes aloof, he seldom tries to ride herd over the Legislature. Hawaii law bestows upon the governor considerable discretionary power over the budget, but Ariyoshi often has appeared reluctant to use it.

Ariyoshi has responded firmly to downturns in state revenues, imposing limits on state agency spending for the 1983 fiscal year. But he has had less success over the past several sessions convincing the Legislature to pass his Functional Plans, which are detailed blueprints for the state's future development.

Discord Among Democrats

Opposition to Ariyoshi's Functional Plans is focused in the Hawaii Senate, a body rife with independent-minded members who often have trouble reaching any consensus on how to deal with the state's problems. The discord was evident during the opening session of the 12th Legislature in 1983, when intraparty squabbling rocked the upper chamber.

A dispute over budget proposals put forth by some Senate committees triggered a division in the Democratic ranks. Complaining that leadership figures had made changes in those budget recommendations without consulting the committees, a group of six maverick Democrats sought to oust the chairman of the Ways and Means Committee. Senate President Richard S. H. Wong viewed the move as a threat to his leadership, and stripped the six of key committee assignments and chairmanships.

Considered a maverick himself at the outset of his legislative career, Wong rose to prominence in the Senate by attacking its old guard. Proclaiming the need for a "new politics," he criticized then-President John T. Ushijima for holding power too closely, and urged that influence in the chamber be spread around.

The dissidents, led by Sens. Benjamin J. Cayetano and Neil Abercrombie, both of Oahu, were former Wong allies. But they now claim that Wong has betrayed his earlier promises of open, decentralized government, and

---

STATE LEADERSHIP

Gov. George Ariyoshi (D)

Born: March 12, 1926, Honolulu, Hawaii.
Home: Honolulu, Hawaii.
Education: Mich. State U., B.A. 1949; U. of Mich., J.D. 1952.
Military Career: Army, 1945-46.
Occupation: Lawyer.
Family: Wife, Jean Hayashi; three children.
Religion: Protestant.
Political Career: Hawaii territorial House, 1954-58; territorial Senate, 1958-59; Hawaii Senate 1959-70, majority leader, 1965-66, 1969-70; lieutenant governor, 1970-73; acting governor, 1973-74; elected governor 1974, 1978, 1982; term expires Dec. 1986.

LEGISLATURE

SENATE

20D, 5R

Richard S. H. Wong (D)
President

HOUSE

43D, 8R

Henry Haalilio Peters (D)
Speaker

has taken up the very brand of secretive, patronage politics he once attacked.

Things are more placid in the House, where Speaker Henry Haalilio Peters enjoys practically undisputed control. A low-key leader without prominent ideological convictions, Peters benefits from a heavy Democratic majority and the lack of any enduring factions. He also has few senior colleagues to worry about. Roughly 40 percent of the House membership turned over in the 1982 elections, and the current floor and majority leaders both were newly selected for their positions in 1983.

The Republican Party in Hawaii has shrunk virtually into oblivion. Hurt by redistricting and the decision of two leading GOP legislators to seek other office, Republicans saw their ranks depleted in the 1982 elections to five seats from eight seats in the 25-member Senate and to eight seats from 12 seats in the 51-member House.

Before 1982, the existence of a bipartisan coalition in the Senate gave Republicans a piece of the political action. But that coalition has since dissolved, and the 1983 GOP support for the dissident Senate Democrats yielded no improvement in the minority party's fortunes.

Republican leaders hope the state's Reapportionment Commission will improve their prospects for the future. A court-imposed redistricting plan replaced Hawaii's traditional multi-member district system with single-member districts in 1982, a step that made it even harder for Republicans to win than in past years. The GOP is counting on the commission to restore the old arrangement, under which Republicans could finish behind their Democratic opponents and still win one of several seats in a given district.

Ethnic Politics

While the Democrats' grip on state politics has grown tighter, power among Hawaii's diverse ethnic groups is growing more diffuse. Caucasians (called *haoles*) still hold the economic reins, and Japanese-Americans, bolstered by strong voter turnout, continue to have a disproportionate share of statewide political power. But Japanese dominance is hardly absolute. House Speaker Peters is an ethnic Hawaiian, and the election of a significant number of Filipinos in the 1982 House freshman class bodes well for further ethnic diversification in state government.

Relations between the various communities generally have been good; Hawaii prides itself on maintaining a spirit of racial harmony. That spirit has been tested, however, by the demands of ethnic Hawaiians in recent years for greater political and economic clout.

Although Caucasian corporate interests no longer maintain an iron grip on Hawaii's economy, several of the original companies still exercise substantial influence. Castle & Cooke and Alexander & Baldwin remain powerful spokesmen for the pineapple and sugar industries; they often join forces with financial interests based in downtown Honolulu's Merchant Street to lobby against land-use planning laws they view as obstacles to development.

But the most prominent interest group in postwar Hawaii has been the International Longshoremen's and Warehousemen's Union (ILWU). Organizing the majority of the state's crop workers, the ILWU traditionally has maintained close ties to legislators from Hawaii's outlying "neighbor islands." But slumps in the sugar and pineapple industries — together with a general shift in power toward the Honolulu area — have combined to chip away at the group's muscle.

A PROFILE OF

Hawaii

PEOPLE

Total Population: 964,691 (39th). White 33%, Black 2%, Asian and Pacific Islander 61%. Spanish origin 7%.

Urban:	87%
Rural:	13%
Born in state:	58%
Foreign-born:	14%

MAJOR CITIES

Honolulu (365,048), Pearl City (42,575), Kailua (35,812), Hilo (35,269), Aiea (32,879)

LAND

Farm	48%
Forest	48%
Federally owned	19%

WORK

Occupations: 56% white-collar; 23% blue-collar; 18% service workers

Government workers: 26,050 federal 45,959 state 12,344 local

Unemployment rate: 7%

MONEY

Median family income (1980)	$22,750	(5th)
Tax burden per capita (1982)	$1,105	(3rd)

EDUCATION

Spending per pupil through grade 12	$2,604	(19th)
Persons with college degrees	20%	(5th)

CRIME

Violent crime rate: 248 per 100,000 (40th)

POLITICS

1980 Presidential Vote: Carter 45%, Reagan 43%, Anderson 11%

Turnout rate in 1980:	56%
Turnout rate in 1982:	54%

U.S. House Delegation: 2D

IDAHO:

Moderate Republican Faction At Center of Power Balance

Despite overwhelming Republican majorities in the Legislature, Idaho is currently something of a three-party state.

The GOP is plagued by deep divisions, especially in the state House, and moderate Republican members have positioned themselves as swing votes willing at times to form legislative coalitions with the Democrats.

This coalition group, aided by Democratic Gov. John V. Evans, has been able to push forward numerous proposals that the conservative Republican leadership has opposed. In the face of a substantial deficit in 1983, the Legislature approved an increase in spending for education, which is one of Evans' priorities.

To reduce the deficit, Evans proposed a one-cent increase in the state sales tax. The conservative Republicans immediately rejected his suggestion, insisting that the governor should cut spending instead. But when the smoke cleared, the two sides reached a compromise — the governor won his tax increase, but it will be rolled back if the Legislature fails to renew it.

The moderate GOP bloc in the House has the advantage of being well-placed in the committee system. Rep. Steve Antone, regarded as the leader of the moderates, chairs the Revenue and Taxation Committee. Another moderate leader, Kathleen W. Gurnsey, is co-chairman of the Appropriations Committee, a joint House-Senate panel that has seen the vast majority of its bills in the last several years pass with few changes.

Still, in many cases the conservatives have the upper hand. Senate Majority Leader Mark G. Ricks, besides serving as the floor leader, sits on the Finance Committee, which draws up the budget. And although committee chairmen have a good deal of autonomy, the floor agenda is set by the conservative leadership.

Shrewd Use of Veto

Evans' role is crucial. Unable to initiate much legislation because of his minority status, the governor has been able to get some of what he wants by making shrewd use of his veto powers. Although Senate Republicans are much more cohesive — and more conservative — than those in the House, their majority is not large enough to override gubernatorial vetoes. Once an Evans veto is upheld, the Legislature is forced to rewrite legislation to make it more to his liking.

Evans is only the third Idaho governor to take the oath of office for a third time. In 1977, he was named acting governor to fill the unexpired term of Cecil D. Andrus, who left to become secretary of the interior. In 1978, Evans was elected to his first full term, and in 1982 he was narrowly re-elected.

Largely because of their small numbers, Democrats in the Legislature are generally a cohesive group. House Minority Leader Mel Hammond, a 16-year veteran, can usually count on his caucus to vote with him when he needs it. Partisanship in the Senate, however, has been muted in recent years.

Besides the ideological division, the Legislature frequently splits along rural-urban lines. When that split occurs, the rural side usually wins, as it has in recent years on water use issues. Another such division is on education; urban legislators of both parties tend to favor more spending for schools than do those from rural areas.

Another important aspect of Idaho politics is the long-standing rivalry between the northern and southern sec-

---

STATE LEADERSHIP

Gov. John V. Evans (D)

Born: Jan. 18, 1925, Malad City, Idaho.
Home: Malad City, Idaho.
Education: Stanford U., B.A. 1951.
Military Career: Army, 1945-46.
Occupation: Farmer; rancher.
Family: Wife, Lola Daniels; five children.
Religion: Mormon.
Political Career: Idaho Senate, 1953-59, 1967-75; mayor, Malad City, 1960-66; lieutenant governor, 1975-77; assumed governorship Jan. 1977 upon the appointment of Gov. Cecil Andrus as secretary of the interior; elected governor 1978, 1982; term expires Jan. 1987.

LEGISLATURE

SENATE
14D, 21R

James Risch (R)
President pro tem

HOUSE
19D, 51R

Tom W. Stivers (R)
Speaker

tions of the state. The two regions are distinctly different: The south is mainly irrigated farm land, with a conservative Mormon population. The northern panhandle, by contrast, is mainly mountains, forests, lakes and mines, with few Mormons and many Democrats. Most of the Democrats in the Legislature come from northern Idaho.

These two diverse regions rarely find much to agree about at the polls, but Evans has been politically successful largely because he can appeal to both areas — he is a Mormon from southern Idaho and a Democrat as well. That was Evans' victory formula in 1982, when he faced a challenge from Republican Lt. Gov. Philip Batt.

Evans ignited a political debate over a geographical issue in 1983, when he vetoed a bill allowing election officials to release results in statewide elections as soon as they are available. Democrats in the north, in the Pacific time zone, were worried that early returns from the south, in Mountain time, showing Republican victories would influence potential Democrats in northern counties not to go to the polls at the end of the day.

Rep. Tom W. Stivers

One of the most important alliances for conservative Republicans in Idaho is with private power companies. Three major power companies serve the state, and they have been successful in pushing for dams, rate increases, and favorable tax rates. Other major businesses have formed the Idaho Association of Commerce and Industry.

Waning Unions

One reason the business lobbies do so well is the relative weakness of labor unions. Idaho's history is full of militant unionism — the radical Industrial Workers of the World were strong here at the beginning of the century — but in recent years the industries in which they organized have declined.

Idaho's unions were strong in the northern part of the state, where mining and timber were crucial industries. But recently, many of the mines have closed, and timber is nowhere near as large an industry as it was. The unions representing those industries have seen their political fortunes fall along with the economic fortunes of their workers. Nevertheless, the legacy has endured enough to produce some legislative victories. The coalition of Democrats and moderate Republicans has been able to hold off conservative attempts to impose a "right-to-work" law.

One area of continuing labor influence is in education. The Idaho Education Association, which represents teachers in the state, helped Evans increase school appropriations by holding rallies and lobbying.

The current three-way dynamic in the Legislature could change, depending on the outcome of a reapportionment suit currently in the courts. The plaintiffs in the suit charge that the current set of state legislative districts violates the state constitution, which requires the use of county boundaries. If the courts hold with the plaintiffs, the state will have to hold an election in November 1983, and the makeup of the Legislature will be altered. ∎

A PROFILE OF

Idaho

PEOPLE

Total Population: 943,935 (41st).
    White 96%, Black 0.3%, American
    Indian, Eskimo and Aleut 1%, Asian and
    Pacific Islander 1%. Spanish origin 4%.

Urban:	54%
Rural:	46%
Born in state:	49%
Foreign-born:	3%

MAJOR CITIES

Boise (102,451), Pocatello (46,340), Idaho Falls (39,590), Lewiston (27,986), Twin Falls (26,209)

LAND

Farm	29%
Forest	41%
Federally owned	65%

WORK

Occupations: 50% white-collar; 29% blue-collar; 13% service workers

Government workers: 11,405 federal
18,908 state
38,263 local

Unemployment rate: 10%

MONEY

Median family
    income (1980) $17,492 (36th)
Tax burden
    per capita (1982) $613 (34th)

EDUCATION

Spending per pupil
    through grade 12 $1,878 (43rd)
Persons with
    college degrees   16% (25th)

CRIME

Violent crime rate: 283 per 100,000 (38th)

POLITICS

1980 Presidential Vote: Reagan 66%,
    Carter 25%, Anderson 6%

Turnout rate in 1980:   70%
Turnout rate in 1982:   57%

U.S. House Delegation: 2R

ILLINOIS:

Madigan Helps Democrats Put New Stamp on Policy

To a degree unmatched since the post-Watergate session of 1975, when they held the governor's mansion and a strong majority in the Legislature, Illinois Democrats are in a position to put their stamp on state policy.

Although Republican Gov. James R. Thompson was  re-elected in 1982, and has the power to veto part or all of legislation passed by the Legislature, the 1982 election gave the House of Representatives a 70-48 Democratic majority, a stark contrast to the slim Republican majorities of recent sessions. And Democrats picked up three seats in the state Senate, giving them more breathing room than their one-seat majority allowed going into the elections.

The party's new success in the Legislature results in large part from a dramatic change in the size of the House, and in the way its members are chosen. A state constitutional amendment cut the size of the House by a third and did away with the old system of multi-member districts. Before 1982, when the amendment took effect, voters were allowed to choose three candidates to fill three seats in each district. The weaker party in a given area — such as the GOP in Chicago — generally could count on winning one of the three. In 1982, with single-member districts and head-to-head competition, the Republicans were virtually wiped out in Chicago, losing all but one of their seats. The result was a massive loss of Republican power in the House as a whole.

The switch to single-member districts did not have as dramatic an effect downstate, but even there Democrats helped themselves in 1982 because they controlled the reapportionment commission that drew up the new House districts. Democratic Rep. Michael J. Madigan of Chicago, then minority leader, pushed through a map that gave his party the advantage in several downstate districts.

Madigan at the Helm

To a great extent, the story of the Legislature this year has been Madigan's story. Made House Speaker by the new Democratic majority, he has stepped into a leadership vacuum. Traditionally, the bulk of the Democratic delegation, which comes from Cook County, has been controlled by the mayor of Chicago, while downstate Republicans have responded to governors of their own party. But while Democrat Harold Washington, Chicago's new mayor, has influence with the delegation of Chicago blacks and handful of white liberals, he has virtually none with Cook County's white, ethnic Democrats. Similarly, the GOP in the Legislature is dominated by conservatives from the Chicago suburbs and downstate, none of whom feels particularly warm toward Thompson. When Thompson proposed a $2.1 billion tax package early in 1983 to rescue the state's ailing finances, he was unable to mobilize his own party on its behalf.

Republican involvement in the tax issue was due largely to Madigan. In order to keep members of his party from bearing most of the political burden of a tax increase, the House Speaker insisted that whatever came out of the Legislature have Republican support in proportion to GOP voting strength. The issue went nowhere until the closing weeks of the session, when House GOP leader Lee A. Daniels presented a scaled-down package of tax increases. It passed with the aid of mixed Democratic and Republican backing.

But Democratic control of the Legislature has not resulted in any bonanza for the party's traditional constituencies. In 1975, freed from decades of GOP control, the new Democratic majority pushed through a sweeping set of labor-oriented legislation, including the state's liberal unemployment and workers' compensation programs. In 1983, although the Legislature did deal with such issues as unemployment compensation and utility rate increases, the results often disappointed labor and consumer advocates.

Much of the explanation lies with Madigan. A long-time presence in state politics whose political alliances are with the now-fragmented Cook County Democratic orga-

STATE LEADERSHIP

Gov. James R. Thompson (R)

Born: May 8, 1936, Chicago, Ill.
Home: Chicago, Ill.
Education: Washington U., B.A. 1956; Northwestern U., J.D. 1959.
Occupation: Lawyer.
Family: Wife, Jayne Carr; one child.
Religion: Presbyterian.
Political Career: U.S. attorney for the Northern District of Ill., 1971-75; elected governor 1976, 1978, 1982; term expires Jan. 1987.

GENERAL ASSEMBLY

SENATE

33D, 26R

Philip J. Rock (D)
President & Majority Leader

HOUSE

70D, 48R

Michael J. Madigan (D)
Speaker

nization headed by Chicago Alderman Edward R. Vrdolyak, Madigan has used his power to force competing interests to reach compromises. "On issue after issue," the *Chicago Tribune* reported in a review of the 1983 session, "Madigan puts all the parties in one room, tells them to work out an agreement and not to bother him until they have."

Many Democrats have found the resulting orderliness — something new for the House — politically useful.

Speaker Michael J. Madigan

Madigan's consensual style shelters them from outside interests; if all parties to an issue have contributed to its resolution, the interests cannot turn around and criticize a legislator for voting for the result. In the words of one Democratic representative, "You don't have to have all the businessmen writing you and saying what a putz you are."

But liberal Democratic elements in both houses complain that Madigan's way of running things has made life too easy for the business community. Madigan's politics of consensus, they say, gives business and professional interest groups a role out of proportion to their political strength.

Early in 1983, consumerist legislators sought to create a Citizens' Utility Board to fight rate increases. Anxious utilities used their access to water down the bill to the point where disgusted consumer advocates have labeled the new board useless. In another example, labor partisans felt they had the votes to force employers to contribute 70 percent of the money needed to keep the state's unemployment insurance program solvent. But when Madigan called labor and business representatives into his office on the issue, the resulting package assessed employers for only 60 percent of its financing, with the rest coming from benefit reductions.

Both Madigan and his Senate counterpart, Senate President Philip J. Rock, have had to grapple with a deeply divided Democratic Party. In both houses, the traditional division between Chicago-area Democrats and their downstate counterparts — who tend to side with neighboring Republicans on such issues as funding for highway maintenance over mass transit — has been overshadowed by fractures among Cook County Democrats. All but monolithic during the days of Chicago Mayor Richard Daley, Chicago-area Democrats broke openly into warring camps with the bitter primary for Chicago mayor between eventual winner Washington, then-Mayor Jane M. Byrne, and Cook County State's Attorney Richard M. Daley, the late mayor's son.

Despite Madigan's ties to Vrdolyak, his speakership has given him considerable independence, and he has had some success at brokering between the various factions. When black legislators joined with downstate Republicans — whose constituents were unaffected — to push through a bill increasing the property tax in Chicago to pay for public school funding, the move was fought by Chicago Democrats from white ethnic wards, many of whose constituents' children attend parochial schools. Madigan made sure there were enough votes for the measure, then voted against it. ∎

A PROFILE OF

Illinois

PEOPLE

Total Population: 11,426,518 (5th).
   White 81%, Black 15%, Asian and Pacific Islander 1%. Spanish origin 6%.

Urban:	83%
Rural:	17%
Born in state:	69%
Foreign-born:	7%

MAJOR CITIES

Chicago (3,005,072), Rockford (139,712), Peoria (124,160), Springfield (99,637), Decatur (94,081)

LAND

Farm	81%
Forest	11%
Federally owned	2%

WORK

Occupations: 54% white-collar; 31% blue-collar; 13% service workers

Government workers: 100,453 federal
151,916 state
476,120 local

Unemployment rate: 13%

MONEY

Median family income (1980)	$22,746	(6th)
Tax burden per capita (1982)	$650	(29th)

EDUCATION

Spending per pupil through grade 12	$2,720	(13th)
Persons with college degrees	16%	(24th)

CRIME

Violent crime rate: 444 per 100,000   (24th)

POLITICS

1980 Presidential Vote: Reagan 50%, Carter 42%, Anderson 7%

Turnout rate in 1980:	66%
Turnout rate in 1982:	55%

U.S. House Delegation: 12D, 10R

INDIANA:

Cautious But Partisan GOP Controls Conservative State

Indiana remains what it has been throughout this century — a cautious and conservative state not preoccupied with being at the cutting edge of events. The pressure groups that promote political change in other major industrial states are not as much of a factor in Indiana, even though it is a heavily industrialized state.

The Indiana spirit of caution and conservatism is represented well by Republican Gov. Robert D. Orr, whose habit is to take plenty of time testing the political winds, not venturing too far in front on any issue.

In many states, governors are demanding more money for education in order to produce a more sophisticated work force that will lure industry. But in Indiana, anyone seeking more money for education (or health or welfare or prisons) bears a heavy burden of proof. Orr has done little to alter that point of view. Some localities seeking more revenue to spend on schools have asked the Legislature to allow the levying of a local-option income tax. While Orr has expressed his approval, he has not twisted legislators' arms to pass the proposal, which faces strong opposition from business groups.

Business' point of view usually gets a sympathetic ear from Indiana Republicans, who have held the governorship for the past 14 years and dominated the Legislature during much of that period. Action in the 1983 legislative session illustrated the ability of one business lobby — the utilities — to block legislation repugnant to it.

In this case, a groundswell of outrage over rising utility costs generated support for a bill designed to limit rate increases. The legislation included a provision preventing utilities from assessing customers for construction work in progress (CWIP) at power plants. The CWIP assessments were strongly opposed by environmentalists, consumer advocates and other groups, such as senior citizens and local governments, that are particularly sensitive to utility rate increases.

The rate-control bill passed the House. But it ran into problems in the Senate, largely because of the efforts of Republican John M. Guy of Monticello, chairman of the Commerce and Consumer Affairs Committee and former Senate majority leader. After revising the measure in a way that assuaged utilities' objections, Guy and his allies pushed it through the full Senate. Although the House disliked the Senate action, the conference committee on the bill dropped the CWIP ban. So the final version did not rankle the utilities, and failed to satisfy any of the consumer groups.

Fierce Partisanship

The salient feature of Indiana politics is fierce partisanship, more pronounced here than almost anywhere else in the country. This is the state whose Legislature practiced gerrymandering to near perfection in its 1981 congressional redistricting bill, which was designed to convert a 6-5 Democratic U.S. House delegation into a 7-3 Republican one. Because 1982 was a bad year for the GOP, the party managed only a 5-5 split. The reapportionment map for the Legislature also was gerrymandered. Because of it, Republicans were able to limit their losses to just a handful of seats even though there was an upsurge of anti-GOP sentiment among voters.

Another example of Indiana-style partisan maneuvering came in the 1982 election season. Democrats claimed that the state's fiscal condition had weakened so much under Republican rule that a sizable budget deficit could not be avoided. Estimating that the shortfall could go as high as $400 million, the Democrats demanded that Orr call a special session of the Legislature to address the problem.

STATE LEADERSHIP

Gov. Robert D. Orr (R)

Born: Nov. 17, 1917, Ann Arbor, Mich.
Home: Indianapolis, Ind.
Education: Yale U., B.A. 1940; Harvard U., M.A. 1942.
Military Career: Army, 1942-46.
Profession: Recreational products manufacturer.
Family: Wife, Joanne Wallace; three children.
Religion: Presbyterian.
Political Career: Indiana Senate, 1969-73; lieutenant governor, 1973-81; elected governor 1980; term expires Jan. 1985.

GENERAL ASSEMBLY

SENATE

18D, 32R

Robert D. Garton (R)
President pro tem

HOUSE

43D, 57R

J. Roberts Dailey (R)
Speaker

Orr rejected those demands, but managed to avoid giving specific figures on the condition of the budget. After the election, Orr announced that the state faced a $450 million deficit. He called a special session in December, and legislators raised the income and sales taxes.

In some states, a governor who appeared to make such an abrupt turnaround on an important issue would have risked being labeled as deceitful. While some such criticism has been leveled at Orr, the prevailing opinion in passionately partisan Indiana seems to be that he did what any politician would rightfully be expected to do — protect the interests of party, first and foremost.

Indiana Republicans have a meticulous, precinct-by-precinct organization that is a living political legend. This is the only large state in which Republicans control both Senate seats, the governorship and both chambers of the Legislature.

A number of key players in the Indiana GOP have moved on to play a role in national politics. Sen. Richard G. Lugar now chairs the National Republican Senatorial Committee (NRSC). Indianapolis lawyer L. Keith Bulen, who gets much of the credit for rebuilding the state party in the mid-to-late 1960s, directed Ronald Reagan's Midwestern efforts in 1976 and 1980 and likely will play an important role if Reagan runs in 1984. NRSC Executive Director Mitchell E. Daniels Jr. also was active in Indiana politics.

Warring Democrats

Democratic disunity is an important contributing factor in Republican success. There are two warring camps in the state Democratic Party. One is the urban, liberal, labor-oriented faction, dominant in northwestern Indiana and strong in Indianapolis, Muncie, South Bend and several other industrial centers. Competing with them is the moderate-to-conservative Democratic faction based in the small towns and rural areas of southern Indiana.

A Democratic candidate for statewide office must have strong personal appeal if he is to span the ideological division within his party. Sen. Birch Bayh successfully combined a folksy style and liberal voting record for nearly two decades, but his luck ran out in 1980.

But there are deep-seated reasons why Democrats have so much trouble in Indiana. Blacks, for example, are only 8 percent of the population, and the bulk of them live in just two places — Lake County (Gary), at the far northwest corner of the state, and Indianapolis, the state capital. Ethnic groups have not been politically crucial. Most immigrants from Europe to the Midwest in years past were drawn to Detroit, Chicago, or Milwaukee, not to Indiana.

The AFL-CIO and individual labor unions such as the United Auto Workers and the United Steelworkers of America play a significant role in municipal and legislative elections in Gary, Indianapolis, Muncie, South Bend and some of the other smaller manufacturing cities. But the foundation of Indiana's working class was native-born white farm boys and Southerners. Those people — and their children now following them into the work force — view some of national labor's social goals as extreme.

Finally, there is no tradition of anti-establishment farm radicalism in Indiana, as there is in some states west of it. Much of the land is fertile and productive, and most farmers believe they can get along well without government hovering closely over them. There are some differences of opinion between the state Farm Bureau and Chamber of Commerce, both influential lobbies in the Legislature. But they share a fear of government heavy-handedness. ∎

A PROFILE OF

Indiana

PEOPLE

Total Population: 5,490,224 (12th). White 91%, Black 8%. Spanish origin 2%.

Urban:	64%
Rural:	36%
Born in state:	71%
Foreign-born:	2%

MAJOR CITIES

Indianapolis (700,807), Fort Wayne (172,196), Gary (151,953), Evansville (130,496), South Bend (109,727)

LAND

Farm	74%
Forest	17%
Federally owned	2%

WORK

Occupations: 47% white-collar; 38% blue-collar; 13% service workers

Government workers:	40,127	federal
	91,819	state
	209,019	local

Unemployment rate: 10%

MONEY

Median family income (1980)	$20,535	(18th)
Tax burden per capita (1982)	$558	(43rd)

EDUCATION

Spending per pupil through grade 12	$2,008	(38th)
Persons with college degrees	13%	(45th)

CRIME

Violent crime rate: 342 per 100,000 (32nd)

POLITICS

1980 Presidential Vote: Reagan 56%, Carter 38%, Anderson 5%

Turnout rate in 1980:	62%
Turnout rate in 1982:	55%

U.S. House Delegation: 5D, 5R

IOWA:

Cities, Unions Challenge Rural Hold on Legislature

After GOP Gov. Terry Branstad ignited a furor in Iowa in 1983 with his proposal to use the slogan, "A State of Minds" on car license plates, one wag suggested as an alternative — "Iowa: Gateway to Nebraska."

As a crack at the state's seeming blandness, it was largely unwarranted. Iowa is more complicated than that, at least in its politics. Despite the state's Republican image, its politically volatile farm population and blue-collar vote in medium-sized manufacturing cities have kept the GOP from growing too comfortable. In 1982, while Republican Branstad was winning his first term easily, Democrats were taking both chambers of the Legislature out of GOP hands.

But there is no denying a measured, middle-of-the-road quality to government in Iowa. In the absence of the deep ethnic and regional rivalries that divide neighboring states, Iowa seems downright placid by comparison. Its citizens pride themselves on running a clean and open government, and state legislators are careful not to be seen as beholden to any particular interest. The rural areas still have the upper hand in the Legislature, although their hold has been weakened by reapportionment and the slow growth of new political forces, especially the League of Municipalities and two unions — the United Auto Workers and the United Food and Commercial Workers (formerly the Amalgamated Meatcutters).

Branstad's Surprises

Many Iowans expected a change from the middle-of-

the-road tone of Iowa politics when Branstad took office earlier in 1983.

Branstad had carried a reputation as a down-the-line conservative ever since his days as a member of the GOP's right wing in the state Legislature. A leader of Ronald Reagan's Iowa campaigns in 1976 and 1980, he had campaigned in 1982 against Democrats' proposals for a tax increase. At one point he indicated that he might donate the proceeds from an inaugural fund-raiser to an anti-abortion group.

But once in office, Branstad began surprising people. His inaugural speech called for checking rising utility rates — a favorite Democratic topic during the election campaign — and proposed higher taxes on employers to meet debts faced by the state's unemployment fund. His budget called for funding of such state programs as aid to children of unemployed parents, and boosted finances for Medicaid and mental health. To the distress of his fellow Republicans, Branstad proposed a one-cent increase in the state sales tax to help the state's ailing treasury.

Branstad explained his new image by pointing out that in the Legislature he had represented a conservative rural district, and that now he had the entire state to worry about. But he was also recognizing a political fact — that the 1982 elections had turned control of both houses of the Legislature over to the Democrats. For the four previous years, during his time as lieutenant governor, the Legislature had been Republican-held.

Branstad's initial spurt of activism, in which he proposed policies that Democrats had traditionally considered their own, was in large part pre-emptive. It allowed him to be seen setting the Legislature's agenda and establishing guidelines for what he would find acceptable. It also gave him a legislative session that was remarkably tension-free. House Speaker Don Avenson and Senate Majority Leader Lowell Junkins, both Democrats, gladly steered the governor's sales tax through, without help from their Republican counterparts. They also went along with most of Branstad's budget proposals.

Whether they will feel as accommodating in 1984 is unclear. After the session ended, Branstad vetoed a bill, backed by some Democrats, that would have set up a state

---

STATE LEADERSHIP

Gov. Terry Branstad (R)

Born: Nov. 17, 1946, Leland, Iowa.
Home: Lake Mills, Iowa.
Education: U. of Iowa, B.A. 1969; Drake U. Law School, J.D. 1974.
Military Career: Army, 1969-71.
Occupation: Lawyer; farmer.
Family: Wife, Christine Johnson; two children.
Religion: Roman Catholic.
Political Career: Iowa House, 1973-79; lieutenant governor, 1979-83; elected governor 1982; term expires Jan. 1987.

GENERAL ASSEMBLY

SENATE

28D, 22R

Charles Miller (D)
President pro tem

HOUSE

60D, 40R

Don Avenson (D)
Speaker

lottery. He also angered Democrats generally by vetoing major portions of a jobs package.

In addition, the two Democratic leaders have higher political ambitions. With comfortable majorities to work with in their respective chambers, both are in a position to make names for themselves by taking a more confrontational attitude toward Branstad in the future.

That may be particularly true for Avenson, who generally sides with his party's liberal wing. His openly partisan leadership style seemed well-suited to the 1983 House, where 28 of the body's 60 Democrats were new to the Legislature and usually amenable to strong direction from the top. Under Avenson's leadership, the more partisan-tinted pieces of legislation in 1983, such as utility rate controls and the unemployment insurance package, tended to originate in the House.

Senate Democrats tend to be more cautious and conservative than those in the House. Senate Majority Leader Junkins takes a low-key, consensus approach, often showing a willingness to cooperate with the chamber's Republican leader, Calvin Hultman. The Senate tends to take the more partisan bills crafted by the House and recast them in a form acceptable to a broader range of interests.

When Democrats found Branstad's unemployment insurance proposal inadequate, for example, the House passed an alternative package requiring employers to pay an additional $255 million in taxes while benefits were cut by $58 million. The governor made it plain that those figures were unacceptable, and it was the Senate that eventually lowered the employers' new burden to $220 million and trimmed workers' benefits by $93 million.

Disappointed Unions

In general, given Democratic control of the Legislature, unions did not fare as well as might have been expected. The problem was in part one of labor's own making. During debate over unemployment insurance, the United Auto Workers and other unions maintained stiff opposition to any cuts in benefits. In doing so, the unions annoyed allies who were convinced of the need to make some cuts to shore up the program.

State employees and teachers also failed to win consideration of a bill expanding the scope of subjects covered by collective bargaining. With a Branstad veto certain, the leadership of both houses wanted to be sure the legislation had significant support before bringing it to a vote; it did not. The Iowa Education Association, one of the best organized lobbying groups in the state, did succeed in winning passage of a bill setting up a system of appeals for teachers who had been fired. But it was vetoed by Branstad.

Organized labor's difficulties also stem from its base in urban areas in a state where rural interests still hold the balance of power. Even the Democratic majority in the House is made up of numerous rural members.

Not surprisingly, the pre-eminent special interest in Iowa historically has been the Iowa Farm Bureau, which has one of the most effective lobbying organizations in the state. Rural Iowans have tended to take a more active interest in legislative affairs than have urbanites.

While Iowa's farm population is shrinking, the bureau's membership has expanded to include small-town merchants and bankers, as well as farm equipment dealers and other agriculture-related retailers. Legislators continue to pay close attention to the bureau's stands on issues directly affecting farmers. But they have grown less willing to go with the bureau on other matters. ∎

A PROFILE OF

Iowa

PEOPLE

Total Population: 2,913,808 (27th). White 97%, Black 1%. Spanish origin 1%.

Urban:	59%
Rural:	41%
Born in state:	78%
Foreign-born:	2%

MAJOR CITIES

Des Moines (191,033), Cedar Rapids (110,243), Davenport (103,264), Sioux City (82,003), Waterloo (75,985)

LAND

Farm	94%
Forest	4%
Federally owned	1%

WORK

Occupations: 47% white-collar; 30% blue-collar; 14% service workers

Government workers: 18,654 federal
53,528 state
129,265 local

Unemployment rate: 8%

MONEY

Median family income (1980)	$20,052	(20th)
Tax burden per capita (1982)	$685	(22nd)

EDUCATION

Spending per pupil through grade 12	$2,343	(23rd)
Persons with college degrees	14%	(37th)

CRIME

Violent crime rate: 204 per 100,000 (42nd)

POLITICS

1980 Presidential Vote: Reagan 51%, Carter 39%, Anderson 9%

Turnout rate in 1980: 68%
Turnout rate in 1982: 56%

U.S. House Delegation: 3D, 3R

KANSAS:

East and West Wage Battles Over Energy, Water Issues

Kansas government is split between a Democratic chief executive and a Republican Legislature, but when controversy arises these days, factors more basic than partisanship are often the root cause. Regional rivalry — between east and west — is the crucial divider in Kansas

politics. On a wide range of issues, loyalty to region turns Republican against Republican and Democrat against Democrat.

Presenting a united front has been a particular problem for Republicans. Voters in rural and small-town western Kansas are the backbone of the state GOP. But their interests often differ from eastern Kansas' suburban Republicans, who are clustered in the part of the state where most of the state's major cities are located.

The Democratic Party also has wide ideological gaps to span — from its minority and blue-collar urban factions in Kansas City and Wichita to the more conservative, Southern-oriented rural wing based in southeast Kansas. But Democrats have cooperated well enough to hold the governorship for all but four years since 1967, even though the GOP is numerically superior statewide and usually manages to control the Legislature and the congressional delegation.

Severance Tax Fight

The regional rivalry in Kansas politics was evident in the acrimonious severance tax debate that preoccupied state politics for several years. The issue, which finally was settled in 1983, led many legislators from both sides of the aisle to oppose their own party's position.

Though most Kansas counties produce some oil and

gas, the bulk of the drilling is done in the thinly settled central and western areas of the state. The rural and small-town conservatives there did not want to see their energy production taxed to provide money they felt would be spent wastefully in the cities of eastern Kansas.

Working together, western Republicans and Democrats provided the staunchest opposition to Democratic Gov. John Carlin's severance tax proposal. Also pressuring the Legislature to defeat the tax was the Kansas Independent Oil and Gas Association, a powerful lobby group that represents most oil and gas producers.

Carlin said the severance tax money was needed for education aid and highway maintenance. He warned that rejection of the tax would force localities to raise property taxes to meet education costs and other service demands. Dread of higher property taxes spurred strong severance tax support from eastern Kansas suburbanites, many of whom live in affluent Johnson County, a heavily Republican area south of Kansas City. The tax also was endorsed by some rural GOP voters in southeast Kansas; people there have seen coal companies extract great wealth from the land while paying relatively little in taxes.

One of the Johnson County suburban Republicans, then-House Speaker Wendell Lady of Overland Park, was a key Carlin ally in the governor's first two attempts to pass the tax, in 1981 and 1982. Even though about a dozen House Democrats (mostly westerners) bucked Carlin and opposed the tax, Lady persuaded twice that many Republicans (mostly easterners) to vote for it, and it cleared the House both years.

But the tax met fierce resistance in the Senate, where the leadership is conservative and western-oriented. Senate President Ross O. Doyen of Concordia and Vice President Charlie L. Angell of Plains, both Republicans, led the efforts that killed the tax in 1981 and 1982. They were assisted by several Democrats, including Sen. Frank D. Gaines of Augusta, probably the chamber's most influential conservative Democrat. Nearly all these tax opponents are small-town products — Doyen's Corcordia and Gaines' Augusta have fewer than 7,000 residents apiece.

Carlin made the severance tax the major issue of his 1982 re-election campaign, and his vote divided along regional lines. Carlin carried only five of 54 counties in western Kansas. But three-fourths of the 51 eastern counties

STATE LEADERSHIP

Gov. John Carlin (D)

Born: Aug. 3, 1940, Salina, Kan.
Home: Topeka, Kan.
Education: Kan. State U., B.S. 1962.
Occupation: Dairy farmer.
Religion: Lutheran.
Family: Wife, Karen Bigsby; four children.
Political Career: Democratic nominee for Kan. House, 1968; Kan. House, 1971-79, minority leader, 1975-77, Speaker, 1977-79; elected governor 1978, 1982; term expires Jan. 1987.

LEGISLATURE

SENATE

16D, 24R

Ross O. Doyen (R)
President

HOUSE

53D, 72R

Mike Hayden (R)
Speaker

Sen. Pres. Ross O. Doyen   **House Speaker Mike Hayden**

voted for him, including Johnson County, Sedgwick County (Wichita) and all other major population centers.

The Legislature interpreted Carlin's comfortable 1982 victory as a mandate to pass the severance tax in 1983. House Speaker Mike Hayden, R, opposed the tax, but he and the Doyen-Angell-Gaines Senate coalition decided against resorting to obstructionist tactics. The tax cleared the House and Senate by comfortable margins.

Reapportionment Ahead?

A new topic on the political agenda could deepen the regional split and work to the advantage of Democrats. This time the issue is legislative reapportionment; leading protagonists likely will be the Senate leadership and a Senate Republican from Johnson County, Norman E. Gaar, who two years ago was deposed as majority leader largely because Doyen and Angell found him too liberal.

Gaar has filed a court suit asking that legislative districts be redrawn using 1980 federal census data. The Legislature last redrew boundaries in 1979, using data from a 1978 state census. The suit claims the state tally was inaccurate because it counted Kansas students as living with their parents and did not count the military population. Thus, Gaar says, current boundaries under-represent places such as Lawrence (with a large student population at the University of Kansas) and Manhattan (which has both Kansas State University and Fort Riley).

If Gaar's suit succeeds in forcing reapportionment based on the federal census, Republicans may lose several legislative seats to Democrats, since the alleged under-counts mostly occurred in urban centers of northeast Kansas where Democratic candidates stand a good chance of success. The arrival of more urban-oriented members in the Senate would shift power from west to east.

The touchy issue of water management is another east-west polarizer. Farmers in the arid west depend on an underground aquifer for irrigation, but the aquifer is being depleted. Unless the west secures an alternate water source, farmers there could be forced to revert to farming without irrigation, a step that would bring dramatic changes to Kansas' agriculture and economy.

Some westerners have suggested embarking on a dam-building program in their region to collect water from the rivers that flow west-to-east across the state. That proposal is sure to upset east Kansans — both rural and urban — who rely on the rivers for their water. A state agency is now trying to develop a water management plan, but the task requires such delicate handling of competing regional viewpoints that it may take years to complete. ∎

A PROFILE OF

Kansas

PEOPLE

Total Population: 2,363,679 (32nd).
   White 92%, Black 5%, American Indian, Eskimo and Aleut 1%, Asian and Pacific Islander 1%. Spanish origin 3%.

Urban:	67%
Rural:	33%
Born in state:	63%
Foreign-born:	2%

MAJOR CITIES

Wichita (279,272), Kansas City (161,087), Topeka (115,266), Overland Park (81,784), Lawrence (52,738)

LAND

Farm	93%
Forest	3%
Federally owned	1%

WORK

Occupations: 51% white-collar; 30% blue-collar; 13% service workers

Government workers:	22,295	federal
	53,225	state
	110,693	local

Unemployment rate: 6%

MONEY

Median family income (1980)	$19,707	(26th)
Tax burden per capita (1982)	$610	(35th)

EDUCATION

Spending per pupil through grade 12	$2,251	(28th)
Persons with college degrees	17%	(22nd)

CRIME

Violent crime rate: 369 per 100,000 (31st)

POLITICS

1980 Presidential Vote: Reagan 58%, Carter 33%, Anderson 7%

Turnout rate in 1980:	64%
Turnout rate in 1982:	54%

U.S. House Delegation: 2D, 3R

KENTUCKY:

Legislature's Leaders Seek Share of Governor's Power

Governors traditionally have held the power in Kentucky; the 1891 constitution virtually forces state legislators into a position of subservience. The Legislature meets every other year for no more than 60 days, and only the governor can authorize a special session. The situation may

be about to change, depending on a crucial court ruling expected late in 1983, but for now, the system of 1891 remains in effect.

Legislators' attempts to change the system have been a fact of Kentucky political life for the past decade. Their frustration grew during the 1970s, but efforts to get a stronger hand in managing state affairs were contained by Democratic Govs. Wendell H. Ford (1971-74) and Julian Carroll (1974-79), both veteran officeholders who kept tight control over the Legislature through their many friends there.

Executive-legislative relations have been quite different under the tenure of Democratic Gov. John Y. Brown, whose style differs markedly from those of Ford and Carroll. A businessman with no previous political experience, Brown has run Kentucky as an executive would run a corporation, delegating authority to agency heads and seldom even dealing with the Legislature.

Feeling little personal kinship to Brown, legislators have renewed their drive for more authority. The peak of this effort came in the 1982 session, when the Legislature expanded the authority of its interim committees, panels which meet between regular legislative sessions.

Those committees are about the only weapon the legislators have during the 20-month periods when they are out of session. The committees were envisioned as study groups when established in the late 1960s, but bills approved in 1982 gave them oversight power over a wide range of executive actions. Brown balked, insisting that once the Legislature adjourns, it cannot constitutionally operate through interim committees as if it were in session.

But rather than embark on a spree of vetoes that would provoke acrimonious legislative override attempts, Brown and the leadership of the Legislature agreed to let the courts decide the dispute. A lower court ruled in favor of the governor; the matter came before the state Supreme Court, which was expected to issue a ruling in fall 1983.

Legislature's Growing Prestige

The Legislature's aggressive push for more power and Brown's dislike for political deal-making already have altered the rules for some of the state's traditionally powerful interest groups — whiskey distillers, racehorse breeders, coal producers and their arch-enemies, the miners' unions. Before Brown, the interest groups spent most of their energy and money vying for access to the governor, whose influence was paramount in pushing or blocking legislation. But in the Brown era, lobbyists have been devoting more time to legislators, a clear sign that the Legislature is coming to be viewed as more influential.

No matter how the state Supreme Court rules, the Legislature may continue to gain prestige and power simply because the quality of its membership is improving. The Legislature is starting to attract more capable people than it did when it was mostly an appendage of the governor. Members such as Democratic Rep. Joe Clarke, chairman of the House Appropriations and Revenue Committee, and Democratic Sen. Michael R. Moloney, chairman of the counterpart Senate panel, have developed considerable expertise in their areas; they are not likely to tolerate a return to the days when lawmakers were spoon-fed information by the governor.

Still, the Legislature will have to struggle to avoid slipping back into its old ways when it confronts a future governor who knows the lawmakers and leans on them more vigorously than Brown has. Such a governor could be Martha Layne Collins, winner of the May 1983 gubernatorial primary. As lieutenant governor, she has built close personal contacts with Democratic officeholders and party

---

STATE LEADERSHIP

Gov. John Y. Brown (D)

Born: Dec. 28, 1933, Lexington, Ky.
Home: Lexington, Ky.
Education: U. of Ky., B.A. 1957, LL.B. 1960.
Military Career: Army Reserve, 1959-65.
Occupation: Restaurateur; sports entrepreneur.
Family: Wife, Phyllis George; four children.
Religion: Baptist.
Political Career: Elected governor 1979; term expires Dec. 1983.

GENERAL ASSEMBLY

SENATE

29D, 9R

Joseph W. Prather (D)
President pro tem

HOUSE

75D, 24R

1 vacancy

Bobby H. Richardson (D)
Speaker

officials. If elected in November, she may be the type of chief executive who can move some of the lobbyists back from the Capitol's third floor (where the Legislature meets) to their traditional perch on the first floor (where the governor's office is located).

Brown's Legacy

John Y. Brown, recovering in 1983 from heart surgery that incapacitated him for several months, seems destined to be one of the most "cussed and discussed" governors in Kentucky history. His preference for running the state as a chairman of the board — a dramatic break from the past — has not been well-received in some quarters.

Since the days when Henry Clay prowled the Capitol corridors in Frankfort, more than 150 years ago, Kentucky has taken great pleasure in the practice of raw politics — the person-to-person, patronage-promising, deal-cutting, smoke-filled room sort of politics for which the state is famous. Brown's failure to embrace that style has left some Democratic legislators, county chairmen and precinct operators grumbling about his aloofness. Dissatisfaction with Brown was partly responsible for the 1981 defeat of a proposal he favored that would have allowed the governor two consecutive terms.

The value of Brown's contribution to the long-term economic health of Kentucky is hard to assess. Few chief executives in the country have taken as high a profile in business recruitment as Brown has. He claims to have brought more business investment to Kentucky than was attracted during the entire decade of the 1970s.

But Kentucky has not emerged from dependence on its longtime economic linchpins — mining, manufacturing and agriculture — and has not lured many high-technology businesses. Brown's critics say that is because he has not stressed the state's education system, which is important to high-technology employers seeking a literate labor pool.

Yet despite the criticisms, there is widespread bipartisan sentiment that Brown has performed a valuable service by streamlining the state goverment. By bringing in skilled managers who cut back patronage-bloated bureaucracies, Brown reduced the cost of government and improved its efficiency. Also, his fiscal acumen is credited with helping keep Kentucky solvent at a time when neighboring states were plunging deep into debt.

Democrats in Kentucky are a diverse bunch — from inner-city Louisville's black liberals and blue-collar Catholics to western Kentucky's Deep South-oriented white farmers. For a time in the early 1970s, bitter rivalry between factions supporting and opposing Governor Ford threatened to disrupt the party's majority. In recent years, however, the Democrats generally have been able to settle their differences and prosper at the polls.

Because the national Democratic Party is perceived as too liberal by many Kentucky Democrats, the GOP has enjoyed considerable success in contests for federal office. It has some localized power bases — in suburban areas and in the mountainous southeast, for example — but at the state level, the GOP is weak. Since 1968, the Democrats have won every gubernatorial contest, and the GOP controls only one-fourth of the seats in the Legislature.

Republican Party leaders in 1983 met repeated refusals from people they sought as gubernatorial candidates, until finally Senate Minority Leader James P. Bunning (who had once declined) changed his mind when it seemed the party might not be able to field any serious candidate for the office.

A PROFILE OF

Kentucky

PEOPLE

Total Population: 3,660,777 (23rd). White 92%, Black 7%. Spanish origin 1%.

Urban:	51%
Rural:	49%
Born in state:	79%
Foreign-born:	1%

MAJOR CITIES

Louisville (298,451), Lexington-Fayette (204,165), Owensboro (54,450), Covington (49,563), Bowling Green (40,450)

LAND

Farm	57%
Forest	48%
Federally owned	6%

WORK

Occupations: 46% white-collar; 37% blue-collar; 13% service workers

Government workers:	31,216 federal
	65,434 state
	107,656 local

Unemployment rate: 11%

MONEY

Median family income (1980)	$16,444	(45th)
Tax burden per capita (1982)	$681	(25th)

EDUCATION

Spending per pupil through grade 12	$1,835	(45th)
Persons with college degrees	11%	(48th)

CRIME

Violent crime rate: 290 per 100,000 (37th)

POLITICS

1980 Presidential Vote: Reagan 49%, Carter 48%, Anderson 2%

Turnout rate in 1980:	57%
Turnout rate in 1982:	36%

U.S. House Delegation: 4D, 3R

LOUISIANA:

With Few Republican Allies, Treen Struggles to Govern

For most of the half-century since Huey P. Long's reign, Louisiana has been a "strong governor" state. Long, who was in office from 1928 to 1932, used to appear on the floor of the state House and Senate and harangue the legislators until they saw things his way. Many of his successors took after him, if not quite as aggressively. Until recent years, nearly every governor could count on getting most of what he wanted from the Legislature.

That relationship has changed somewhat since David C. Treen was elected governor in 1979. The state's first GOP chief executive in this century, Treen has had to confront a Legislature in which his party is virtually unrepresented. While there are enough conservative Democratic legislators to give him a bloc of potential sympathizers, Treen has not shown much inclination to press hard for his initiatives. A veteran of seven years in the U.S. House, he seems genuinely to believe in legislative independence.

The governor has had most of his confrontations with the state Senate. Even when he has convinced the House to go along with him, the Senate often has been reluctant to do so. It is laced with supporters of Democrat Edwin W. Edwards, who preceded Treen as governor and will challenge him for re-election in November 1983.

Another reason the Senate has been such an obstacle for Treen is that power there, at least until recently, has been tightly controlled. Until he was convicted early in

1983 for mail fraud, Senate President Michael H. O'Keefe Jr. ruled the chamber with an iron hand. After his conviction, he gave up his presidency, but he is running for re-election to his Senate seat. Samuel B. Nunez Jr., formerly president pro tem, took over as president, but he has not controlled the Senate the same way. Partly this has been his own choice; he prefers a more open style of leadership.

B. B. Rayburn, the dean of the Senate, is another key figure. Rayburn chairs the joint House-Senate committee that reviews the governor's budget, so his views are important. He also chairs the Senate Finance Committee, although that confers less power than it once did.

In the House, Speaker John J. Hainkel Jr. is well-liked, even by liberals who consider him too conservative. If Edwards wins and Hainkel is re-elected as Speaker, it will mark a milestone in the relationship between the governor and the Legislature: Hainkel will become the first Speaker to survive a change in administrations.

The politics of the House revolves around the activities of a variety of regional and ethnic caucuses, all clamoring for legislative influence. The largest such group, representing suburban New Orleans, is the Jefferson Parish caucus, headed by Edward J. D'Gerolamo; others are the rural, black and conservative caucuses.

Business Lobby Strengthened

Outside the Legislature and the governor's office, the key political figure in the state is Ed Steimel, head of the Louisiana Association of Business and Industry (LABI — pronounced "lobby"). Steimel was formerly the director of the Public Affairs Research Council, a group focusing on business issues. Well-versed on those issues, and possessing a good organizing ability, Steimel formed LABI in the mid-70s to lobby on behalf of businesses.

Steinmel's first major effort was for a "right-to-work" law. Prior to that, organized labor had been a major force — some would say the major force — in state politics. It was centered around the oil and petrochemical industries, and strong among state workers. Union backers had blocked every attempt to impose such a statute. But, after

---

STATE LEADERSHIP

Gov. David C. Treen (R)

Born: July 16, 1928, Baton Rouge, La.
Home: New Orleans, La.
Education: Tulane U., B.A. 1948; LL.B. 1950.
Military Career: Air Force, 1950-52.
Occupation: Lawyer.
Family: Wife, Dolores Brisbi; three children.
Religion: Methodist.
Political Career: Republican nominee for U.S. House, 1962, 1964, 1968; Republican nominee for governor, 1972; served in U.S. House, 1973-80; elected governor 1979; term expires March 1984.

LEGISLATURE

SENATE
38D, 1R
Samuel B. Nunez Jr. (D)
President

HOUSE
94D, 9R, 1 Ind.
1 vacancy
John J. Hainkel Jr. (D)
Speaker

one of the most acrimonious sessions in state history, the Legislature passed the right-to-work law in 1976.

That event seemed to be a turning point in recent state politics. Since then, LABI, with sizable campaign contributions helping elect pro-business members to the Legislature, has successfully pushed several more initiatives, and has become more than competitive with unions. In recent sessions, the Legislature has passed several business-sponsored changes in the workmen's compensation and unemployment benefit systems.

As recently as the early 1970s, lobbying was not very subtle in Louisiana — lobbyists for traditional economic interests were allowed in the legislative chambers and did everything but vote. The process is still as intense as ever, but it is more complex, with broad coalitions forming and breaking up on an issue-by-issue basis.

Rep. John J. Hainkel Jr.

That was evident in 1983 as the Legislature debated Treen's proposal to create a separate Cabinet department of environmental protection. The governor wanted to take some functions away from the natural resources department, which was viewed by many as a captive of the oil industry.

But the state constitution limits the total number of Cabinet departments, so one had to be eliminated if the new environmental agency was to be created. Treen chose the Urban and Community Affairs Department, an agency close to New Orleans urban interests and to former Gov. Edwards. A coalition of urban legislators and blacks blocked that plan. Then Treen proposed to abolish the Culture, Recreation and Tourism Department. Cities again objected, bringing arts groups along with them.

Finally, the governor and the legislators agreed to merge the Department of Corrections into the Department of Public Safety, despite opposition from police, in order to create the Environmental Protection Department. But the oil industry still managed to win an important victory by seeing to it that coastal zone management remained under the jurisdiction of the Department of Natural Resources.

The two-party system has yet to come to the Louisiana Legislature. Although the governor is a Republican, there is only one Republican in the state Senate, and only nine Republicans in the 105-member House. In addition, Louisiana's Democrats have given themselves an institutional advantage. Under a 1975 law, primaries are open to candidates of all parties. If a candidate wins 50 percent or more of the vote in the primary, no general election is held. This prevents Republicans from appealing to supporters of the loser in a divisive Democratic primary.

Geography remains a key factor in state politics. The southern parishes are for the most part Cajun and Catholic; the northern part of the state is Anglo-Saxon and Protestant. The two blocs have fought for control of state politics in every election. But the division means less in the Legislature now than it once did, since southerners increasingly outnumber those from the north. Speaker Hainkel and most of the other members of the legislative leadership come from the south. ∎

A PROFILE OF

Louisiana

PEOPLE

Total Population: 4,205,900 (19th).
   White 69%, Black 29%, Asian and
   Pacific Islander 1%. Spanish origin 3%.

Urban:	69%
Rural:	31%
Born in state:	78%
Foreign-born:	2%

MAJOR CITIES

New Orleans (557,515), Baton Rouge (219,419), Shreveport (205,820), Lafayette (81,961), Lake Charles (75,226)

LAND

Farm	35%
Forest	51%
Federally owned	4%

WORK

Occupations: 50% white-collar; 34% blue-collar; 13% service workers

Government workers: 31,927 federal
94,582 state
151,666 local

Unemployment rate: 13%

MONEY

Median family income (1980)	$18,088	(33rd)
Tax burden per capita (1982)	$744	(19th)

EDUCATION

Spending per pupil through grade 12	$2,002	(39th)
Persons with college degrees	14%	(38th)

CRIME

Violent crime rate: 638 per 100,000 (9th)

POLITICS

1980 Presidential Vote: Reagan 51%, Carter 46%, Anderson 2%

Turnout rate in 1980:   64%
Turnout rate in 1982:   26%

U.S. House Delegation: 6D, 2R

MAINE:

Democrats' Power Increases While State GOP Languishes

Thirty years ago, when Maine was second only to Vermont in its dedication to Republicanism, few Democrats permitted themselves even the fantasy that the state's political structure would ever look the way it does today. The 1982 election placed the final touches on the Democratic revolution that had gathered strength over the preceding generation. With the Democratic takeover of the state Senate in 1982, the party holds the governorship and both houses of the Legislature for the first time in more than 70 years.

It is the GOP that is languishing, at least at the state level. Its organization has little of its former vitality; the party's three members of Congress — Sen. William S. Cohen and Reps. Olympia J. Snowe and John R. McKernan Jr. — have bypassed it to build their own political networks. The other traditional sources of Republican power, the big timber companies and paper mills, the power companies and manufacturing firms, have lost a good portion of the political clout they once exercised.

The most visible beneficiary of the lopsided Democratic majorities in both houses of the Legislature has been Democratic Gov. Joseph E. Brennan. During his first term, which started in 1979, Brennan got along fairly well with both the Democratic House and the Republican Senate, steering a course that took careful account of the conservative sentiment dominating the Senate on fiscal matters. Now, however, with Democrats holding a better than 2-to-1 majority in the Senate and close to that in the House, he

has a freer hand.

Brennan began his second term by pushing successfully for partial repeal of a tax indexing initiative passed by Maine voters the previous year — a step he probably would have been reluctant to take with a GOP-held Senate. He also saw his proposal for hospital cost controls enacted with minimal change despite a forceful lobbying effort against it by private health care interests in the state.

The governor also has benefited from the Legislature's apparent willingness to leave policy initiatives up to him and his administrators. That is something relatively new. During the 1970s, it was the Legislature that was the site of battles over issues such as environmental regulation, worker compensation and social welfare spending. But with those programs enacted, the focus has shifted to the bureaucracy that administers them.

Martin Ascendancy

The other major political figure to benefit from the Democratic takeover of the Senate has been House Speaker John L. Martin, now in his fifth term in that post. A plain-talking insurance agent from a tiny village near the Canadian border, Martin has never been reticent about using or threatening to use the prerogatives of his office — to name and remove committee chairmen and members, for example — as a way of bringing House members into line.

Before 1983, Martin had to make constant compromises with the Republican Senate, especially on fiscal matters. Now, however, the additional Democratic legislative strength gives him influence even in the Senate, where he sometimes seems to eclipse that chamber's low-key president, Gerard P. Conley.

Despite the Democrats' overwhelming numbers, GOP legislators have retained some influence. One such case came during Brennan's effort to repeal the portion of the income tax initiative that made indexing retroactive to 1981. House Republican opposition delayed the measure, which required a two-thirds majority vote in each house, until a compromise could be reached. Still, the GOP victory was largely symbolic — the new version placed a retroactive tax on 1981 and 1982 returns equal to the amount the

---

STATE LEADERSHIP

Gov. Joseph E. Brennan (D)

Born: Nov. 2, 1934, Portland, Maine.
Home: Portland, Maine.
Education: Boston College, A.B. 1958; U. of Maine Law School, J.D. 1963.
Military Career: Army, 1953-55.
Occupation: Lawyer.
Family: Divorced; two children.
Religion: Roman Catholic.
Political Career: Maine House, 1965-71; Maine Senate, 1973-75; sought Democratic gubernatorial nomination, 1974; Maine attorney general, 1975-77; elected governor 1978, 1982; term expires Jan. 1987.

LEGISLATURE

SENATE
23D, 10R

Gerard P. Conley (D)
President

HOUSE
92D, 59R

John L. Martin (D)
Speaker

initiative forced the state to return to taxpayers.

Internal dissension has been a more potent check on the power of the majority. Blessed with the luxury of lopsided majorities, Democrats are splitting along ideological and regional lines that rarely showed up in past years. During the 1983 session, a proposal to increase the state's minimum wage to a level several cents above the national minimum passed the House, but failed narrowly in the Senate. The crucial votes against it were cast by Democrats representing coastal districts dependent on tourism and inland districts tied to traditional low-wage industries such as shoes and textiles.

The divisions within the Legislature reflect the state's political variations. The belt of industrial cities that stretches north along Interstate 95 through Biddeford, Portland, Lewiston and Waterville is the center of moderate-to-liberal Democratic sentiment. The growth of the I-95 corridor, which now has about half the state's population, gave its representatives and their pro-labor, pro-social spending views corresponding legislative clout during the 1970s. However, recent migration from the cities to small towns surrounding them was reflected in legislative reapportionment in 1983, and may tilt the area's delegations in a more conservative direction in the future.

Rep. John L. Martin

Southeast of I-95 is the small cluster of coastal counties where Maine's small-town tradition of fiscal conservatism still flourishes. In these counties, the age-old suspicion of government, particularly state government, has begun to clash with the views of newcomers who want more government services. But many of the area's small towns still refuse to join the regional planning commissions that were set up several years ago, and their voters continue to elect conservative legislators.

The rest of Maine, to the west, north and east of the I-95 corridor, is a mix of vast forests, the potato farms of sprawling Aroostook County, rural towns, and small mill and factory towns. Although residents often share the same skeptical attitude toward the state government as the coastal towns, rural Maine's poverty has led many to welcome involvement in economic development by the state.

Still, towns throughout Maine hold tenaciously to a say in what shape development will take, and there seems to be little disagreement about holding industries to tough standards on pollution, even at the cost of jobs. Local opposition scuttled the latest proposal for an oil refinery and deep-water terminal for supertankers in poverty-stricken Washington County.

Local control is limited somewhat by the reach of the state's paper companies, which own enormous tracts of land throughout the state. Most of their land is outside local jurisdiction. Although they lost the environmental battles of the early 1970s, the companies still command attention. Brennan's program for controlling the use of specific segments of the state's rivers left open for development portions of rivers on which two of the paper giants, Great Northern and St. Regis, want to build dams. ∎

A PROFILE OF
Maine

PEOPLE

Total Population: 1,124,660 (38th).
White 99%, Black 0.3%. Spanish origin 4%.

Urban:	47%
Rural:	53%
Born in state:	73%
Foreign-born:	4%

MAJOR CITIES

Portland (61,572), Lewiston (40,481), Bangor (31,643), Auburn (23,128), South Portland (22,712)

LAND

Farm	8%
Forest	89%
Federally owned	1%

WORK

Occupations: 46% white-collar; 37% blue-collar; 13% service workers

Government workers: 8,918 federal
22,780 state
45,573 local

Unemployment rate: 9%

MONEY

Median family income (1980)	$16,167	(47th)
Tax burden per capita (1982)	$650	(30th)

EDUCATION

Spending per pupil through grade 12	$1,985	(41st)
Persons with college degrees	14%	(34th)

CRIME

Violent crime rate: 196 per 100,000 (43rd)

POLITICS

1980 Presidential Vote: Reagan 46%, Carter 42%, Anderson 10%

Turnout rate in 1980:	68%
Turnout rate in 1982:	63%

U.S. House Delegation: 2R

MARYLAND:

Suburbs Consolidate Control In Heavily Democratic State

Partisan politics has little practical meaning in Maryland, where Democrats reign virtually unchallenged and preside over routine gubernatorial landslides every four years. The important divisions are those of geography.

Legislators from rural western Maryland join col-

leagues from the Eastern Shore, along Chesapeake Bay, in fighting a common enemy — their party colleagues from inner-city Baltimore and the suburbs surrounding both Baltimore and Washington, D.C. They consider the suburbanites their special enemies. Branding them the "Beltway bullies," the rural legislators

decry suburban and urban success in garnering state funds for the two metropolitan area subway systems — neither of which is of much use to residents of western Maryland or the Eastern Shore.

Despite complaints from the hinterlands, however, it is the suburbs that are coming to define the state politically, through the sheer force of numbers. Nearly 30 percent of Maryland's population lives in the Washington suburbs of Montgomery and Prince George's counties; more than 15 percent are in Baltimore County, which surrounds the city of Baltimore but does not include it. Anne Arundel County, within commuting distance of both metropolitan areas, contributes another 9 percent. The result is that Mary-

land has a clear suburban majority — the only state in the country that can make that claim.

Baltimore County is overwhelmingly white and middle class, faintly Southern in outlook and generally conservative on social issues. Montgomery is an upper middle-class white-collar area, liberal and nominally Democratic but highly independent. It sends to Annapolis aggressive, reform-minded legislators who frequently seem outraged by the horse-trading practiced by colleagues from other parts of the state.

Prince George's County used to be something like Baltimore County, but an influx of blacks in recent years has helped pull its politics leftward and firmly into the Democratic column. Its legislators tend to side with the city of Baltimore in battles to protect allocations for social welfare programs.

The city of Baltimore has seen its legislative stature diminished by shrinking population. It lost two seats in the Senate and six in the House of Delegates as a result of the 1980 census. But it remains an influential force. The city maintains a lobbying office in the state capital of Annapolis, and Mayor William Donald Schaefer uses his personal and political popularity as leverage in winning for Baltimore a healthy share of the state's revenues.

Mandel and Hughes

It was Baltimore that produced the dominant statewide political figure of the past generation. Former Gov. Marvin Mandel was a brilliant streetwise politician who ran state government with an iron fist for nearly a decade before being convicted and sentenced to prison on corruption charges in 1977.

Despite his legal troubles, Mandel has left an enduring imprint on Maryland politics; there are still in the Legislature many old-line Democratic admirers of his rough-and-tumble style. But they have had some trouble adjusting to Mandel's successor, Gov. Harry R. Hughes — a quiet lawyer from the Eastern Shore who shuns the spotlight and

---

STATE LEADERSHIP

Gov. Harry R. Hughes (D)

Born: Nov. 13, 1926, Easton, Md.
Home: Baltimore, Md.
Education: U. of Md., B.S. 1949; George Washington U. Law School, J.D. 1952.
Military Career: Navy Air Corps, 1944-45.
Occupation: Lawyer.
Family: Wife, Patricia Donoho; two children.
Religion: Episcopalian.
Political Career: Md. House of Delegates, 1955-59; Md. Senate, 1959-71; Democratic nominee for U.S. House, 1964; secretary of Md. Dept. of Transportation, 1971-77; elected governor 1978, 1982; term expires Jan. 1987.

GENERAL ASSEMBLY

SENATE
41D, 6R

Melvin A. Steinberg (D)
President

HOUSE
124D, 17R

Benjamin L. Cardin (D)
Speaker

Speaker Benjamin L. Cardin   **Sen. Pres. Melvin A. Steinberg**

prides himself on his political independence.

Hughes got off to a rocky start in his first term. Legislators accustomed to Mandel's backslapping politics were stunned to find the new governor encouraging them to assert their independence. But Hughes since has forged a closer working relationship with the Legislature, distributing patronage and playing the pork-barrel politics he once disdained. During the 1983 session, Hughes worked closely with legislative leaders in producing a package of unemployment compensation and job training initiatives.

Leadership in the House of Delegates is monopolized by Speaker Benjamin L. Cardin. Heir to a Maryland tradition of powerful House Speakers, Cardin is a veteran legislator with allies throughout the state. He is said to be considering running for governor in 1986.

The power structure in the state Senate has recently undergone change. Democratic Sen. James Clark Jr., a farmer from rural Howard County, was ousted from his post as Senate president at the outset of the 1983 session, amid criticism that the upper chamber had fallen into disarray under his weak stewardship. Urban and suburban legislators lined up behind Sen. Melvin A. Steinberg of Baltimore County as a replacement.

As rural legislators rallied around Clark, Steinberg gathered support throughout the chamber with promises of attractive committee assignments and leadership posts. Several black legislators from the city of Baltimore helped swing the final vote to Steinberg.

The new president took to his duties forcefully, imposing a dress code for the Senate floor and even ejecting one reporter from the chamber for not wearing a necktie. Soon after, Steinberg pushed through a measure making substantial cutbacks in pension benefits to teachers and public employees, many of whom had been strong suporters of his in the past. Although the bill drew a backlash from several unions, Steinberg won high marks from colleagues who regarded the move as an act of striking political independence. The bill died in the House.

Despite that setback, organized labor remains a powerful interest group in Maryland, and a vital ally for any Democrat with statewide ambitions. Among the most influential unions in the state are the Maryland affiliate of the AFL-CIO and the Maryland Classified Employees Association.

Blacks, who comprise 23 percent of the state's population, are a significant force in Maryland politics. The efforts of several black organizations in Baltimore helped boost black voter turnout in 1982; buoyed by such efforts, a black won election as state's attorney in the city. ∎

A PROFILE OF
Maryland

PEOPLE

Total Population: 4,216,975 (18th).
   White 75%, Black 23%, Asian and
   Pacific Islander 2%. Spanish origin 2%.

Urban:	80%
Rural:	20%
Born in state:	54%
Foreign-born:	5%

MAJOR CITIES

Baltimore (786,775), Rockville (43,811),
   Hagerstown (34,132), Bowie (33,695),
   Annapolis (31,740)

LAND

Farm	45%
Forest	42%
Federally owned	3%

WORK

Occupations: 61% white-collar; 25% blue-collar; 13% service workers

Government workers: 128,493 federal
                      84,768 state
                      166,342 local

Unemployment rate: 7%

MONEY

Median family income (1980)	$23,112	(3rd)
Tax burden per capita (1982)	$757	(16th)

EDUCATION

Spending per pupil through grade 12	$2,998	(6th)
Persons with college degrees	20%	(4th)

CRIME

Violent crime rate: 887 per 100,000 (4th)

POLITICS

1980 Presidential Vote: Carter 47%,
                     Reagan 44%, Anderson 8%

Turnout rate in 1980:	59%
Turnout rate in 1982:	47%

U.S. House Delegation: 7D, 1R

MASSACHUSETTS:

'New' Dukakis Rules State With Help of 'Old' Politics

Politics in Massachusetts is played — and watched — with an intensity matched only by the state's obsession with the Red Sox. *The Boston Globe* and its chief competitor, the *Boston Herald*, deluge their readers with article after article on the intricacies of maneuvering in the Legis-

lature, strategy for upcoming elections and speculation about power plays among state administrators. The personal enmities and tactical ploys beneath the surface of public issues are the coin of political talk statewide.

There is no question that the political atmosphere has changed from the time when urban ethnic political machines dominated the state. Many Bostonians today are clearly uncomfortable with the personal machine built during the 1970s by Mayor Kevin White. Former Gov. Edward J. King lost his 1982 Democratic primary battle with Michael S. Dukakis in part because voters were upset by the aura of corruption and raw patronage that hung around his administration. The newest political force in the state — high-tech managers, engineers, scientists — wants little to do with the urban ethnic style of governing.

But Massachusetts state government is still a realm of clout and political *quid pro quo*, as Dukakis seems to have learned. First elected governor in 1974, he entered office with an agenda born of the "New Politics" reform move-

ment and a casual disregard for patronage etiquette. Over four years in office, Dukakis alienated not only conservatives but the more traditional labor-oriented "lunch bucket" Democrats who controlled the Legislature. The acrimony that developed gave King the chance to bind together the conservative Democratic coalition that toppled Dukakis in 1978.

Dukakis' Adroit Maneuvers

But the Dukakis who took control of the governorship again in 1983 has had a different way of operating. He used one adroit series of maneuvers to gain control of the board that oversees Boston's Logan Airport, deposing its chairman, a King ally and a friend of Democratic House Speaker Thomas W. McGee. Then, to soothe McGee's feelings, he gave the ousted chairman a less influential post in the state transportation department. That was a move the earlier Dukakis would not have bothered with.

The "new" Dukakis has made a point of ensuring that legislators are lined up before an issue is put to a vote. In preparing legislation giving workers and communities access to information about hazardous materials and work conditions, Dukakis aides and House leaders have met with representatives of smokestack and high-tech industries, as well as organized labor and community groups. The bill that eventually emerges almost certainly will have solid support on the House floor, even if it does not please all the interest groups.

As his relatively easy first months back in office have demonstrated, Dukakis' care in dealing with McGee and Senate President William M. Bulger — both of whom supported King in the 1982 primary — is prudent. Bulger in particular wields enormous influence over what comes out of his chamber. Bright, witty, and possessing a long memory for slights, he has sole power to appoint and dismiss committee chairmen, who earn some $7,000 a year more than rank-and-file legislators. With 26 committees and four leadership positions to fill, he is able to take care of all but three of the 33 Democrats in the Senate. Those

---

STATE LEADERSHIP

Gov. Michael S. Dukakis (D)

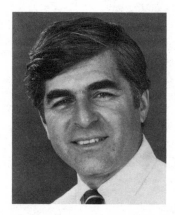

Born: Nov. 3, 1933, Brookline, Mass.
Home: Brookline, Mass.
Education: Swarthmore College, B.A. 1955; Harvard U. Law School, J.D. 1960.
Military Career: Army, 1956-58.
Occupation: Lawyer; television commentator.
Family: Wife, Katharine Dickson; three children.
Religion: Greek Orthodox.
Political Career: Mass. House, 1963-71; Democratic nominee for lieutenant governor, 1970; governor, 1975-79; defeated for renomination, 1978; re-elected governor, 1982; term expires Jan. 1987.

GENERAL COURT

SENATE

33D, 7R

William M. Bulger (D)
President

HOUSE

129D, 29R
2 vacancies

Thomas W. McGee (D)
Speaker

who oppose him consistently run the risk of becoming part of the three, rather than the 30. The GOP, which has only seven senators, lacks the strength to force roll-call votes; senators' accountability is to Bulger, not to the public.

McGee has the same institutional powers as Bulger. But with a far larger chamber to preside over, he has to work harder to line up votes, and allows more independence among the rank-and-file. Still, maverick status in the House is a luxury enjoyed by a minority of liberals and conservatives who come from well-to-do districts that do not need much in the way of state funds.

Insurgencies do succeed, but they tend to do so only on high-visibility issues where the political cost of going along with the leadership may be greater than deserting it. House liberals finally succeeded in placing a nuclear freeze referendum on the 1982 statewide ballot, after months of stalling on McGee's part, by having members of the state's congressional delegation bring pressure on legislators.

In 1983, Dukakis worked out a plan to allow 11 towns and cities to spread out over two years property tax reductions required by 1980's tax-slashing Proposition 2½. The Senate leadership quickly lined up votes for the proposal, and it sailed through that chamber with no trouble. But in the House, a small group of dissidents fought it until a tidal wave of public opinion against the step forced a number of representatives to back off. Dukakis eventually withdrew the proposal.

The legislative mavericks tend to be identified with their battles against the leadership over process rather than substance. They resent the tight control exercised by Bulger and McGee and their loyalist chairmen. Reform-minded Democratic legislators have joined in an odd coalition with the GOP, liberal community organizations and the state's leading anti-tax group to develop a statewide initiative campaign for changes in the legislative rules.

Chablis and Brie

But the Legislature is also split by the two political cultures that have coalesced around King and Dukakis. Named "Joe Six-Pack" and the "Chablis and Brie crowd" by the press, they represent two wings of the Democratic Party in Massachusetts — the GOP being little better than a token presence in state politics.

King's core vote was in the old industrial cities and working class, ethnic neighborhoods of Boston. Descendants of the Irish, Italian, Polish and Portuguese workers who built the party as a counter to the statewide economic control of Yankee Republicans, the King supporters endorse a New Deal approach toward government relief, but tend to oppose busing, abortion and gun control.

Despite the "Chablis-and-Brie" label, Dukakis' constituency is highly varied. It includes poor people, union activists and the elderly, as well as the more conspicuous young professionals, teachers and veterans of the reform movements of the 1960s. Dukakis' new pragmatism in dealing with members of the business community and with the leaders of the Legislature has caused some concern among his liberal supporters.

The high-tech community, which is the newest political force in Massachusetts, has held itself separate from traditional business interests and the entrenched Democratic coalition of labor and urban legislators. Although its membership is diverse, it tilts toward liberal social and conservative fiscal views. The Massachusetts High Technology Council played an important role in pushing the tax cuts of Proposition 2½. ∎

A PROFILE OF

Massachusetts

PEOPLE

Total Population: 5,737,037 (11th).
   White 94%, Black 4%, Asian and
   Pacific Islander 1%. Spanish origin 3%.

Urban:	84%
Rural:	16%
Born in state:	72%
Foreign-born:	9%

MAJOR CITIES

Boston (562,994), Worcester (161,799), Springfield (152,319), New Bedford (98,478), Cambridge (95,322)

LAND

Farm	13%
Forest	59%
Federally owned	2%

WORK

Occupations: 58% white-collar; 28% blue-collar; 13% service workers

Government workers:	55,923 federal
	85,479 state
	233,308 local

Unemployment rate: 8%

MONEY

Median family income (1980)	$21,166	(14th)
Tax burden per capita (1982)	$837	(12th)

EDUCATION

Spending per pupil through grade 12	$2,964	(9th)
Persons with college degrees	20%	(6th)

CRIME

Violent crime rate: 629 per 100,000 (11th)

POLITICS

1980 Presidential Vote: Reagan 42%, Carter 42%, Anderson 15%

Turnout rate in 1980:	66%
Turnout rate in 1982:	54%

U.S. House Delegation: 10D, 1R

MICHIGAN:

Fierce Partisanship Prevails In Declining Industrial State

"If we can't face the facts," Michigan Gov. James J. Blanchard said on taking office in January 1983, "we are going to be a state which time passes by." The facts facing the 40-year-old Democrat were grim: a declining industrial base, dwindling revenues, 700,000 people unemployed and a huge deficit.

Since then, Blanchard has jerked the state back from the brink of bankruptcy. Solving the larger problem — Michigan's economic obsolescence — will be much more difficult. That task requires unprecedented cooperation from legislators, labor and business. But fierce partisanship, rather than cooperation, is the dominant tone of Michigan politics today. Democrats are caught up in the euphoria of controlling both legislative chambers and the governorship for the first time since 1936, and the state lacks a consensus-seeker with the stature of former GOP Gov. William G. Milliken (1969-83).

From the very start, Blanchard quarreled with the Legislature's Republicans. He estimated the budget deficit at $850 million; Republicans said the shortfall was $650 million and predicted a faster economic recovery than the governor did. The final deficit level is still uncertain.

After Blanchard proposed to erase the deficit by raising income tax rates by 38 percent, a diverse coalition of urban, suburban and rural GOP senators indicated they would support a tax increase if it were smaller. But Blanchard declined to compromise and instead sought down-the-line Democratic support for the full 38 percent increase. That approach departed dramatically from the habit of Milliken, who always sought bipartisan support for tax-raising measures.

To bring pressure on the Legislature, Blanchard urged all groups benefiting from Michigan government spending to agitate for passage of his tax increase. The result was lobbying by an unusually broad array of interests — employee unions, teachers, social service workers, families with children in day-care programs and even private colleges, who rely on a state tuition grant program. Blanchard himself played an active role in lobbying for the proposal. He converted one Democratic state senator after showing up at a shower for the man's baby. Democrats united behind Blanchard and approved the tax increase in March. Only one Republican, Battle Creek Sen. Harry A. DeMaso, voted for it.

Now that additional tax revenues are coming in, the short-term fiscal crisis is resolved. Some estimates say the state might even finish fiscal 1983 with a small surplus. But the manner in which Blanchard achieved his tax victory soured his relations with some of the moderate Republicans whose compromise tax proposals were rebuffed. Blanchard needs to be on good terms with those centrist Republicans if he is to resolve future controversial issues. The margin of Democratic control in both the Senate and House is slim, and maintaining strict Democratic unity will become more difficult for Blanchard as the crisis atmosphere of his administration dissipates.

The toughest issue ahead is deciding what can be done to make Michigan economically viable in the future. Blanchard has offered a plan to promote diversification and resource development, but some critics discount it as a reshuffling of Milliken programs, with sweeteners added for traditional Democratic constituencies.

Democratic Divisions

It has been no mean feat for Blanchard to keep the Democratic Party united for as long as he has — from the 1982 election campaign well into his first year in office. There are a host of different groups within the party, each with spokesmen for its interests in the Legislature.

Year after year, the Detroit Democratic delegation meets stubborn resistance when it seeks money for its liberal and heavily black city from the white-dominated Legislature. Rural Democrats — both from the Upper Peninsula and the northern half of the Lower Peninsula — believe Detroit squanders state resources. Their outlook is shared to a lesser degree by Democrats from the state's smaller cities. But the strongest animosity toward Detroit

---

STATE LEADERSHIP

Gov. James J. Blanchard (D)

Born: Aug. 8, 1942, Detroit, Mich.
Home: Royal Oak, Mich.
Education: Mich. State U., B.A. 1964; M.B.A. 1965; U. of Minn. Law School, J.D. 1968.
Occupation: Lawyer.
Family: Wife, Paula Parker; one child.
Religion: Unitarian.
Political Career: U.S. House, 1975-83; elected governor, 1982; term expires Jan. 1987.

LEGISLATURE

SENATE
20D, 18R

Jackie Vaughn III (D)
President pro tem

HOUSE
63D, 47R

Gary M. Owen (D)
Speaker

comes from the city's suburbs, where some Democratic legislators, such as Sen. Gilbert J. DiNello of East Detroit, build their careers around suburbia's distrust of Detroit.

Within Detroit, politics revolves around Mayor Coleman A. Young, who is black and whose organization kept its distance from the state Democratic Party during the Milliken era. Young's good relationship with Milliken produced hefty state aid packages for Detroit, and in return Young provided only lukewarm backing for Milliken's election opponents.

Another easily identifiable faction in the state party is the one from the thinly settled Upper Peninsula (UP), an economically troubled mining area with strong Democratic loyalties. UP Democrats have influence in the Legislature far beyond their relatively small numbers. They tend to settle into safe Democratic seats and hold them year after year, winning re-election repeatedly and using seniority to attain committee chairmanships that give them considerable power statewide. Two UP Democrats in that mold are House Appropriations Chairman Dominic J. Jacobetti of Negaunee and Senate Natural Resources Chairman Joseph S. Mack of Ironwood.

Other Democratic branches include the "kiddie caucus," a group of now-maturing academics, ministers and other ideologically oriented liberals. One of the "kiddie caucus" liberals who has risen to prominence is House Taxation Committee Chairman H. Lynn Jondahl, a Church of Christ minister from East Lansing, home of Michigan State University. The blue-collar faction, which is led by the United Auto Workers (UAW), is concerned with wage rates, unemployment compensation and other bread-and-butter issues.

Speaker Gary M. Owen

The labor-UAW viewpoint, the dominant Democratic influence, has a strong spokesman in House Speaker Gary M. Owen of Ypsilanti, a blue-collar city dominated by autoworkers and devastated by unemployment.

Having lost its 20-year hold on the governorship, the Republican Party lacks a focus and is in the throes of defining its philosophical orientation. But it has not fallen into the disarray that many predicted for the post-Milliken era. Aided by a new reapportionment plan that stressed creation of compact constituencies (thereby packing Democrats into a limited number of urban districts), the GOP gained four Senate seats in 1982, and one seat in the House. They could gain more ground in upcoming months; efforts are under way in several districts to recall Democratic legislators who made campaign promises not to increase taxes, then supported Blanchard's bill.

There has been no GOP blood bath in the wake of the gubernatorial defeat. While Milliken and moderates did not exert themselves on behalf of party nominee Richard H. Headlee, a conservative devotee of supply-side economics, tensions have been eased by the new state GOP chairman, Spencer Abraham. In the future, the GOP center seems likely to lie somewhere to the right of where Milliken stood, but there is little sentiment that the party should move all the way to Headlee-style conservative ideology. ∎

A PROFILE OF

Michigan

PEOPLE

Total Population: 9,262,078 (8th).
   White 85%, Black 13%, Asian and
   Pacific Islander 1%. Spanish origin 2%.

Urban:	71%
Rural:	29%
Born in state:	72%
Foreign-born:	5%

MAJOR CITIES

Detroit (1,203,339), Grand Rapids (181,843), Flint (159,611), Lansing (130,414), Ann Arbor (107,966)

LAND

Farm	32%
Forest	53%
Federally owned	10%

WORK

Occupations: 51% white-collar; 34% blue-collar; 14% service workers

Government workers: 53,767 federal
153,065 state
371,917 local

Unemployment rate: 15%

MONEY

Median family income (1980)	$22,107	(8th)
Tax burden per capita (1982)	$681	(24th)

EDUCATION

Spending per pupil through grade 12	$2,652	(18th)
Persons with college degrees	14%	(35th)

CRIME

Violent crime rate: 642 per 100,000 (7th)

POLITICS

1980 Presidential Vote: Reagan 49%,
      Carter 43%, Anderson 7%

Turnout rate in 1980:   64%
Turnout rate in 1982:   54%

U.S. House Delegation: 12D, 6R

MINNESOTA:

Parties Becoming Polarized Under Stress of Budget Crisis

For years the two political parties in Minnesota have operated on virtually the same wavelength, creating a bipartisan consensus that enhanced the state's reputation for "good government." But under the weight of a state budget crisis, the Minnesota consensus has begun to unravel.

Since 1981, a series of shortfalls in government revenue has sent Democrats and Republicans scurrying in different directions for a solution. Democrats have emphasized the need for both tax increases and spending cuts to balance the budget, while Republicans have stressed only spending cuts.

Six special sessions were needed in the last two-year Legislature to deal with the budget crisis. By the time the sixth special session met in December 1982, partisan lines were clearly drawn. Outgoing GOP Gov. Albert H. Quie had to negotiate a bailout package with the Democrats over the opposition of Republican legislative leaders. The resulting combination of tax increases and spending cuts was passed almost exclusively with Democratic votes.

The partisan wrangling continued in 1983. But since Democrats regained the governorship in November 1982 and rebuilt comfortable majorities in both houses of the Legislature, GOP assent is less vital. Gov. Rudy Perpich and his party's legislative leaders have formed an uneasy, but so far effective, alliance.

Populist Perpich

A populist from the hard-scrabble Iron Range of northeastern Minnesota, Perpich is clearly of a different world from that of the cosmopolitan liberals of Minneapolis and St. Paul. He antagonized many legislators in 1982 by challenging, and then defeating, the gubernatorial choice of the party's state convention.

But Perpich has overcome the image of the amiable eccentric that characterized his first term as governor (1976-79). No longer does he jump into a state car and drive alone to a trouble spot to get a firsthand impression. Instead, he sought in 1983 to be the pragmatic team player, negotiating the outlines of his legislative package with the leadership. As a result, he has received most of what he publicly asked for, including a new $70 million jobs program and extensions of temporary increases in the state sales and income taxes. However, the legislative leadership squelched some of his other ideas, such as a sales tax on clothing.

Historically, the Legislature has held the upper hand in its dealings with the governor. But a series of assertive Democratic governors, from Orville L. Freeman (1955-61) to Wendell R. Anderson (1971-76), have broadened the influence of the governor and given Perpich more room in which to maneuver. He controls appointments in the executive branch and proposes the state budget from which the Legislature works.

To his advantage, he is not pitted against an entrenched "Old Guard." Both House Speaker Harry A. Sieben Jr. and Senate Majority Leader Roger Moe are under 40. Like Perpich, they are from outside the party's liberal stronghold, the Twin Cities. The soft-spoken, politically astute Sieben is from one of the distant suburbs; Moe, regularly mentioned as a possibility for statewide office, is from rural northwest Minnesota.

They preside over a legislative majority dominated by a labor-liberal axis based in the Twin Cities area and Duluth. The smaller rural component is more conservative, but has a strong populist streak. The combination enables the Democrats to produce a working majority on most economic issues, although the harmony is shattered on controversial social questions.

Debates on abortion have bitterly divided party gath-

STATE LEADERSHIP

Gov. Rudy Perpich (D)

Born: June 27, 1928, Carson Lake, Minn.
Home: Hibbing, Minn.
Education: Hibbing Junior College, A.A. 1950; Marquette U., D.D.S. 1954.
Military Career: Army, 1946-47.
Occupation: Dentist.
Family: Wife, Delores Simich; two children.
Religion: Roman Catholic.
Political Career: Hibbing Board of Education, 1956-62; Minn. Senate, 1963-71; lieutenant governor, 1971-76; governor, Dec. 1976-Jan. 1979; re-elected governor, 1982; term expires Jan. 1987.

LEGISLATURE

SENATE
42D, 25R

Jerome M. Hughes (D)
President

HOUSE
77D, 57R

Harry A. Sieben Jr. (D)
Speaker

erings in recent years. But a number of Minnesota's law-makers, such as freshman Democratic congressmen Gerry Sikorski and Timothy J. Penny (both former state sena-tors), have managed to bridge the gap by opposing abortion while voting with legislators from the Twin Cities on other issues.

But with the state's budget problems pushing other issues into the background, Democratic legislators in recent years have presented a reasonably united front. The only major defections in 1983 came when a group of rural Demo-crats known as the "Wood Ticks" — a Minnesota version of the congressional Boll Weevils — bolted to join the Republicans and pass a workmen's compensation law that was less expensive for businesses.

Otherwise, the Democrats got their way on practically every vote in the regular legislative session of 1983. While conservative Republican legislators put up vocal opposi-tion, they drew criticism — even from some party officials — for extreme partisanship. Their critics contend that while the anti-tax theme is an ideal stance in time of prosperity, it is ill-suited for a major budget crisis.

Republican 'Turks'

But there are many other Republicans who do not regret the polarized environment. Since 1978, when the party won the governorship and gained an even split in the state House, the GOP has moved steadily away from bipar-tisan consensus. That year saw the election of a large new class of Republicans to the Minnesota House. Known as the "Turks," they made an immediate impact on Minne-sota government. More conservative, more militant and more partisan than their GOP colleagues, they now hold the party's major leadership positions in the lower cham-ber.

But the Republican role in state government is limited by the absence of major outside allies. The most politically active interest groups — the AFL-CIO and the public employees' and teachers' unions — are almost exclusively allied with the Democrats. Neither agriculture nor the business community, which could provide sources of con-servative strength in state politics, is so intensely involved.

Although corn, wheat and other agricultural commod-ities provide about half of Minnesota's gross state product, farm interests in recent years have not had leverage in the Legislature to match their economic importance. The three major farm organizations within Minnesota — the state Farm Bureau, the Farmers Union and the National Farm-ers Organization — have their own separate agendas.

The same can be said for the state's two major busi-ness lobbies. The Minnesota Association of Commerce and Industry promotes the interests of smaller businesses. The Minnesota Business Partnership provides a forum for the chief executives of the state's major corporations, such as Honeywell and Control Data Corporation. A diverse group politically, the Partnership was headed early in 1983 by Ken Dayton, executive in a family department store empire and uncle of Mark Dayton, the liberal Democratic U.S. Senate candidate in 1982. Dayton's group has been active on several fronts. Besides developing close ties to Perpich, it mounted an expensive advertising campaign during the 1983 legislative session that helped blunt efforts to repeal the indexing of state income taxes.

While Republicans are locked out of the Minnesota power structure at present, their future is not bleak. The population in recent years has been shifting from the Dem-ocratic cities to the politically marginal suburbs. ∎

A PROFILE OF

Minnesota

PEOPLE

Total Population: 4,075,970 (21st).
White 97%, Black 1%, American Indian, Eskimo and Aleut 1%, Asian and Pacific Islander 1%. Spanish origin 1%.

Urban:	67%
Rural:	33%
Born in state:	75%
Foreign-born:	3%

MAJOR CITIES

Minneapolis (370,951), St. Paul (270,230), Duluth (92,811), Bloomington (81,831), Rochester (57,855)

LAND

Farm	60%
Forest	33%
Federally owned	7%

WORK

Occupations: 53% white-collar; 27% blue-collar; 14% service workers

Government workers:	29,604	federal
	73,273	state
	191,183	local

Unemployment rate: 8%

MONEY

Median family income (1980)	$21,185	(13th)
Tax burden per capita (1982)	$932	(6th)

EDUCATION

Spending per pupil through grade 12	$2,698	(15th)
Persons with college degrees	17%	(20th)

CRIME

Violent crime rate: 229 per 100,000 (41st)

POLITICS

1980 Presidential Vote: Carter 47%, Reagan 43%, Anderson 9%

Turnout rate in 1980:	73%
Turnout rate in 1982:	67%

U.S. House Delegation: 5D, 3R

MISSISSIPPI:

Rural Power Base Weakened By Integration, Urbanization

No state has undergone a more dramatic transformation in recent years than Mississippi. From a racially segregated, rural backwater, it has become an integrated, increasingly urbanized part of the Sun Belt.

Locked out of political power in the old Mississippi,  blacks and Republicans have begun flexing their muscles in recent federal elections. But state government has been slower to change, remaining the bailiwick of the conservative white, rural Democrats who have ruled the Magnolia State for a century.

Their power is enshrined in the state's archaic constitution of 1890, a document written by rural interests to perpetuate rural control. It enabled the development of a near-feudal system of government, centered at the local level in the powerful county board of supervisors. Each supervisor has his own little fiefdom in the county, wielding power through control of road construction and maintenance.

At the state level, power is centralized in a Legislature dominated by a conservative "Old Guard" from the Delta. Through its control of the leadership positions, the Old Guard has maintained a tight rein over state government for years.

The most powerful figure in the Legislature — some say in the whole state — is House Speaker C. B. "Buddie" Newman, a 35-year legislative veteran from the Delta village of Valley Park. He controls all committee assignments in the House and his friends chair the key committees. Probably his closest confidant is H. L. "Sonny" Merideth, a 23-year House veteran from Greenville who chairs the Ways and Means Committee. He is considered to be Newman's heir apparent as Speaker.

In the Senate, Lt. Gov. Brad Dye is trying to build a power base to rival Newman's. The lieutenant governor has the right to appoint committee chairmen in the Senate, but few have accumulated much power in the job because few have kept it very long. Dye will try; he is running for re-election in 1983.

The governor is at a distinct disadvantage in dealing with the Legislature. While legislative leaders have been able to cement their power through long tenure, the governor is a lame duck from the start of his four-year term. He cannot run for re-election.

To make his situation worse, power within the executive branch is badly fragmented. Many posts that governors of other states can fill by Cabinet appointment are elected offices in Mississippi; their occupants may or may not be the governor's allies. And the Legislature has made inroads of its own, stocking numerous boards and commissions in the executive branch with sitting members of the House and Senate.

Winter's Education Program

But a resourceful governor can succeed even in the face of his institutional disadvantages; William Winter, the current Democratic incumbent, has proved that. Winter coordinated a massive effort that culminated in December 1982 with legislative passage of a landmark education reform bill. Key features included teacher pay raises, creation of free public kindergartens and the establishment of tougher standards for school accreditation, teacher certification and student compulsory attendance.

The Legislature had rejected major education measures for years. Free kindergartens, many white legislators claimed, would be no more than a baby-sitting service for

STATE LEADERSHIP

Gov. William Winter (D)

Born: Feb. 21, 1923, Grenada County, Miss.
Home: Jackson, Miss.
Education: U. of Miss., B.A. 1943, LL.B., 1949.
Military Career: Army, World War II.
Occupation: Lawyer.
Family: Wife, Elise Varner; three children.
Religion: Presbyterian.
Political Career: Miss. House, 1948-56; State tax collector, 1956-64; state treasurer, 1964-68; sought Democratic gubernatorial nomination, 1967, 1975; lieutenant governor, 1972-76; elected governor 1979; term expires Jan. 1984.

LEGISLATURE

SENATE

48D, 4R

William B. Alexander (D)
President pro tem

HOUSE

116D, 4R, 2 Ind.

C. B. Newman (D)
Speaker

blacks. But Winter made an end run around the Legislature in 1982, selling his package to the public on the grounds that it made economic sense. Mississippi was the poorest and least-educated state in the nation, he argued, and could not hope to compete with other Sun Belt states in attracting new industry until the quality of its public education was improved dramatically.

Winter organized his lobbying effort like a political campaign. He, his wife and staff crisscrossed the state giving speeches and holding forums to call attention to the education issue. A network of allies was formed to help build grass-roots support. Some of the allies were natural, such as the teachers. But Winter also received help from business groups and the state's major newspaper, the *Jackson Clarion-Ledger.*

Long a quiet voice for the status quo when owned by the conservative Hederman family, the *Clarion-Ledger* was sold to the Gannett chain in 1982 and has become an outspoken proponent of government reform. Its steady drumbeat of articles and editorials in support of Winter's education package won the paper a Pulitzer Prize.

Rep. C. B. "Buddie" Newman

Once the groundwork was laid, Winter called a special session of the Legislature. The leadership at first balked at considering the package, but as outside support for the measure intensified, they gradually gave in.

But it was not a total victory. The state's oil interests won a key victory over Winter when it came time to fund the education package. As a means of paying for the improvements, the governor wanted to raise the severance tax on oil and gas for the first time since 1944. But when oil lobbyists warned that a severance tax increase might force their industry to leave the state, the Legislature backed down and increased sales and income taxes instead.

Regardless of who occupies the governorship in future years, the Legislature's era of unrivaled dominance is likely to come to a gradual close. Mississippi's shifting population is slowly draining power from the rural Old Guard. The main problem for the leadership is the erosion of its Delta base. Not only has the Delta lost population, but the region's conservative white legislators can no longer count on building power through seniority. Since passage of the 1965 Voting Rights Act, the Old Guard has faced increasing competition from blacks, who represent a majority of the population in most Delta counties.

Mississippi's population growth in recent years has primarily been along the Gulf Coast, in metropolitan Jackson and in scattered urban centers around the state where a more modern brand of legislator is being elected.

While changing demographics are propelling a quiet evolution in state government, a separation of powers suit could bring a dramatic realignment overnight. The suit, brought by the state attorney general, challenges the right of legislators to sit on executive branch boards and commissions. If the suit is upheld by the state Supreme Court, it would immediately expand the governor's appointment power.

A PROFILE OF

Mississippi

PEOPLE

Total Population: 2,520,638 (31st).
　　White 64%, Black 35%. Spanish
　　origin 1%.

Urban:	47%
Rural:	53%
Born in state:	79%
Foreign-born:	1%

MAJOR CITIES

Jackson (202,895), Biloxi (49,311), Meridian (46,577), Hattiesburg (40,829), Greenville (40,613)

LAND

Farm	48%
Forest	55%
Federally owned	6%

WORK

Occupations:　45% white-collar; 38% blue-collar; 12% service workers

Government workers:　25,119　federal
　　　　　　　　　　44,577　state
　　　　　　　　　　101,519　local

Unemployment rate:　14%

MONEY

Median family income (1980)	$14,591	(50th)
Tax burden per capita (1982)	$580	(40th)

EDUCATION

Spending per pupil through grade 12	$1,685	(50th)
Persons with college degrees	12%	(46th)

CRIME

Violent crime rate:　305 per 100,000 (35th)

POLITICS

1980 Presidential Vote:　Reagan 49%,
　　　　　　Carter 48%, Anderson 1%

Turnout rate in 1980:　67%
Turnout rate in 1982:　52%

U.S. House Delegation:　3D, 2R

MISSOURI:

St. Louis, Kansas City Battle For State's Power and Money

Missouri has always been conservative Democratic territory, and that tradition remains intact even though Republican Christopher S. "Kit" Bond has won two gubernatorial terms. Democrats still outnumber Republicans by better than 2-to-1 in the state House, and nearly that much in the Senate. A majority of the Democratic legislators stand to the right of their national party.

But the structure of Democratic control is gradually changing. Rural legislators are losing their numbers, due to reapportionment, and those from metropolitan St. Louis and Kansas City have the opportunity to replace them as leaders. But, while the two metropolitan areas have enough voting strength to dominate the Legislature as an alliance, they generally do not do so because their relationship is marked more by conflict than by cooperation.

Tension between St. Louis and Kansas City was evident in the 1983 legislative session, in which Bond and the Legislature worked to distribute benefits from a $600 million state bond issue. Virtually from the outset, Kansas City-area legislators complained that St. Louis was getting more than its fair share.

Legislators from the St. Louis area also argue with each other. Local politics often spills over onto the legislative agenda. Since Civil War days, for example, the Legislature has controlled pay raises for the St. Louis police force — an issue that turns black north St. Louis against the white South Side and frustrates legislators from other areas, who feel they have more important business.

Rural legislators complain frequently these days that both metropolitan areas receive too much of the Legislature's attention, and they push to divert state funds toward their own regions. They often benefit from the division between St. Louis and Kansas City by providing the votes necessary to swing an issue to one side or the other, and bargaining for benefits in the process.

Senate Power Play

The complexity of regional politics in Missouri was demonstrated early in 1981, when a liberal Democratic bloc dominated by Kansas City legislators organized to take control of the state Senate. The bloc lined up enough votes to elect its candidate for Senate president pro tem in the Democratic caucus. But the liberals were outvoted on the Senate floor by a rival coalition made up of conservative Republicans (and some Democrats) from suburban St. Louis and Democrats from Missouri's southeastern Bootheel, northeastern Little Dixie and other rural regions.

A key player in that struggle was Republican Sen. Richard M. Webster of rural southwest Missouri, who helped gather the votes that swung the election to Norman L. Merrell, another rural conservative. Merrell has since stepped down from the presidency to prepare a gubernatorial campaign, but Webster remains one of the foremost powers in the Senate. Officially the minority floor leader, Webster is a vital part of an informal bipartisan coalition of conservatives that effectively runs the Senate.

Party-line votes are relatively rare in the Senate, a body dominated by senior members whose personal friendships and political alliances often take precedence over partisan identification. Some younger members have managed to carve out influence in the Senate, however. One of them, Democrat John E. Scott of St. Louis, currently is serving in his first term as Senate president pro tem. Scott is credited with helping paper over some of the cracks exposed by the 1981 leadership clash. But critics claim that his errors in predicting the outcome of floor votes show that he does not have the chamber under his control.

Party politics is more important in the Missouri House, and political power is more centralized there. Issues often are worked out in private session or in the Demo-

---

STATE LEADERSHIP

Gov. Christopher S. "Kit" Bond (R)

Born: March 6, 1939, St. Louis, Mo.
Home: Kansas City, Mo.
Education: Princeton U., A.B. 1960; U. of Va. Law School, LL.B. 1963.
Occupation: Lawyer.
Family: Wife, Carolyn Reid; one child.
Religion: Presbyterian.
Political Career: Republican nominee for U.S. House, 1968; assistant Mo. attorney general, 1969-70; state auditor, 1971-73; elected governor 1972; defeated for re-election, 1976; re-elected 1980; term expires Jan. 1985.

GENERAL ASSEMBLY

SENATE
22D, 12R

John E. Scott (D)
President pro tem

HOUSE
110D, 53R

Bob F. Griffin (D)
Speaker

Sen. Richard M. Webster   **Rep. Bob F. Griffin**

cratic caucus, led by Speaker Bob F. Griffin of Cameron. Griffin has undergone a political transformation since he first took over as Speaker in 1981. Considered somewhat liberal by Missouri standards — he won his post in part through support from the increasingly influential black delegations from St. Louis and Kansas City — he pushed at the outset for a tax increase. But Griffin eventually backed down after losing several preliminary votes on the matter, and has maintained a lower profile on most issues ever since. During this year's session, Griffin was instrumental in steering through a measure calling for the conservative goal of a constitutional convention to deal with the subject of balancing the federal budget.

GOP Quest

Griffin was one of more than 50 Democratic legislators targeted for defeat by the Missouri Republican Party in 1982, as part of the state GOP's quest for greater power. Although the party has developed a well-funded and well-structured organization over the last decade, the 1982 offensive did not appreciably increase Republican ranks in the Legislature.

The GOP's one source of power at the state level is the governorship, wrenched from the Democratic column for the first time in over a quarter century when Bond won his initial Statehouse term in 1972. Bond fell victim to Democrat Joseph P. Teasdale in 1976, losing in one of the notable upsets of the year. But he avenged his loss in 1980.

In his second term, Bond has warmed up to the task of playing politics with the Legislature. He is much more accessible to legislators now than he was during his first term. But Bond is not a highly visible or activist governor; beyond his longstanding opposition to a tax increase, he has done little to attract attention. State law prevents Bond from seeking a third term, and many feel the governor is lying low in an effort to improve his political stock for a possible 1986 U.S. Senate candidacy.

Among interest groups that lobby the Legislature, teachers are coming to rival organized labor in visibility and influence. The Missouri State Teachers Association (MSTA) claims credit for placing on the ballot and helping to pass an initiative boosting the state sales tax by one cent, and earmarking a sizable chunk of the revenues for educators' salaries. The MSTA frequently feuds with the state chapter of the National Education Association.

Although lobbyists for the State Labor Council have had little success in seeking collective bargaining legislation, they scored significant increases in workers' compensation benefits in 1983. ∎

A PROFILE OF

Missouri

PEOPLE

Total Population: 4,916,686 (15th).
   White 88%, Black 11%, Asian and
   Pacific Islander 1%. Spanish origin 1%.

Urban:	68%
Rural:	32%
Born in state:	70%
Foreign-born:	2%

MAJOR CITIES

St. Louis (453,085), Kansas City (448,159), Springfield (133,116), Independence (111,806), Columbia (62,061)

LAND

Farm	73%
Forest	29%
Federally owned	5%

WORK

Occupations: 51% white-collar; 31% blue-collar; 14% service workers

Government workers:	65,810	federal
	69,045	state
	192,065	local

Unemployment rate: 9%

MONEY

Median family income (1980)	$18,784	(31st)
Tax burden per capita (1982)	$470	(48th)

EDUCATION

Spending per pupil through grade 12	$2,197	(30th)
Persons with college degrees	14%	(39th)

CRIME

Violent crime rate: 540 per 100,000 (15th)

POLITICS

1980 Presidential Vote: Reagan 51%,
   Carter 44%, Anderson 4%

Turnout rate in 1980:	67%
Turnout rate in 1982:	51%

U.S. House Delegation: 6D, 3R

MONTANA:

Unions, Environmentalists Keys to Democratic Control

Montana is not only the closest thing to a Democratic state in the Mountain West, it is about the only state in the region where Democrats can win without repudiating liberal politics. In striking contrast to its early history, in which it was virtually a captive of the Anaconda Copper  Company and other corporate interests, Montana is a state where labor is more than equal to business in legislative influence.

Environmental regulation is generally more strict in Montana than in other Mountain states. The state's coal severance tax is by far the highest in the nation, and Democratic Gov. Ted Schwinden vigorously defends it.

Labor influence on the Legislature is a Montana tradition that grew out of hard-won union success organizing the copper miners. It continues even though the industry itself is in decline. The state AFL-CIO is effective at all political levels; its director, Jim Murry, has been widely mentioned as a future congressional candidate.

Unions joined with environmentalists to pass some of the critical environmental legislation of the 1970s. The coalition has been successful since then in fighting off efforts to repeal the laws. The pro-business side in environmental arguments is often led by utility companies, especially Montana Power Company, which was formerly associated with Anaconda Copper. But business has failed to organize effectively to counter the environmental-labor co-alition's efforts.

Recently, women's groups have joined that liberal-oriented coalition. With help from Sen. Pat Regan, a well-respected Democrat from Billings, the women's groups were able to push for a measure prohibiting sex discrimination in insurance.

Legislature Meets Infrequently

Montana's Legislature has to do its work quickly — it meets for only 90 days every two years. The 1972 state constitution instituted annual legislative sessions, but an initiative to restore the biennial sessions passed overwhelmingly, and subsequent attempts to impose annual sessions have been decisively defeated.

When in session, the Legislature is productive. Some 1,600 bills are introduced every session, and under the rules, all have to receive a hearing. In the House, the Speaker's role is decisive. In 1983, the Speaker was Dan Kemmis, a liberal 38-year-old lawyer from the university town of Missoula.

Kemmis is highly regarded by most members, but he was unable to prevent serious factionalism from developing among House Democrats during the 1983 session. On one measure that highlighted the division in the Democratic Party, Kemmis broke with Schwinden over the governor's plan to sell water to other states. While Schwinden backed the plan as a way of raising money, Kemmis objected to it on environmental grounds. Kemmis won, but the split hurt chances for concerted Democratic action on other issues in the rest of the session.

Reapportionment should affect the House before the next session. Democrats, particularly urban Democrats, are expected to pick up seats when lines are redrawn for the 1984 elections. Because the Senate has staggered terms, half the Senate seats will be up for election in reapportioned districts in 1984, and half in 1986.

A major figure in the 1983 session of the Senate was Republican Jean A. Turnage. Although he is not currently a member of the leadership, Turnage is a former Senate

---

STATE LEADERSHIP

Gov. Ted Schwinden (D)

Born: Aug. 31, 1925, Wolf Point, Mont.
Home: Helena, Mont.
Education: Attended Mont. School of Mines, 1946-47; U. of Mont., B.A. 1949, M.A. 1950; Attended U. of Minn., 1950-54.
Military Career: Army, 1943-46.
Occupation: Farmer and rancher.
Family: Wife, Jean Christianson; three children.
Religion: Lutheran.
Political Career: Mont. House, 1959-61; commissioner of state lands, 1969-76; lieutenant governor, 1977-81; elected governor 1980; term expires Jan. 1985.

LEGISLATURE

SENATE
24D, 26R
Stan Stephens (R)
President

HOUSE
55D, 45R
Daniel Kemmis (D)
Speaker

Speaker Daniel Kemmis   **Sen. Jean A. Turnage**

president who functions as a gray eminence in the party.

Control of the Democrats in the Senate rested with floor leader Chet Blaylock. Blaylock showed some political courage in 1980 when, as minority leader, he backed then-Lt. Gov. Schwinden in a primary against incumbent Gov. Thomas L. Judge. Schwinden won, and he and Blaylock have been allies ever since.

Because the Legislature meets so infrequently, the governor is the only visible year-round presence in state government. Schwinden is highly conscious of that visibility, and has cultivated a public image as a sort of Western Harry S Truman. The first working farmer to occupy the Statehouse, Schwinden talks in the earthy language of the eastern Montana plains. The governor chooses his issues carefully, and he is successful more often than not. In 1981, his first legislative session, Schwinden had his difficulties with the Legislature. But he was far more successful in 1983.

Either the governor or the Legislature can call a special session. Two were called after the 1981 session, and at least one is expected before 1985. Schwinden called one after a disturbance at the state prison, proposing to build new minimum- and maximum-security facilities. The Legislature balked, however, and proposed instead to conduct its own study of the question.

Initiative Process

The slow legislative pace is in part responsible for the frequent use of the state's initiative law, under which it is relatively easy to bring measures to a popular vote. A part of the constitutional revision of 1972, the initiative process generally has helped Democrats and liberals more than their conservative opposition, which has been slow to take advantage of it. In 1981, when Republicans had majorities in both the House and Senate, several GOP members introduced bills to restrict the initiative process. These met substantial resistance from constituents, and were soundly defeated. No such bills were introduced in 1983.

Initiatives also affect the work of the Legislature. In 1983, much of the Legislature's time was devoted to implementing an economic development plan passed by the voters in a 1982 initiative. The plan, which required one-fourth of the coal tax trust fund to be invested within the state, was a joint project of Schwinden and Kemmis.

In addition, the Legislature has passed bills to head off possible initiatives. Common Cause, the self-styled citizens' lobby, planned an initiative campaign for 1984 to limit money from political action committees in state campaigns. But the Legislature passed its own limitation first. ∎

A PROFILE OF

Montana

PEOPLE

Total Population: 786,690 (44th).
   White 94%, Black 0.2%, American Indian, Eskimo and Aleut 5%. Spanish origin 1%.

Urban:	53%
Rural:	47%
Born in state:	57%
Foreign-born:	2%

MAJOR CITIES

Billings (66,798), Great Falls (56,725), Butte-Silver Bow (37,205), Missoula (33,388), Helena (23,938)

LAND

Farm	68%
Forest	24%
Federally owned	30%

WORK

Occupations: 50% white-collar; 26% blue-collar; 15% service workers

Government workers:	12,501 federal
	20,135 state
	35,623 local

Unemployment rate: 8%

MONEY

Median family income (1980)	$18,413	(32nd)
Tax burden per capita (1982)	$672	(26th)

EDUCATION

Spending per pupil through grade 12	$2,727	(12th)
Persons with college degrees	18%	(18th)

CRIME

Violent crime rate: 253 per 100,000 (39th)

POLITICS

1980 Presidential Vote: Reagan 57%, Carter 32%, Anderson 8%

Turnout rate in 1980:	68%
Turnout rate in 1982:	61%

U.S. House Delegation: 1D, 1R

NEBRASKA:

Individualism Is Supreme In Non-Partisan Legislature

Nebraska's Legislature is unique in two ways. It is the nation's only one-house Legislature, and the only one to which members are elected on a non-partisan basis. The casual attitude toward party labels is at least as important as the unicameral structure. There is no party leadership to

discipline the 49 Nebraska senators. Individualism reigns supreme.

Although none of the senators run on a party label, it is generally agreed that 31 of the current ones are registered Republicans, and 18 are registered Democrats. It is unusual, however, for senators to vote along party lines. Rural and

urban coalitions emerge with more frequency; the state's population is about evenly divided between the eastern metropolitan areas of Omaha and Lincoln and the rural "outstate" areas. But more than in other Legislatures, voting blocs shift with the issues. Anybody who can put together an ad hoc majority of 25 senators is the leader of the day.

The man who is getting what he wants out of the Legislature most these days is Nebraska's new governor, Democrat Bob Kerrey. Kerrey was narrowly elected in November 1982 in an upset over GOP Gov. Charles Thone, who had a reputation for indecision. Kerrey, by contrast, is an aggressive Vietnam veteran who departs from the mold of conservative Nebraska politicians.

Kerrey gained a celebrity reputation in 1983 by dating movie star Debra Winger, whom he met while Winger was acting in a movie in Lincoln. At a meeting of the National Governors' Association in August, Kerrey drafted a widely publicized letter blasting President Reagan's economic program.

The unicameral system magnifies the influence of Ne-

braska's governor, allowing him to absorb some of the power of a second legislative chamber. The threat of a gubernatorial veto seems to be more effective in dealing with a single legislative body. In behind-the-scenes negotiations with the Legislature on budget issues this year, Kerrey dangled the veto threat successfully to help accomplish his goals. In the end, his approach was a public relations success. Rather than seeming negative, he gave the impression of an activist governor who worked in tandem with the Legislature to resolve issues that had dragged on for years.

Early in 1983, for example, Kerrey and the Legislature hammered out a liberalized banking law that allows multibank holding companies in Nebraska. It settled a long-standing fight between large and small banks, with the large banks winning the right to expand into new areas. Another long-running issue was resolved by the Legislature's decision to repeal the sales tax on food. Kerrey signed the bill, pushed by liberals who said the tax was regressive, at the risk of alienating municipal officials who complained about losing an important source of local revenue.

Budget Woes

The state's budget was the overriding issue in 1983. Kerrey faced a large deficit, brought on partly by reduced revenues from the state's depressed farm economy and partly by a ripple effect from the federal income tax cut. (Nebraska income taxes are calculated as a percentage of a taxpayer's federal bill, and the three-year federal tax reduction bit into state revenues).

Kerrey pushed through the Legislature a package of spending cuts and a 2 percent income tax increase. Some of the cuts surprised the governor's supporters, particularly his recommendation to deny a pay raise this year to state employees, who backed him in last year's campaign. Boosters of the University of Nebraska, a sacred cow in the eastern part of the state, also were annoyed that Kerrey's budget did not give the university as large an increase as it sought.

Despite the lack of party identity in the Legislature, Kerrey generally could count on support from Democratic senators. And he could depend on opposition from a group of about 10 conservative Republicans, dubbed "Thone's Clones" during the previous administration because of

STATE LEADERSHIP

Gov. Bob Kerrey (D)

Born: Aug. 27, 1943, Lincoln, Neb.
Home: Lincoln; Neb.
Education: U. Of Neb., B.S., 1965.
Military Career: Navy, 1966-69.
Occupation: Restaurateur.
Family: Divorced; two children.
Religion: Congregationalist.
Political Career: Elected governor, 1982; term expires, Jan. 1987.

LEGISLATURE

49 non-partisan senators in unicameral assembly

Sen. William E. Nichol
Speaker

their unwavering loyalty to the former governor. To build winning coalitions, Kerrey turned to the moderate Republicans, who supported most of his first-year initiatives.

To achieve his goals in the non-partisan situation, a governor has to recruit individual senators, rather than depending on party leaders who might bring in the rest of the flock in a more partisan Legislature. An example of the importance of individuals is the power ascribed to Sen. John DeCamp, chairman of the Legislature's Banking Committee. An independent man who is now a Republican but once was a Democrat, DeCamp often aligns himself with the side that looks like it might win. Individuals like DeCamp can provide the swing votes on legislation.

With each senator following his or her own instincts, Lincoln would seem to be a tough place for a lobbyist to operate. But lobbyists like it, largely because it is a unicameral body. There is only one set of lawmakers to cajole, and no risk that a bill will fall victim to disagreement between two chambers.

The statewide teachers' union, an affiliate of the National Education Association, is a key liberal influence in Lincoln, especially with its generous campaign finance treasury. For a state so heavily dependent on agriculture, the farm lobby is surprisingly weak. This is because it is so splintered, with different commodity groups often squabbling with each other.

Although Kerrey and the Legislature were applauded for their cooperation in 1983, some of the state's most difficult issues lie just ahead. A large problem is how to meet Nebraska's future water needs. Although much of the farm land already is irrigated, development interests say more water projects are needed to sustain economic growth. They are at odds with environmentalists, who are concerned about endangered species, groundwater pollution and overdevelopment of the state's water resources.∎

A PROFILE OF
Nebraska

PEOPLE

Total Population: 1,569,825 (35th).
White 95%, Black 3%, American Indian, Eskimo and Aleut 1%. Spanish origin 2%.

Urban:	63%
Rural:	37%
Born in state:	70%
Foreign-born:	2%

MAJOR CITIES

Omaha (314,255), Lincoln (171,932), Grand Island (33,180), North Platte (24,479), Fremont (23,979)

LAND

Farm	97%
Forest	2%
Federally owned	1%

WORK

Occupations: 49% white-collar; 27% blue-collar; 14% service workers

Government workers: 15,273 federal
32,101 state
83,336 local

Unemployment rate: 6%

MONEY

Median family income (1980)	$19,122	(29th)
Tax burden per capita (1982)	$548	(45th)

EDUCATION

Spending per pupil through grade 12	$2,445	(20th)
Persons with college degrees	16%	(26th)

CRIME

Violent crime rate: 182 per 100,000 (45th)

POLITICS

1980 Presidential Vote: Reagan 66%, Carter 26%, Anderson 7%

Turnout rate in 1980: 63%
Turnout rate in 1982: 56%

U.S. House Delegation: 3R

NEVADA:

Reno 'Reformers' Confront 'Old Guard' Conservatives

Nevada is a state whose politics and economics never seem to match. Its economy is heavily dependent on gambling and a frisky tourist trade, but its politics are rooted in the conservative traditions and philosophy that dominate the whole Rocky Mountain region.

Democrats control the governorship and both houses of the Legislature, but Gov. Richard H. Bryan is the only well-known state political figure who could be considered a "national" Democrat. While pro-labor Democrats from Las Vegas and reformist "good government" advocates from the Reno area dot the Legislature, the top leadership positions are dominated by a conservative "Old Guard" that allies with Republicans to produce a working majority on most issues.

The embodiment of the Old Guard is Senate Majority Leader Jim Gibson, who has served 25 years in the Legislature, seven as majority leader. He has developed a power base to rival anyone in state government. An engineer by trade, Gibson has steadily accrued influence through perseverance and a knack for detail. He served nearly 20 years on the Senate Finance Committee, and has a key ally there now in committee Chairman Floyd Lamb.

Together, Lamb and Gibson form a Nevada version of "the odd couple." As a longtime officer of the Mormon Church in the Las Vegas area, Gibson has a reputation for being strait-laced on ethical matters. Lamb does not; he recently was indicted on public corruption charges.

There is no similar power focus in the Assembly, where it has been traditional for the Speaker to serve only one term. A lame duck from the start, any Speaker must watch aspirants scheme openly to replace him.

In recent years Republicans have steadily increased their numbers in the Assembly, adding an element of partisanship that was absent in the Legislature when Democrats enjoyed large majorities in both chambers. Republicans held 19 of the 42 Assembly seats in 1983 and used the session to develop campaign themes for 1984.

With the agenda dominated by budget questions, GOP legislators presented a united front in opposing major tax increases. Bryan managed to scuttle the "Tax Shift," an ill-fated plan through which the previous Republican governor, Robert F. List, reduced property taxes and increased the sales tax. But when Bryan offered his own proposal, to increase funding for education through new property tax levies, Republican legislators joined with a few Democratic defectors to defeat it.

Assembly Republicans, however, were not Bryan's only headache. He also had to contend with the machinations of his lieutenant governor, Bob Cashell, an ally of Gibson and the conservative coalition in the Legislature. Many Democrats complained that Cashell, a wealthy Reno businessman, actually preferred List for governor in 1982, even though he himself was on the Democratic statewide ticket. In 1983, while Gibson and other conservative Democrats in the Legislature were giving at least lukewarm support for the Bryan tax plan, Cashell was lobbying successfully for its defeat.

To the chagrin of Bryan, Cashell also outmaneuvered him on the creation of two new commissions on economic development and tourism. Bryan had wanted his office to control the composition of both commissions, but Cashell

STATE LEADERSHIP

Gov. Richard H. Bryan (D)

Born: July 16, 1937, Washington, D.C.
Home: Carson City, Nev.
Education: U. of Nev., B.A. 1959; U. of Calif., Hastings College of Law, LL.B. 1963.
Military Career: Army, 1959-60.
Occupation: Lawyer.
Family: Wife, Bonnie Fairchild; three children.
Religion: Episcopalian.
Political Career: Deputy district attorney, Clark County, 1964-66; Nev. Assembly, 1969-73; Democratic nominee for Nev. attorney general, 1974; Nev. Senate, 1973-79; Nev. attorney general, 1979-83; elected governor 1982; term expires Jan. 1987.

LEGISLATURE

SENATE
17D, 4R

Keith Ashworth (D)
President pro tem

ASSEMBLY
23D, 19R

John M. Vergiels (D)
Speaker

persuaded the Legislature to designate the lieutenant governor as the chairman of both. Cashell's sparring with Bryan spurred talk that he would switch parties and try for the governorship as a Republican in 1986. In mid-August 1983, Cashell announced that he was changing parties and becoming a Republican.

'Reform' Faction

Whatever the current dominance of the conservative Democratic bloc, however, the balance of power is likely to change over the 1980s. A rival faction of "reform" Democrats currently holds about one-third of the seats in the Assembly, and a slightly larger percentage in the Senate. Their numbers are steadily growing as Nevada's population boom brings an influx of relatively liberal, highly educated newcomers from neighboring California and from the East.

Fueled by a series of "good government" editorials from the Gannett-owned Reno newspapers, the Reno area has emerged as the center of a government reform movement. The group includes Bryan's major Democratic supporters, assistant Senate Majority Leader Thomas "Spike" Wilson and Assembly Majority Whip Robert Sader. There is also one prominent Republican — state Sen. Sue Wagner, a former reporter and teacher who is among only four GOP members of the upper chamber. All three are part of the recent emigration to Nevada: Wilson and Sader are from California, and Wagner is from Maine.

The Reno bloc frequently is outvoted, but it has made inroads in tightening Nevada's lax campaign finance laws.

The group spearheaded passage of legislation in 1983 requiring candidates to report contributions collected in the calendar year prior to the election. Previously, only money received in the election year had to be disclosed. But Nevada still has some of the weakest ethics laws in the country.

Sen. Jim Gibson

Gambling interests — "gaming" by Nevada political euphemism — enjoy the most influential lobbying position. Not only are they Nevada's major revenue producers, but they are widely accepted as a vital and legitimate part of the state economy. The Republican state convention in 1982 was held at Caesars' hotel and casino resort on Lake Tahoe.

The growth of gambling operations in other states has strengthened the demands of the gaming interests for favorable treatment. The casinos were largely untouched by the 1983 round of tax increases and successfully blunted a legislative proposal to create a state lottery.

Cattle and mining interests are no longer the dominant forces they were before gambling was legalized in Nevada a half century ago. Their natural allies, legislators from the Cow Counties, also have lost clout. Before one-man, one-vote, each county had its own Senate seat. That meant that while populous Clark County (Las Vegas) and Washoe County (Reno) each had one seat, the sparsely populated Cow Counties, which make up the rest of the state, had more than a dozen. Reapportionment has eliminated this disparity, but Cow County legislators still have considerable influence due to seniority and ties to the leadership. ∎

A PROFILE OF
Nevada

PEOPLE

Total Population: 800,493 (43rd).
White 87%, Black 6%, American Indian, Eskimo and Aleut 2%, Asian and Pacific Islander 2%. Spanish origin 7%.

Urban:	85%
Rural:	15%
Born in state:	22%
Foreign-born:	7%

MAJOR CITIES

Las Vegas (164,674), Reno (100,756), North Las Vegas (42,739), Sparks (40,780), Carson City (32,022)

LAND

Farm	13%
Forest	11%
Federally owned	82%

WORK

Occupations: 50% white-collar; 23% blue-collar; 26% service workers

Government workers:	9,085	federal
	14,433	state
	33,792	local

Unemployment rate: 9%

MONEY

Median family income (1980)	$21,311	(11th)
Tax burden per capita (1982)	$932	(7th)

EDUCATION

Spending per pupil through grade 12	$2,069	(34th)
Persons with college degrees	14%	(33rd)

CRIME

Violent crime rate: 896 per 100,000 (3rd)

POLITICS

1980 Presidential Vote: Reagan 63%, Carter 27%, Anderson 7%

Turnout rate in 1980:	49%
Turnout rate in 1982:	42%

U.S. House Delegation: 1D, 1R

NEW HAMPSHIRE:

Population Boom Reinforces Anti-Tax Conservative Rule

One learns a lot about New Hampshire from the state's motto, "Live Free or Die." It conveys a sense of combative independence and feisty self-sufficiency.

Nowhere is this more evident than in the Granite State's approach to taxes. For generations, residents have

forsaken a variety of state-supported services in order to preserve one of the lowest levels of taxation in the country. New Hampshire is the only state without either a state sales or income tax, and candidates for governor routinely "take the pledge" not to impose either in order to stand a chance to win.

In the 1970s, New Hampshire grew at a faster pace than any state east of the Mississippi River except Florida. But rather than mellowing New Hampshire's flinty brand of fiscal conservatism, the population boom has served to reinforce it. Many of the newcomers, especially those from neighboring Massachusetts, were attracted to New Hampshire by its low taxes. While they have provided votes for liberal Democratic candidates in congressional elections, they usually vote in state and local contests to preserve the status quo.

And in New Hampshire, the status quo is a moderate to conservative brand of pro-business Republicanism. The business community is the dominant influence on the Legislature. Besides its low tax rate, New Hampshire is one of the least unionized states outside the South. The hospitable business climate has enabled the thriving southern tier of the state to make the transition from agriculture and textiles to high technology.

Many southern New Hampshire locals decry the suburbanization of their once pastoral region, but the area from Manchester and Nashua east to the coast has become the center of political power within the state. It is home for Gov. John H. Sununu and Senate President Vesta M. Roy. Both are Republicans from Salem, a bustling town on the Massachusetts border that forms one corner of New Hampshire's "high-tech" golden triangle.

Sununu is a good match for modern New Hampshire. A one-time energy consultant and mechanical engineering professor at Tufts University in Massachusetts, he knows how to speak the language of the business world. His governorship, he says, is a two-year management consultancy. Sununu has sought to bridge the traditional gap between the GOP's conservative and moderate wings by portraying himself as a business-oriented pragmatist rather than a conservative ideologue like New Hampshire's last Republican governor, Meldrim Thomson Jr. (1973-79).

Thus far, Sununu has succeeded. With unabashed self-confidence and Republican majorities at all levels of government, Sununu largely had his way during his first year in office. To meet a $44 million budget deficit, the governor proposed spending cuts and revenue measures that were generally palatable to the business community. But balancing the budget is always difficult without a sales or income tax, and Sununu was forced to rely on what the *Concord Monitor* has described as revenue sources "that rank only a cut above bake sales and car washes."

Checks and Balances

If Sununu had wanted to make any significant changes in the tax structure, he would have faced an elaborate system of checks and balances that has long frustrated reformers and perpetuated the status quo.

As the only statewide elected official in New Hampshire, the governor is the focal point of political power. But he has no appointive Cabinet to help him and serves only a two-year term. The executive branch is a rambling collection of departments, boards and commissions. Some are run by the governor's appointees, but in many cases they are dominated by the choices of his predecessor. Most of the appointments are for three to six years.

Within the executive branch, the governor also must confront an independently elected executive council that approves state contracts and appointments. That has been a greater problem for past governors than for Sununu, since the current council has a 4-1 GOP majority.

STATE LEADERSHIP

Gov. John H. Sununu (R)

Born: July 2, 1939, Havana, Cuba.
Home: Salem, N.H.
Education: M.I.T., B.S. 1961, M.S. 1962, Ph.D. 1966.
Profession: Engineer.
Family: Wife, Nancy Hayes; eight children.
Religion: Roman Catholic.
Political Career: N.H. House, 1973-75; sought Republican nomination for U.S. Senate, 1980; elected governor, 1982; term expires Jan. 1985.

GENERAL COURT

SENATE

9D, 15R

Vesta M. Roy (R)
President

HOUSE

158D, 237R, 2 Ind.
3 vacancies

John B. Tucker (R)
Speaker

Equally Republican is New Hampshire's House of Representatives, whose 400 members make it by far the largest such legislative body in the country and allegedly the third largest in the free world (behind only the U.S. House and the British House of Commons). Its supporters refer to it as a "citizen" Legislature, since virtually every neighborhood in the state is represented. Critics prefer the word "amateur." With legislators drawing a salary of $100 a year plus mileage, there is an immense turnover. Each session about one-third of the members are newcomers.

The sheer size of the House makes it difficult for an individual to stand out. An exception is Everett Sackett, a former dean at the University of New Hampshire who became a legislator at age 73. Now an octogenarian, he introduces a bill each session to create a state income tax.

But most legislators are not so visible as Sackett and look to the leadership for guidance. Essentially the leadership amounts to Republican House Speaker John B. Tucker, a haberdasher from the Connecticut River Valley town of Claremont. Tucker controls committee appointments and bill referrals, and is assisted by a small coterie of middle-aged businessmen who anchor the key committees.

The close link between the Legislature and the business world is illustrated by the career of Tucker's predecessor, former Speaker George B. Roberts. After losing the Republican U.S. Senate primary in 1980, he became one of the state's leading lobbyists. Among his clients are liquor and horse-racing interests, which are typical targets of the "sin" taxes that provide a large portion of the state's revenue.

Senate: Focus for Lobbying

For the most part, business interests spend their time working the New Hampshire Senate. Less than one-tenth the size of the House, it is compact enough so that lobbyists can defeat or pass a bill with only a handful of supporters. In many cases, business representatives are lobbying their own. Insurance agents, trucking company owners and real estate developers are well represented in the Legislature.

Senate President Roy succeeded Robert B. Monier, who unsuccessfully sought the GOP gubernatorial nomination in 1982. Roy is not as militant a conservative as the crusty Monier, and she needed Sununu's support to surmount conservative resistance to her candidacy for the post in 1983. Roy gained a spot in New Hampshire history at the end of 1982 by serving several days as acting governor after the outgoing chief executive, Democrat Hugh Gallen, died in December.

Democrats have minimal influence in the Legislature. The party is rooted in the cities and academic communities, but often there is a broad gap between liberal academics and conservative ethnics. The Democratic legislative leaders are both from Manchester and represent two of the leading ethnic communities in New Hampshire's largest city. The House minority leader, Chris Spirou, is of Greek descent; the more conservative Senate Minority Leader Norman Champagne is of French-Canadian ancestry.

Republicans are the party of Yankee New Hampshire, the smaller towns and rural areas. The GOP has a strong moderate wing, especially in the House, but the influence of the *Manchester Union Leader* keeps the party from drifting very far to the left. There have been fewer front-page diatribes in the paper since the death in 1981 of its acerbic publisher, William Loeb. But as the state's largest paper, the *Union Leader* is still capable of energizing conservatives in both parties.

A PROFILE OF
New Hampshire

PEOPLE

Total Population: 920,610 (42nd).
White 99%, Black 0.4%. Spanish origin 1%.

Urban:	52%
Rural:	48%
Born in state:	49%
Foreign-born:	5%

MAJOR CITIES

Manchester (90,936), Nashua (67,865), Concord (30,400), Portsmouth (26,254), Dover (22,377)

LAND

Farm	10%
Forest	87%
Federally owned	13%

WORK

Occupations: 52% white-collar; 35% blue-collar; 12% service workers

Government workers: 15,469 federal
18,225 state
33,379 local

Unemployment rate: 5%

MONEY

Median family income (1980)	$19,723	(25th)
Tax burden per capita (1982)	$353	(50th)

EDUCATION

Spending per pupil through grade 12	$2,256	(27th)
Persons with college degrees	18%	(13th)

CRIME

Violent crime rate: 147 per 100,000 (47th)

POLITICS

1980 Presidential Vote: Reagan 58%, Carter 28%, Anderson 13%

Turnout rate in 1980:	68%
Turnout rate in 1982:	50%

U.S. House Delegation: 1D, 1R

NEW JERSEY:

Delicate Balance of Parties Adds to Legislative Tension

New Jersey politics is based on a taut partisan equilibrium that makes legislating a precarious business and leaves neither party very comfortable for very long. A switch of one seat would cost Democrats control of the state Senate; a switch of three would cost them the House.

Republican Gov. Thomas H. Kean won his first term in 1981 by fewer than 2,000 votes out of 2.3 million cast.

Things are especially tense in 1983 because the entire Legislature is up for election in November. With the prospect of a more sympathetic Legislature dangling before him, Kean is gearing up to lead an all-out partisan campaign. Democrats, in turn, hope to use the governor as a campaign issue, portraying him as a drifting, ineffectual leader.

The style of New Jersey politics has changed dramatically in the past generation, with the old-fashioned county machines seeing their influence in state politics fall victim to campaign reforms and federal prosecution. But the century-old tradition of close partisan competition has survived. New Jersey's political leadership has simply passed from party bosses to elected officials with statewide roles, such as Kean and House Speaker Alan J. Karcher, D.

The base of Democratic strength in New Jersey has spread with the state's suburbanization. The old manufacturing cities of Newark, Jersey City, Camden and Trenton continue to anchor a solid and traditional Democratic vote. But as blue-collar and lower middle-class whites have left the cities for the older suburbs that ring them, and affluent young professionals have arrived from Manhattan, the Democratic vote has moved with them. In the process, it has grown somewhat more conservative — suburban Democrats in the Legislature take a relatively hard line against tax increases, although they often side with their urban brethren on spending issues. The most serious split between urban and suburban Democrats has come on education issues, with urban representatives pushing for heavier taxes to support public education, and for an aid distribution formula that would favor the cities.

Despite the Democratic inroads, however, Republicans remain the majority party in most suburban areas, and this virtually guarantees that they will be competitive in the Legislature and in most statewide elections. Republicans win the bulk of the seats based in the fast-growing outer suburbs, which have attracted corporate managers and other upper-income residents: the hunt country of Morris County, and the wealthier communities of Somerset and Bergen counties. The GOP still can rely on votes from the rural northwest counties, and from rural and coastal South Jersey.

Regional Coalitions

Although the prime split within the Legislature is between Democrats and Republicans, some issues bring out bipartisan coalitions. There are only about 8,000 farms left in the state, concentrated in the northwest and in the inland counties of South Jersey. But some astute vote-trading with suburban delegations has allowed the farm bloc to stave off labor-backed attempts to win new rights for migrant farm workers.

North Jersey and South Jersey have been fighting for decades, but only recently has an informal, bipartisan South Jersey caucus shown up in the Legislature. The southern part of the state, far less crowded and developed

---

STATE LEADERSHIP

Gov. Thomas H. Kean (R)

Born: April 21, 1935, New York, N.Y.
Home: Livingston, N.J.
Education: Princeton U., B.A. 1957; Columbia U., M.A. 1963.
Miltary Career: New Jersey National Guard.
Occupation: High school teacher; real estate executive.
Family: Wife, Deborah Bye; three children.
Religion: Episcopalian.
Political Career: N.J. Assembly, 1968-77, Speaker, 1972-74; sought Republican nomination for U.S. House, 1974, and for governor, 1977; elected governor, 1981; term ends Jan. 1986.

LEGISLATURE

SENATE
21D, 19R
Carmen A. Orechio (D)
President

GENERAL ASSEMBLY
43D, 37R
Alan J. Karcher (D)
Speaker

than the north, has long felt dominated by North Jersey urban and suburban interests. When former Democratic Gov. Brendan T. Byrne (1974-82) proposed protecting a large area of the Pine Barrens wilderness from development, local resentment flared up. In 1983, tempers were again aroused when legislators from the northern suburbs pushed a statewide ban on leg-hold traps, contending that they were a danger to wandering pets. South Jerseyites in the Legislature, whose constituents used the traps to catch muskrat and other animals, banded together in a losing fight against the ban.

New Jersey politics has developed an image as a stronghold of special interests, from corrupt union officials to polluting industries and the Mafia. As a spate of newspaper articles and prosecutions in the 1970s demonstrated, powerful interests often could find a welcoming ear — and pocket — among local officials. At the state level, however, matters are not so simple.

The Legislature has long had a pro-business climate, dating from the days at the turn of the century when it created a haven from the regulations governing New York financial institutions. Corporations such as the Prudential Insurance Company and Johnson & Johnson can still bring considerable weight to bear on lawmakers. But despite a hefty lobbying effort by the state's manufacturers in 1983, the Legislature passed a stringent "right-to-know" bill requiring labeling of substances used in the work place. The legislation represented a major victory for organized labor, which, long dominated by the conservative building trades unions, has been at best a marginal actor in state politics.

Speaker Alan J. Karcher

The Legislature is institutionally weak in New Jersey. The governor is the only statewide elected official, and he has sweeping powers of appointment, a line-item veto and a stock of patronage and pork-barrel levers that few other governors can match. But Kean, so far at least, has not been a particularly strong governor. In pushing the few initiatives he has undertaken, he has tended to rely more on low-key reasoning than on forceful persuasion; Democrats in the Legislature, used to Byrne's arm-twisting ways, have seen little reason to cooperate.

The chief legislative initiative of Kean's first term, an "infrastructure bank" designed to help localities deal with aging roads, sewers and water systems, has been stuck in the Legislature since the governor proposed it not long after taking office. His idea for a gasoline tax to pay for repairs on the state's roads and bridges was voted down in 1982. Not until mid-August 1983, did Kean's first palpable success come, with passage of changes in the state's no-fault auto insurance law.

Still, Kean has fared well in the public eye. Unlike Byrne, who had many fights with the Legislature early in his first term, Kean has avoided offending any major groups in the state. His proclaimed priority for his term, administrative reform, has been non-controversial. His quick reaction in ordering the cleanup of sites contaminated by dioxin has played well with voters. ∎

A PROFILE OF

New Jersey

PEOPLE

Total Population: 7,364,823 (9th).
    White 83%, Black 13%, Asian and
    Pacific Islander 1%. Spanish origin 7%.

Urban:	89%
Rural:	11%
Born in state:	57%
Foreign-born:	10%

MAJOR CITIES

Newark (329,248), Jersey City (223,532),
    Paterson (137,970), Elizabeth (106,201),
    Trenton (92,124)

LAND

Farm	22%
Forest	40%
Federally owned	3%

WORK

Occupations: 59% white-collar; 29% blue-collar; 12% service workers

Government workers:	71,072	federal
	99,988	state
	323,651	local

Unemployment rate: 9%

MONEY

Median family income (1980)	$22,906	(4th)
Tax burden per capita (1982)	$757	(15th)

EDUCATION

Spending per pupil through grade 12	$3,285	(3rd)
Persons with college degrees	18%	(12th)

CRIME

Violent crime rate: 631 per 100,000 (10th)

POLITICS

1980 Presidential Vote: Reagan 52%,
    Carter 39%, Anderson 8%

Turnout rate in 1980:	60%
Turnout rate in 1982:	49%

U.S. House Delegation: 9D, 5R

NEW MEXICO:

Anaya's Liberal Whirlwind Consolidates Urban Control

Long known for its easygoing and relatively conservative state government, New Mexico is being rocked by a political whirlwind in the form of Democratic Gov. Toney Anaya. The course of the year 1984 will determine whether the assertively liberal Anaya has launched a revolution in New Mexico politics or has merely offered a colorful interlude.

An unabashed activist, he transformed the office of state attorney general in the mid-1970s from a political backwater into one of the most visible positions in New Mexico. He developed a crusading image by fighting corruption and championing consumer and environmental issues. That frequently led him to confront the Democratic Party's conservative "Old Guard" and the business community, two groups that have formed a working relationship with Anaya in the Statehouse but still view him warily.

Anaya did not change his politics when he arrived at the governor's office in Santa Fe. He staffed his administration with perhaps the most liberal state Cabinet in the country, one that included four women and four Hispanics. The executive branch is laced with environmentalists, including a former national president of the Sierra Club as head of the natural resources department.

But the ultimate legacy of Anaya may be in sealing the transformation of political power from rural New Mexico to the booming Albuquerque-Santa Fe axis. For years, ranching interests dominated the Legislature. In the person of Democrat Bruce King, they controlled the governor's office

for much of the 1970s. But the influence of conservative rural forces is now in eclipse in the Legislature, and it has been broken in the executive branch. Virtually all of Anaya's major appointees are people from Albuquerque or Santa Fe.

Executive-Legislative Harmony

Critics have complained that Anaya has overloaded his administration with liberal young lawyers, many of them comparatively recent arrivals in the state. But while this is a source of potential friction with the more conservative Legislature — dominated by members who have deep roots in New Mexico — the two wings of government operated in relative harmony during the 1983 session.

Facing a one-term limit on his gubernatorial tenure, Anaya moved quickly to put his stamp on state government. Before the 1983 session even began, he took an active role in steering the New Mexico House in a more liberal direction. Retirements and election defeats in 1982 had softened up the House's ruling coalition of Republicans and conservative Democrats, many of whom are from the "Little Texas" region of southeastern New Mexico.

Anaya helped deliver the coup de grace, actively lobbying several legislators to leave the coalition and join the group of more liberal Democratic "loyalists." The key break came when Max Coll, a Republican legislator from Santa Fe, not only switched sides but changed parties. For joining the loyalists, he was rewarded with the chairmanship of the House Taxation and Revenue Committee.

With a slim majority, the Anaya loyalists were able to install liberal Albuquerque lawyer Ray Sanchez as Speaker to replace Gene Samberson, a conservative Democrat. Samberson remains the head of the "government in exile," eclipsing Republican Minority Leader Hoyt Pattison, a farmer from Little Texas and an outspoken critic of Anaya. Pattison's GOP colleagues currently make up about three-fourths of the conservative coalition.

The situation in the Senate is more fluid. On paper, Democrats have a four-vote majority, but many of their legislators are conservatives. Still, they were slow to buck Anaya in 1983, and efforts to form a conservative coalition

---

STATE LEADERSHIP

Gov. Toney Anaya (D)

Born: April 29, 1941, Moriarty, N.M.
Home: Santa Fe, N.M.
Education: Attended Highlands U. 1959; Georgetown U., School of Foreign Service, B.A. 1963; American U., J.D. 1967.
Occupation: Lawyer.
Family: Wife, Elaine Bolin; three children.
Religion: Roman Catholic.
Political Career: N.M. attorney general, 1975-79; Democratic nominee for U.S. Senate, 1978; elected governor 1982; term expires Jan. 1987.

LEGISLATURE

SENATE
23D, 19R

I. M. Smalley (D)
President pro tem

HOUSE
46D, 24R

Raymond G. Sanchez (D)
Speaker

in the Senate were blunted.

Anaya has strong allies within the leadership in both chambers: Sanchez in the House; and Majority Whip Tom Rutherford in the Senate. Their help, and the declining influence of the Old Guard, helped Anaya get most of his legislative agenda in 1983.

For years, the important finance committees in the Legislature were chaired by Sen. Aubrey Dunn and Rep. John Mershon, both Democrats from the rural southern part of the state. But by 1983, the two had retired. A 31-year legislative veteran, I. M. Smalley, remains as president pro tem of the Senate. But nearing 80, he lacks the vitality to marshal the conservative forces.

Anaya interjected himself into the Senate's power vacuum as much as he could. He frequently met with legislators of both parties during the 1983 session, but coupled an open-door policy with warnings that he would not take opposition lightly. When conservative legislators attacked his budget program, Anaya went to their home base in southern New Mexico to criticize them.

That scene might be repeated more often in 1984 than it was in 1983. Absorbed in balancing the budget, the 1983 session avoided pitched battles on controversial new projects. Anaya got the funding he wanted for some economic development programs as well as legislative approval to reorganize part of the executive branch. But he was forced to focus most of his attention on finding the right combination of spending cuts and tax increases. These were needed to offset a rare budget deficit caused by the effect of the recession on the state's extractive industries — uranium, copper, coal and especially oil and gas.

Fireworks in 1984

The real fireworks between Anaya and the Legislature are expected to come in 1984. The governor has already promised that the 1984 session will focus on education. The Legislature rebuffed him on the issue twice in 1983 — once on a proposed constitutional amendment to establish a state Office of Education; the other time on salary increases for teachers and public employees. To lay the groundwork for 1984, Anaya named former U.S. Sen. Fred Harris, D-Okla., to head a commission on higher education.

Any proposal that involves a major tax increase would likely activate a network of business lobbyists. Mining interests and the New Mexico Association of Commerce and Industry are well represented in Santa Fe. But the oil and gas industry is widely regarded as having the most formidable lobbying operation. New Mexico is one of the leading states in the production of oil and gas, and industry sources claim that as recently as 1981 the industry provided the state more than $1 billion in direct revenue.

But the oil and gas interests do not always get their way. Anaya's 1983 budget bailout included increased taxes on oil and gas production. Not only are oil and gas operations concentrated in several sparsely populated counties, but the prominent involvement of several out-of-state companies makes the oil and gas industry a popular political target.

The 1984 election could set the tone of New Mexico politics for years to come. Conservatives hope that voter reaction to Anaya's liberalism and tax increases will restore the conservative coalition in the House. But Democratic loyalists are optimistic that the expected retirement of several veteran conservative senators and the shift of a handful of legislative seats from rural New Mexico to the Albuquerque area will have the opposite effect. ∎

A PROFILE OF

New Mexico

PEOPLE

Total Population: 1,302,894 (37th).
White 75%, Black 2%, American Indian, Eskimo and Aleut 8%. Spanish origin 37%.

Urban:	72%
Rural:	28%
Born in state:	52%
Foreign-born:	4%

MAJOR CITIES

Albuquerque (331,767), Sante Fe (48,953), Las Cruces (45,086), Roswell (39,676), Clovis (31,194)

LAND

Farm	61%
Forest	23%
Federally owned	33%

WORK

Occupations: 54% white-collar; 29% blue-collar; 14% service workers

Government workers: 27,489 federal
41,197 state
48,490 local

Unemployment rate: 11%

MONEY

Median family income (1980)	$16,928	(42nd)
Tax burden per capita (1982)	$942	(5th)

EDUCATION

Spending per pupil through grade 12	$2,178	(32nd)
Persons with college degrees	18%	(16th)

CRIME

Violent crime rate: 672 per 100,000 (6th)

POLITICS

1980 Presidential Vote: Reagan 55%, Carter 37%, Anderson 7%

Turnout rate in 1980: 59%
Turnout rate in 1982: 58%

U.S. House Delegation: 1D, 2R

NEW YORK:

Divergent Political Elements Brought Together by Cuomo

While new governors in other large industrial states have been struggling through their first legislative sessions, New York Democrat Mario M. Cuomo has enjoyed a pleasant honeymoon. Cuomo has presided over sizable tax increases and massive cutbacks in the state bureaucracy in an effort to curb the state's $1.8 billion deficit, but neither has prevented him from winning the praise of legislative leaders in both parties. The national press has given him rave reviews, and there has been speculation about him as a Democratic presidential candidate of the future.

Although New York has a history of strong governors, that sort of praise has not been heard in Albany for some time. Cuomo's predecessor, Democratic Gov. Hugh L. Carey (1975-83), left behind a legacy of bitter executive-legislative relations that often threatened to bring state government to a halt. In that acrimonious environment, leaders of the Republican-controlled Senate and the Democratic Assembly sometimes froze Carey out of decision-making, teaming up to decide issues among themselves.

Cuomo inherited the split Legislature, but he has worked hard to improve ties to its principal players. He met frequently with Republican Senate President Pro Tem and Majority Leader Warren M. Anderson and Democratic Assembly Speaker Stanley Fink during the 1983 session, thrashing out issues over breakfast at the governor's man-

sion. The results were evident when Cuomo signed the state budget into law on schedule for the first time since 1977.

Whatever his skills as a negotiator, however, Cuomo could not have managed his legislative triumphs without the help of both Anderson and Fink, the undisputed power brokers within their respective chambers.

The two leaders represent divergent points on New York's wide-ranging political spectrum. Anderson, a bland fiscal conservative, hails from the state's traditionally Republican southern tier, along the Pennsylvania border. Fink is an aggressively liberal product of Brooklyn's Democratic clubs.

Both leaders are tough legislative veterans with a demonstrated capacity for transcending the needs of their immediate geographic constituencies. Anderson played a vital role in helping to prevent New York City from going bankrupt in the late 1970s. Still, he more typically works to divert state money away from the city and toward rural upstate New York.

The City vs. Upstate

The rift between upstate and metropolitan New York City remains one of the most pervasive features of state political life. Conservative upstate Republicans often join forces to fight increased state funding for New York City's troubled mass transit and school systems.

Traditionally, New York City has been able to win most of its regional skirmishes, with the help of its own influential lobbying operation in Albany. But population losses are reducing the city's influence in the long run, as districts move beyond its limits and into the suburbs and exurbs.

At the same time, however, the urban bloc is finding new allies among legislators from the city's inner suburbs, which are losing population themselves and are facing similar problems of decline. Westchester County, once the archetype of Republican suburbia, is losing population and coming to be defined politically by its middle-income eth-

STATE LEADERSHIP

Gov. Mario M. Cuomo (D)

Born: June 15, 1932, Queens, N.Y.
Home: Queens.
Education: St. John's College, B.A. 1953, LL.B. 1956.
Occupation: Lawyer
Family: Wife, Matilda Raffa; five children.
Religion: Roman Catholic.
Political Career: Sought Democratic nomination for lieutenant governor, 1974; N.Y. secretary of state, 1975-79; sought Democratic nomination for New York City mayor, 1977; Liberal Party nominee for mayor, 1977; lieutenant governor, 1979-83; elected governor 1982; term expires Jan. 1987.

LEGISLATURE

SENATE

26D, 35R

Warren M. Anderson (R)
President Pro Tem and Majority Leader

ASSEMBLY

97D, 52R
1 vacancy

Stanley Fink (D)
Speaker

nic voters. Its legislators, many of them ethnic Democrats themselves, are increasingly likely to side with city liberals on health and welfare issues. People living in the outer ring of suburbs, in Rockland, Putnam and Orange counties, more often share the upstate affinity for the GOP.

Republicans dominate the delegation from Long Island's suburban Nassau and Suffolk counties. They are swing players in the upstate-downstate division. They share city legislators' interest in the Metropolitan Transit Authority, which operates commuter train lines linking Long Island suburbia with midtown Manhattan.

For years, Nassau County politics has been dominated by Republican boss Joseph Margiotta, who ran one of the most powerful machines in the country until his conviction in 1982 on corruption charges. Margiotta was legendary for boosting legislators into office and then traveling north to Albany to make sure they voted his way.

New York City's county organizations remain an important force in legislative politics. Democratic lawmakers from Queens maintain ties to party chief and borough president Donald Manes. Brooklyn Democratic leader Meade Esposito once rivaled Margiotta for influence in legislative politics, but his organization has been weakened by factional dissension. Esposito's party "regulars" have long been under challenge from liberal "reform" Democrats seeking greater clout within the party. Brooklyn's black community has regulars and reformers of its own.

Whatever the influence of local party bosses, however, Democratic lawmakers seeking political help today are more likely to turn to their own legislative leadership. Both Fink and Senate Minority Leader Manfred Ohrenstein have established potent campaign committees to lend financial and organizational help to Democratic candidates and aid in their push to capture the Senate.

Party Divisions

New York City remains the heart and soul of the state's Democratic Party, providing the necessary margin of victory for virtually every statewide Democratic winner. Cuomo lost 52 of the state's 62 counties in his 1982 gubernatorial bid, making up the difference in the city's five boroughs with help from the inner suburbs and the upstate cities of Albany and Buffalo.

In forging his 1982 victory, Cuomo pulled together elements of the party's traditional core. He capitalized on negative feelings toward his Democratic primary opponent, New York City Mayor Edward I. Koch, to assemble a coalition of reform-minded liberals, labor unions and blacks. His general election victory marked the first time since 1964 that a candidate clearly identified with the Democratic Party's liberal wing had won a contest in New York for governor or the U. S. Senate.

Liberals have a strong voice in the Legislature as well. Manhattan routinely sends a left-leaning delegation to both the Senate and the Assembly; many of its strongest legislators, now in their mid-thirties and reaching positions of power, are products of the anti-war movement of the 1960s. The Legislative Black and Puerto Rican Caucus, spanning both chambers to take in 24 members, is influential on issues of concern to minorities.

Under pressure from the insurgent Conservative Party, New York's GOP has moved in a rightward direction in recent statewide elections. Conservatives have made their presence felt in the Legislature as well. All but a handful of the Senate's 35 Republicans also bear the Conservative endorsement. ∎

A PROFILE OF

New York

PEOPLE

Total Population: 17,558,072 (2nd).
  White 80%, Black 14%, Asian and
  Pacific Islander 2%. Spanish
  origin 10%.

Urban:	85%
Rural:	15%
Born in state:	69%
Foreign-born:	14%

MAJOR CITIES

New York (7,071,639), Buffalo (357,870), Rochester (241,741), Yonkers (195,351), Syracuse (170,105)

LAND

Farm	33%
Forest	57%
Federally owned	1%

WORK

Occupations: 59% white-collar; 26% blue-collar; 14% service workers

Government workers: 152,141 federal
  251,268 state
  841,998 local

Unemployment rate: 9%

MONEY

Median family income (1980)	$20,180	(19th)
Tax burden per capita (1982)	$879	(10th)

EDUCATION

Spending per pupil through grade 12	$3,769	(2nd)
Persons with college degrees	18%	(14th)

CRIME

Violent crime rate: 1,070 per 100,000 (1st)

POLITICS

1980 Presidential Vote: Reagan 47%,
  Carter 44%, Anderson 8%

Turnout rate in 1980:	55%
Turnout rate in 1982:	48%

U.S. House Delegation: 20D, 14R

NORTH CAROLINA:

Legislature Reasserts Itself As Hunt Era Draws to Close

As the administration of Democratic Gov. James B. Hunt Jr. comes to an end, North Carolina seems to be leaving a period of strong executive government and moving back to its tradition of legislative control.

The 1983 session of the Legislature showed clear signs of change even though Hunt had more than a year still to serve as governor. The first governor allowed to serve two terms, Hunt has been the dominant figure in state politics virtually from the day he took office in 1977. But he has spent most of 1983 preparing for his expected U.S. Senate challenge to Republican Jesse Helms, and his role in legislative affairs has been modest.

Meanwhile, the state's lieutenant governor, Democrat Jimmy Green, saw his legislative influence decline for an entirely different reason. Indicted in June on bribery charges, his legal problems kept him from playing the strong role as presiding officer in the Senate that he had played in past years.

The combination of Hunt's political concerns and Green's personal problems created a vacuum that members of the Legislature were more than willing to fill. In doing so, they established a style of government that seems likely to continue for at least a few years. While both Democrats and Republicans have a host of candidates for governor, none seems to have the stature or ambition that gave Hunt a commanding presence — and none has the organization Hunt has been able to establish.

Within the Legislature, there are changes as well. The North Carolina House, often in the Senate's shadow in years past, has become the more dominant chamber under the leadership of Speaker Liston Ramsey, who comes from Madison, a small town on the Tennessee border. Only the second Speaker ever to serve two terms, Ramsey has already lined up commitments for an unprecedented third. A retired hardware dealer, the 63-year-old Ramsey spends most of the year in the state capital, making him a virtually full-time practitioner of a traditionally part-time job.

It is generally believed that Ramsey can in fact have the position as long as he wants. The transition to a relatively permanent leadership is expected to give the entire House more influence than it had when it rotated Speakers every two years.

Tax Increase for Education

The clearest sign of legislative activism in 1983 was passage of a tax increase package aimed at financing improvements in higher education. In past years, the Legislature rarely raised taxes without strong backing from the governor. But given Hunt's 1984 political plans, he was not interested in getting involved in a tax fight in 1983, particularly because he had pushed hard the previous Legislature for a gasoline tax increase and found himself in a bitter fight with Helms' political organization, the National Congressional Club.

Ramsey and his close ally, Rep. Allen Adams of Raleigh, who chairs the Base Budget Appropriations Committee, took matters into their hands. They drafted a bill that imposed higher taxes on liquor and video games and eliminated some corporate tax benefits. In addition, the Legislature approved a local-option sales tax to finance water, sewer and local school improvements.

Institutionally, North Carolina has every reason to have a strong Legislature. The governor has no veto power, a situation unique in the country. Strong chief executives such as Hunt have had to work by building support within the legislature, not overpowering it.

The Legislature's wings were clipped slightly in 1982 when the state Supreme Court determined that legislators had overstepped their bounds by serving on an executive branch advisory committee on the environment. But the legislators insisted they still needed to maintain better control over some executive branch functions. The state House passed a bill to let the legislature write the rules that agencies use in making regulatory decisions. That was killed in the Senate, but a compromise was worked out

STATE LEADERSHIP

Gov. James B. Hunt Jr. (D)

Born: May 16, 1937, Greensboro, N.C.
Home: Lucama, N.C.
Education: N.C. State U., B.S. 1959, M.S. 1962; U. of N.C. Law School, J.D. 1964.
Occupation: Lawyer; farmer.
Family: Wife, Carolyn Leonard; four children.
Religion: Presbyterian.
Political Career: Lieutenant governor, 1973-77; elected governor 1976, 1980; term expires Jan. 1985.

GENERAL ASSEMBLY

SENATE
44D, 6R

W. Craig Lawing (D)
President pro tem

HOUSE
102D, 18R

Liston B. Ramsey (D)
Speaker

Sen. W. Craig Lawing

Rep. Liston B. Ramsey

creating a "Governor's Rules Review Committee," which will review all agency regulations. Members appointed by the Legislature will hold a majority on the committee.

Although his eye has been on the Senate campaign, Hunt did have some of his own initiatives in 1983. His major accomplishment was pushing through a tough drunken driving law that stiffened penalties, raised the drinking age for beer and wine to 19, banned plea bargaining and made jail terms mandatory for repeat offenders. Hunt hoped to get political mileage out of the drunken driving bill by picking up support among fundamentalist religious groups and those who historically have opposed the sale of liquor in the state. Both groups in the past have been considered strong Helms allies.

Hunt was less successful with a tough hazardous waste bill he backed. The measure ran into strong opposition from the state's historic business coalition — power companies, timber, textiles and tobacco. This episode was a reminder that industry in North Carolina is not likely to suffer regardless of where the political power lies. No governor or Legislature has ever taken lightly the concerns of the state's major business interests.

Republican Tension

Although North Carolina is represented in the U.S. Senate by two Republicans, the GOP is hardly a factor in state government these days. For the past eight years, since Republican Gov. James C. Holshouser Jr. left office, Republicans have been hopelessly outnumbered in Raleigh. The Congressional Club, the political organization that has made Helms a potent conservative force nationwide, has only marginal influence in the Legislature. The handful of Republicans who serve generally keep their distance from the club. That is especially true for those from the mountain counties of western North Carolina, where GOP legislative representation traditionally has been concentrated.

Tension between the westerners and the Helms Republican faction flares up regularly. In August 1983, as U.S. Rep. James G. Martin was preparing to declare his candidacy for governor, with the support of many of the westerners, the Congressional Club announced it would field its own candidate — William Cobey, former athletic director at the University of North Carolina and an unsuccessful congressional candidate in 1982.

Helms and his lieutenants remain in control of the state party mechanism, and are expected to remain in control at least through 1984. In May 1983, when the party met in Raleigh, two separate challenges were made to Helms' leadership. Both failed decisively. ∎

A PROFILE OF
North Carolina

PEOPLE

Total Population: 5,881,766 (10th).
White 76%, Black 22%, American Indian, Eskimo and Aleut 1%. Spanish origin 1%.

Urban:	48%
Rural:	52%
Born in state:	76%
Foreign-born:	1%

MAJOR CITIES

Charlotte (314,447), Greensboro (155,642), Raleigh (150,255), Winston-Salem (131,885), Durham (100,831)

LAND

Farm	36%
Forest	64%
Federally owned	7%

WORK

Occupations: 45% white-collar; 41% blue-collar; 11% service workers

Government workers:	42,393 federal
	102,350 state
	234,900 local
Unemployment rate:	9%

MONEY

Median family income (1980)	$16,792 (43rd)
Tax burden per capita (1982)	$644 (31st)

EDUCATION

Spending per pupil through grade 12	$2,033 (35th)
Persons with college degrees	13% (43rd)

CRIME

Violent crime rate: 437 per 100,000 (26th)

POLITICS

1980 Presidential Vote: Reagan 49%, Carter 47%, Anderson 3%

Turnout rate in 1980:	52%
Turnout rate in 1982:	39%

U.S. House Delegation: 9D, 2R

NORTH DAKOTA:

Populist Sentiment Survives Despite Republican Control

To an outsider's eye, there is not much left of the agrarian populism that once swept North Dakota. Business-oriented Republicans control the Senate and the governorship and hold most of the numerous statewide offices. The Non-Partisan League (NPL), which in the early de-

cades of the century carried the standard of farm revolt against large business interests, merged in 1956 with the Democratic Party and carries on in name only.

But in less obvious ways, the populist tradition endures. While the Burlington Northern Railroad and Minneapolis-based grain companies and banks carry tremendous economic weight, many North Dakotans still view them with considerable suspicion. The state's rural electric and farmers' cooperatives have the loyalty of much of the rural population. And the remnants of the NPL's heyday — the only state-owned bank in the country, and a state grain mill and elevator — are institutionalized actors on the economic scene.

State government itself bears the marks of the populist tradition. North Dakota has 14 elected, statewide officials — more than any other state. The list of elected officials includes its tax commissioner, three members of the public service commission and the commissioners of agriculture, labor and insurance. The Legislature is strictly a citizens' body — it meets for only three months every two years.

That short time-span would seem to guarantee the bulk of policy-making weight to the governor. But the balance of power in North Dakota lies with the Legislature. Not only does it usually accomplish a great deal in the months allotted to it, it can sometimes afford to do so

without paying much attention to what the governor wants.

In large part, the reason is constitutional. The governor has most of the nominal powers of other chief executives, but he is severely limited in using them. While he can veto legislation, he cannot influence legislators by threatening to veto it; that is an impeachable offense in North Dakota. He is also forbidden from trying to exert legislative control through the use of his appointment power.

As a result of their institutional weakness, North Dakota governors have come to depend on a range of outside allies to help them in dealing with the Legislature. Govs. William L. Guy and Arthur A. Link, who held the Statehouse for the Democrats from 1960 through 1980, relied on the rural electric cooperatives, the Farmers Union, the teachers and North Dakota's small labor community. GOP Gov. Allen I. Olson and Republicans in the Legislature have tended to listen to the Greater North Dakota Association (the state's Chamber of Commerce), the state Farm Bureau and energy companies.

The governor's relatively weak position gives a significant degree of independence to lesser administrative officials. Democrat Byron L. Dorgan used his position as tax commissioner during the 1970s to launch a populist attack on outside business interests, cracking down on companies that were delinquent in tax payments and parlaying his high profile into a congressional seat in 1980. His successor, Democrat Kent Conrad, has taken a similarly activist stance. In 1983, when Democrats in the Legislature wanted the state to bring in more revenue through speeding up tax collections — without raising the rates — Conrad backed up their efforts and helped them shepherd the program through, essentially ignoring Olson's opposition.

'Red Right' Republicans

Republicans have traditionally controlled the Legislature; in 1982, they lost their hold on the House of Representatives for only the second time in North Dakota's history as a state. During the two decades when Guy and Link were in power, Republican legislators obstructed numerous gubernatorial initiatives. Link's efforts to slow down energy resource development showed some results during legislative off-years, but when the Legislature reconvened, it tended to undo them. Republicans, who fa-

STATE LEADERSHIP

Gov. Allen I. Olson (R)

Born: Nov. 5, 1938, Rolla, N.D.
Home: Bismarck, N.D.
Education: U. of N.D., B.S., B.A. 1960; LL.B. 1963.
Military Career: Army Judge Advocate General Corps, 1963-67.
Occupation: Lawyer.
Family: Wife, Barbara Benner; three children.
Religion: Presbyterian.
Political Career: N.D. attorney general, 1973-81; elected governor 1980; term expires Jan. 1985.

LEGISLATIVE ASSEMBLY

SENATE

21D, 32R

Russell Thane (R)
President pro tem

HOUSE

55D, 51R

Tish Kelly (D)
Speaker

vored speedier energy development, pushed legislation granting energy companies favorable tax treatment and allowing them to bill consumers for plant construction. Olson, who also favors rapid development, has let the Legislature take the lead on the issue.

The GOP in North Dakota embraces a divergent set of views. Senate Majority Leader David Nething found his caucus split in 1983 when its more conservative members — who under Democratic governors earned the sobriquet "the Red Right," after the color of the "nay" voting light they were wont to use — took a stand against tax increases that more moderate Republicans felt were necessary.

To a large degree, the divisions within the GOP in the Legislature are regional. Members of the "Red Right" tend to come from the central and southeastern parts of the state, where their resolutions supporting a "human life amendment" or U.S. withdrawal from the United Nations are well received among the prosperous German farmers of the Red River Valley. Business-oriented Republicans who represent the small towns outside that area are more moderate in outlook, although well within the mainstream of Republican thinking.

North Dakota's four major cities also have produced a moderate breed of Republican. A leading example is House Minority Leader Earl Strinden, a hard-working and creative legislator from Grand Forks who during seven years as majority leader was the most influential member of the Legislature. Strinden repeatedly blocked efforts to pass a "human life amendment" and supported the Equal Rights Amendment, while taking a conservative stance on state spending.

Sen. David Nething

Democrats in the Legislature, through years in the minority, have come to develop a cohesiveness on economic issues that the GOP lacks. The roots of the party are in the western two-thirds of the state, where the vast reaches of wheat-growing prairie and semi-arid ranch land made the lot of farmers harder than in the east. Although Democratic candidates — particularly teachers and union activists — have been making headway in the cities, the party's strength continues to lie in rural communities in the central and western parts of the state.

Despite their longtime minority status, Democrats have won significant victories over the years, usually with the help of organizations such as the Farmers Union and the rural electric cooperatives. In 1975, with help from some moderate Republicans and from Dorgan in his role as tax commissioner, the Democratic minority steered through a severance tax on coal. In 1980, the Democrats led a successful statewide campaign for a tax on oil companies.

But when the party's outside allies divide, Democrats have trouble. The predominant source of fuel for the rural electric cooperatives, for example, is lignite, which is strip-mined in the western part of the state. Efforts to force coal companies to clean up strip-mined land have fallen victim to opposition not only from the GOP and allied coal interests, but from the traditionally Democratic cooperatives as well. ∎

A PROFILE OF
North Dakota

PEOPLE

Total Population: 652,717 (46th).
   White 96%, Black 0.4%, American Indian, Eskimo and Aleut 3%. Spanish origin 1%.

Urban:	49%
Rural:	51%
Born in state:	73%
Foreign-born:	2%

MAJOR CITIES

Fargo (61,383), Bismarck (44,485), Grand Forks (43,765), Minot (32,843), Jamestown (16,280)

LAND

Farm	94%
Forest	1%
Federally owned	5%

WORK

Occupations: 46% white-collar; 24% blue-collar; 15% service workers

Government workers: 8,367 federal
16,553 state
33,861 local

Unemployment rate: 5%

MONEY

Median family income (1980)	$18,023	(34th)
Tax burden per capita (1982)	$816	(14th)

EDUCATION

Spending per pupil through grade 12	$2,002	(39th)
Persons with college degrees	15%	(31st)

CRIME

Violent crime rate: 68 per 100,000 (50th)

POLITICS

1980 Presidential Vote: Reagan 64%, Carter 26%, Anderson 8%

Turnout rate in 1980: 72%
Turnout rate in 1982: 64%

U.S. House Delegation: 1D

OHIO:

New Democratic Era Falters In Wake of Big Tax Increase

A new Democratic era has begun in Ohio, with the party in control of the governorship and both legislative chambers for the first time since 1960. But the recession that helped elect Democratic majorities in 1982 has led to painful legislative decisions that could make the era a short and unpleasant one for those in control.

There is no question that Democratic Gov. Richard F. Celeste has brought unabashed activism to a state government long accustomed to maintenance of the status quo. His opening year has been a bittersweet one, however, dotted with legislative success and public relations failure.

The symbol of both the success and the failure is the quick passage in winter 1982-83 of a 27 percent increase in the state income tax. In a state long used to slow-moving government and Band-Aid fiscal measures, Celeste demonstrated unaccustomed energy and a willingness to make major alterations in the tax system. But in moving quickly, he failed to build wide public support for his action. In spite of a projected $500 million budget deficit, the tax increase appeared excessive to much of Ohio's electorate.

The result was an awfully short honeymoon. Barely five months after Celeste had won the governorship in a landslide, his popularity apparently had fallen sharply. Republicans were confident that Celeste had squandered the Democrats' best electoral showing in Ohio since 1958.

But in spite of his sinking popularity, Celeste was able to retain the support of the Democratic Legislature. By developing an effective working relationship with the leadership and by mollifying key interest groups, he was able to win legislative approval for most of his remaining initiatives. These constituted his "action agenda," a wide range of ideas designed to stabilize the state budget and decrease Ohio's reliance on declining "smokestack" industries.

One of the major beneficiaries of the Democrats' 1982 surge was organized labor. After years in the shadow of Ohio's powerful business interests, labor now has ready access to power. Celeste paid off a campaign debt to labor by pushing passage of a landmark collective bargaining law for public employees.

For the business community, Democratic government has not been so favorable. Corporate lobbies simply do not have the same influence they enjoyed during the 16 pro-business years of Republican Gov. James A. Rhodes (1963-71, 1975-83). Part of Celeste's new budget package was a modest reorganization of the tax system, one that included an increase in business taxes. Still, Celeste has been careful not to alienate powerful business lobbies such as the Ohio Manufacturers Association, the Ohio Chamber of Commerce and the Ohio Council of Retail Merchants. They were consulted before his tax reorganization package was unveiled, and were generally supportive of it.

Strong Legislative Leadership

This is a period of unusual partisanship in Ohio. Nearly every major issue in both chambers in 1983 has been decided on a straight party-line vote. Republicans consistently opposed all the tax increases, a stance they hope will help them regain the Legislature in 1984. While Celeste has three years to rebuild his image, most of the Democratic legislators have to face the voters again in 1984.

Strong leadership in both chambers has kept the Democratic majorities in line. In the House, that means Vernal G. Riffe Jr., the latest in a long line of powerful Ohio House Speakers. He has held the post for nearly a decade, adding to his power by raising hundreds of thousands of dollars in each election for Democratic legislative candidates.

Those who are elected find that he demands "team" play and is not afraid to discipline recalcitrant members. When a number of independent-minded House freshmen bolted the leadership in 1983 on an amendment to the collective bargaining bill, he sent them a message by holding up action on their bills.

STATE LEADERSHIP

Gov. Richard F. Celeste (D)

Born: Nov. 11, 1937, Cleveland, Ohio.
Home: Cleveland, Ohio.
Education: Yale U., B.A. 1959.
Occupation: Businessman.
Family: Wife, Dagmar Braun; six children.
Religion: Methodist.
Political Career: Ohio House, 1971-75; lieutenant governor, 1975-79; Democratic nominee for governor, 1978; director of the Peace Corps, 1979-81; elected governor 1982; term expires Jan. 1987.

GENERAL ASSEMBLY

SENATE

17D, 16R

Harry Meshel (D)
President & Majority Leader

HOUSE

62D, 37R

Vernal G. Riffe Jr. (D)
Speaker

At first glance, it would appear that Riffe and Celeste would be frequently in conflict. A Yale graduate and Rhodes scholar, Celeste was weaned on the liberal, pro-labor politics of the Cleveland area. Riffe runs an insurance agency in rural southern Ohio, a conservative region politically closer to Appalachia than to the urban centers of northeastern Ohio.

But Riffe is a pragmatist who endorsed Celeste at an early stage of the 1982 campaign. Celeste cemented the alliance by tapping one of Riffe's closest legislative allies, 70-year-old Myrl H. Shoemaker, as his running mate for lieutenant governor.

While Riffe has operated with a comfortable Democratic majority in the House, Senate President Harry Meshel has been threatened by a "one senator veto." The Democrats hold a 17-16 majority in the upper chamber.

A Youngstown real estate broker, Meshel is in his first term as Senate president and majority leader. But he has held together the tenuous Democratic majority by basically following the same "carrot-and-stick" approach as Riffe.

To Meshel's advantage, most of the Senate Democrats were philosophically in tune with him and Celeste. The bulk of them, including many of the committee chairmen, are from populous northern Ohio, the most liberal part of the state. Marigene Valiquette of Toledo, for example, chairs the Committee on State Government, Health and Human Resources. The professorial, pipe-smoking Marcus Roberto of Ravenna heads the Ways and Means Committee; Oliver Ocasek of the Cleveland suburbs is chairman of the Education and Retirement Committee.

Ocasek was dumped by Meshel as the Democratic leader in the Senate several years ago, and the lingering bitterness from that contest nearly cost the Democrats control of the upper chamber in 1983. When Meshel passed over veteran black state Sen. M. Morris Jackson, an Ocasek loyalist, for a major committee chairmanship, Jackson threatened to bolt to the Republicans in exchange for the post of Senate president. Only pressure from a host of Democratic officials and an offer of the chairmanship of the influential Elections, Financial Institutions and Insurance Committee was able to keep Jackson in line and the Democratic Senate majority intact.

Key Democratic Test

In the last decade there has been a steady exodus of people from Ohio's Democratic central cities to the politically competitive suburbs. But with control of the state reapportionment board, Democrats were able to mute the consequences of demographic change. In 1982 the Republicans lost a handful of seats where the district lines had been revised dramatically. Those losses were enough to cost the GOP control of the Senate.

The first real verdict on Ohio's Democratic stewardship in 1983 will be delivered by the voters in November. They will decide two key ballot questions. One would repeal the changes Celeste and the Legislature made in the state tax system, including the 27 percent increase in the state income tax; the second would require a three-fifths majority in the Legislature to make any future changes in the tax structure.

The campaign on the ballot questions is likely to develop into a sharply partisan fight, with the business community divided. The Ohio Council of Retail Merchants, which fears an increase in the sales tax if the recent tax revisions are repealed, is already in the vanguard of the anti-repeal forces.

A PROFILE OF
Ohio

PEOPLE

Total Population: 10,797,630 (6th).
White 89%, Black 10%. Spanish origin 1%.

Urban:	73%
Rural:	27%
Born in state:	73%
Foreign-born:	3%

MAJOR CITIES

Cleveland (573,822), Columbus (564,871), Cincinnati (385,457), Toledo (354,635), Akron (237,177)

LAND

Farm	62%
Forest	23%
Federally owned	1%

WORK

Occupations: 50% white-collar; 35% blue-collar; 13% service workers

Government workers: 87,583 federal / 151,388 state / 430,407 local

Unemployment rate: 13%

MONEY

Median family income (1980)	$20,909	(16th)
Tax burden per capita (1982)	$539	(46th)

EDUCATION

Spending per pupil through grade 12	$2,321	(24th)
Persons with college degrees	14%	(40th)

CRIME

Violent crime rate: 497 per 100,000 (19th)

POLITICS

1980 Presidential Vote: Reagan 52%, Carter 41%, Anderson 6%

Turnout rate in 1980: 61%
Turnout rate in 1982: 50%

U.S. House Delegation: 10D, 11R

OKLAHOMA:

Vote-Fraud, Kickback Cases Create Chaos in Government

Government in Oklahoma is in shambles. In late summer 1983, the House Speaker and majority leader were convicted on charges of vote fraud and conspiracy. The incident follows closely on the heels of a 1981 corruption case involving two-thirds of the county commissioners. It was reputed to be the most wide-ranging kickback scandal in the nation's history.

What the series of scandals will do to entrenched Democratic power is still unclear. Although Oklahoma has taken to voting Republican in national elections, Democratic control at the state and local levels has been solid. Long accustomed to dominating state government, conservative rural Democrats have stubbornly resisted handing over power.

Republicans never have controlled the Oklahoma Senate; the only time they won the House was in 1920. Democratic margins into the 1980s have remained substantial. Gov. George Nigh, a Democrat who has not been connected to any of the scandals, was re-elected overwhelmingly in 1982.

Whatever its impact on future elections, the current vote fraud incident is crucial because it has cost Oklahoma one of its most powerful political figures. House Speaker Daniel D. Draper Jr. ruled the lower chamber with an iron fist, rewarding his supporters and punishing those who crossed him — sometimes by banishing them to distant offices and denying them key committee assignments.

A Stillwater attorney and twelve-year legislative veteran, Draper sought the speakership in 1978, in part be-

cause of his frustration at the weak leadership of his predecessor, William P. Willis. Draper built his campaign around a promise to make the House a more prominent force in state government. Throughout much of his tenure, he succeeded, chipping away at the Senate's ability to dictate legislative priorities and routinely overshadowing Nigh. Draper was hailed as a progressive leader by the education lobby, and seemed to be settling in for a lengthy tenure.

Draper's influence began to wane, however, as personal problems undermined his credibility. He has apologized publicly for his gambling habits. In March 1983, while he was fighting against a proposal to raise the legal drinking age for beer from 18 to 21, Draper was arrested for drunken driving.

Vote Fraud

Calls for Draper's resignation came following his indictment for vote fraud. Draper was accused, along with Majority Leader Joe Fitzgibbon, of trying to buy votes to elect Draper's father to the Legislature. Draper and Fitzgibbon since have suspended themselves from office, pending appeal of their case. The state House Democratic caucus met in September 1983 and selected Jim L. Barker to succeed Draper.

The mantle of power soon will be passed along in the Senate as well, albeit by less dramatic means. Senate President Pro Tem Marvin York, currently serving his second term, was voted out of his leadership post late in the 1982 session, amid criticism that he had failed to provide centralized authority in the Senate's clubby environment.

York's successor will be Sen. Rodger A. Randle, a Tulsa attorney who began amassing "pledge cards" from supporters of his leadership bid early in 1983. Randall lined up sufficient backing to overtake York in Democratic caucus voting, and is scheduled to assume control of the upper chamber in 1985.

Some of the Senate's most influential members are not part of the formal leadership. A particularly enigmatic personality is veteran Sen. Gene Stipe, who represents a rural "Little Dixie" district in the southeast corner of the state. Called the "Prince of Darkness" by some reporters in Oklahoma City, Stipe is notorious for flashy oratory, politi-

---

STATE LEADERSHIP

Gov. George Nigh (D)

Born: June 9, 1927, McAlester, Okla.
Home: Oklahoma City, Okla.
Education: East Central State Teachers College, B.A. 1950.
Military Career: Navy, 1946-47.
Occupation: High school teacher.
Family: Wife, Donna Skinner Mashburn; two children.
Religion: Baptist.
Political Career: Okla. House, 1951-59; lieutenant governor, 1959-63, 1967-79; sought Democratic gubernatorial nomination, 1962; elected governor 1978, 1982; term expires Jan. 1987.

LEGISLATURE

SENATE
34D, 14R

Marvin York (D)
President pro tem

HOUSE
76D, 25R

Daniel D. Draper Jr. (D)
Speaker
(suspended)

cal horse-trading and the ability to emerge unharmed from journalistic and governmental inquiries into his personal wealth.

While the Legislature is listing from its leadership shake-ups, the Statehouse is on an even keel. Nigh's 1982 victory, in which he carried every county in the state, made him the first Oklahoma governor ever to win two consecutive terms. With a record of nearly 30 years in public office in Oklahoma, Nigh is a household name.

Despite his personal popularity, however, Nigh does not wield a great deal of power. While he has opposed tax increases, he appears content on most other issues to let legislative leaders run their own course. According to one legislator, Nigh "governs by benign neglect."

Oklahoma was sheltered for several years from the recession that stung most of the rest of the country, but it

Rep. Daniel D. Draper Jr.

is no longer immune from economic problems. The 1983 legislative session demonstrated rising tension in the recently booming oil state, which did not expect to be poor again this soon. Shrinking state revenues have forced lawmakers to impose substantial cuts in the budget, and many have found it difficult to adapt to the climate of fiscal austerity. The Legislature took a two-week recess to let tempers cool following one round of budget cutting in March; a protracted battle over funding for the state's Department of Human Services held up work on the budget for fiscal year 1984 until late in the session.

Budget battles have exacerbated tensions between rural and urban legislators. The split is evident in debate over state funding for education — rural members frequently criticize the Tulsa public school system and press for more aid to outlying areas. Rural legislators often are aided in their cause by the potent Oklahoma County Commissioners Association. Despite its scandals, the organization remains a strong voice for county government in the appropriations process. On issues of water conservation and development, the crucial split is between eastern Oklahoma — awash with state and federal water projects — and the state's dusty western plains.

Skirmishes over state funding formulas also break out occasionally between the legislative delegations from Tulsa and Oklahoma City, the state's two major metropolitan areas. Tulsa, the state's traditional Republican hub, sometimes loses out to its southwestern neighbor in allocations for road projects and buildings. Legislators from Oklahoma City's south side band together to help each other in legislative and political campaigns; they are known collectively as the "South Side Mafia," and have strong ties to the city's organized labor community.

Among the other influential lobbies in Oklahoma City are the banking industry, which won a longstanding battle in 1983 to legalize multi-bank holding companies and loosen restrictions on branch banking, and the Malt Beverage Association, which has teamed with fundamentalist Christian groups in blocking efforts to repeal Oklahoma's law banning the sale of hard liquor by the drink. ∎

A PROFILE OF

Oklahoma

PEOPLE

Total Population: 3,025,290 (26th).
  White 86%, Black 7%, American
  Indian, Eskimo and Aleut 6%, Asian and
  Pacific Islander 1%. Spanish origin 2%.

Urban:	67%
Rural:	33%
Born in state:	63%
Foreign-born:	2%

MAJOR CITIES

Oklahoma City (403,213), Tulsa (360,919), Lawton (80,054), Norman (68,020), Enid (50,363)

LAND

Farm	78%
Forest	19%
Federally owned	4%

WORK

Occupations: 51% white-collar; 33% blue-collar; 13% service workers

Government workers:	46,101	federal
	69,595	state
	120,288	local

Unemployment rate: 9%

MONEY

Median family income (1980)	$17,668	(35th)
Tax burden per capita (1982)	$897	(9th)

EDUCATION

Spending per pupil through grade 12	$2,237	(29th)
Persons with college degrees	15%	(28th)

CRIME

Violent crime rate: 427 per 100,000 (28th)

POLITICS

1980 Presidential Vote: Reagan 61%, Carter 35%, Anderson 3%

Turnout rate in 1980:	59%
Turnout rate in 1982:	47%

U.S. House Delegation: 5D, 1R

OREGON:

Weak Leadership, Economy Create Sense of Uncertainty

There is a sense of uncertainty in Oregon these days. A depression in the timber industry has wrenched the state, forcing mill closures and creating high unemployment in its manufacturing sector, which is heavily tied to wood products. Fear that timber companies may move to the South to take advantage of cheaper labor has left some Oregonians worried that the crisis will last beyond the national economic recovery. The industry many Oregonians are looking to for salvation, electronics, is still in no position to take up the slack.

The state's difficulties in coming to grips with its problems have been exacerbated by its open style of government. Ideological divisions within each party make it difficult to develop a consensus.

The "Oregon system," established by reformers during the first decade of this century, gave voters a sweeping ability to use initiatives and referendums. It made them the final arbiters on major issues dealt with by the Legislature. It also broke the power of the political parties, leaving legislators free of much peer pressure on their actions. Factions in the Legislature shift according to the issue; without a strong party structure, leadership is a matter of personality and persuasion. When there is no individual capable of handling this system, the state tends to drift.

Republican Govs. Mark O. Hatfield (1959-67) and Tom McCall (1967-75) maneuvered their way through the system skillfully and placed their stamp on state government for years to come. In the later 1970s, under the less forceful leadership of Democratic Gov. Robert Straub, the momentum shifted over to the Legislature and its Democratic Senate president, Jason Boe.

Currently, there is a common perception that no party or branch of government is providing much leadership. While given high marks for personal integrity, GOP Gov. Victor G. Atiyeh has been criticized for holding too firmly to his convictions and for a reluctance to compromise. Once he has presented his policy on a given issue, critics say, he shows little willingness to deal with the Legislature in shaping the eventual outcome. For its part, the Democratic Legislature has been unable to seize the opportunity to set policy itself.

Tax Stalemate

The problem was apparent during the 1983 legislative session, in which lawmakers failed to agree on any approach to Oregon's tax woes. Trying to head off a likely 1984 ballot initiative slashing property taxes, Atiyeh and the Legislature spent most of the session trying to find a way to provide some property tax relief without bankrupting the state treasury. Atiyeh's solution, an increase in the state's income tax, was highly unpopular with the business community and a broad range of legislators of both parties; Oregon already ranked second in the country in its personal income tax rate, and it was argued that an increase would frighten away potential new businesses.

The alternative favored by some legislators was a sales tax, a move Oregon voters have rejected six times — the last time, in 1969, by an 8-to-1 margin. Despite this lesson of history, the House decided by one vote, over the personal opposition of Speaker Grattan Kerans, to place a new sales tax proposal before the electorate. In the Senate, however, President Edward N. Fadeley refused to allow the tax proposal even to reach the floor. The measure's failure forced Atiyeh to call a special session of the Legislature for September. Late in August, he and the two legislative leaders arrived at a potential compromise package to put before the voters.

Neither Fadeley nor Kerans, however, has yet been able to step in for Boe, who was widely seen as the anchor of state government until his retirement in 1980. Kerans, a liberal from Eugene, has been given high marks for his consensual style of leadership — in contrast to his highly partisan manner in earlier years as majority leader — and

STATE LEADERSHIP

Gov. Victor G. Atiyeh (R)

Born: Feb. 20, 1923, Portland, Ore.
Home: Salem, Ore.
Education: Attended U. of Ore., 1941-43.
Occupation: Rug company executive.
Family: Wife, Dolores Hewitt; two children.
Religion: Episcopalian.
Political Career: Ore. House, 1959-65; Ore. Senate, 1965-79; Republican nominee for governor, 1974; elected governor 1978, 1982; term expires Jan. 1987.

LEGISLATIVE ASSEMBLY

SENATE

21D, 9R

Edward N. Fadeley (D)
President

HOUSE

36D, 24R

Grattan Kerans (D)
Speaker

Speaker Grattan Kerans   **Sen. Edward N. Fadeley**

has begun to develop personal stature in the House. Fadeley's position is more precarious. Initially a dark-horse candidate for the Senate presidency, he narrowly emerged as the consensus choice after conservative Democrats and Republicans combined to keep the leading contender, a Portland Democrat, from winning the position. Fadeley's loner style and rigid manner, however, have kept him from giving the Senate direction.

Power Shifts to Cities

The Republicans and conservative rural Democrats — descendants of immigrants from the South who settled southern Oregon between the two world wars — are the remnant of an alliance that held sway for years in Salem, giving disproportionate influence to the state's farm and timber communities. The hold of that coalition on legislative matters was broken in the 1970s, as population growth in the cities of the Willamette Valley — Portland, Eugene and Salem — caught up with the Legislature. But the rural bloc still is able to keep any Portland liberal from winning the leadership of the Senate, and it forms a significant force opposing efforts to strengthen environmental laws.

Still, boosted by the growth of Portland and the other cities of the Willamette Valley, liberals and moderates have gained the upper hand in the Legislature. The liberal vote in the Legislature is anchored by representatives from the two ends of the valley: Portland, with its young professionals, blue-collar whites, blacks and elderly; and Eugene, home of the University of Oregon.

The state government community in Salem tends to follow a more moderate politics, and sometimes sends Republicans to the Legislature. The farming communities and sawmill towns between the Willamette Valley cities tend to go Republican despite a Democratic registration edge. The GOP also draws strength from the wealthy suburbs of Portland in Washington and Clackamas counties.

Despite its reputation as an oasis of "clean government," Oregon's Legislature has always paid generous attention to the lobbyists and special interests that move in Salem legislative circles. The Legislature meets for only about six months every two years, and has few permanent staff members. Legislators often have to rely on lobbyists for their information, and to some extent for an institutional memory. That has dealt tremendous influence to the banks, utilities and timber companies that can afford to keep representatives in Salem and contribute to campaigns. In 1981, when banks pushed for repeal of the limit on interest rates they could charge, the measure sailed through the House with only two dissenting votes. ∎

A PROFILE OF

Oregon

PEOPLE

Total Population: 2,633,105 (30th).
White 95%, Black 1%, American Indian, Eskimo and Aleut 1%, Asian and Pacific Islander 1%. Spanish origin 3%.

Urban:	68%
Rural:	32%
Born in state:	44%
Foreign-born:	4%

MAJOR CITIES

Portland (366,383), Eugene (105,624), Salem (89,233), Springfield (41,621), Corvallis (40,960)

LAND

Farm	30%
Forest	48%
Federally owned	49%

WORK

Occupations: 53% white-collar; 29% blue-collar; 14% service workers

Government workers:	28,836 federal
	52,839 state
	117,256 local

Unemployment rate: 9%

MONEY

Median family income (1980)	$20,027	(21st)
Tax burden per capita (1982)	$590	(38th)

EDUCATION

Spending per pupil through grade 12	$3,130	(4th)
Persons with college degrees	18%	(15th)

CRIME

Violent crime rate: 479 per 100,000 (20th)

POLITICS

1980 Presidential Vote: Reagan 48%, Carter 39%, Anderson 10%

Turnout rate in 1980:	66%
Turnout rate in 1982:	62%

U.S. House Delegation: 3D, 2R

PENNSYLVANIA:

Business-Labor Cooperation Provides Hope for Economy

Steel, coal, railroads and Pennsylvania's other once-burly industries are in decline, and the state's work force, heavily dependent on manufacturing, is plagued by joblessness. But in spite of these and other difficulties, there are signs of optimism in Harrisburg that are absent in other capitals of industrial America.

For much of this century, the Legislature was essentially the instrument of the corporate community — steel, coal and other industrial giants organized through the wealthy and much-feared Pennsylvania Manufacturers Association. In the past generation, labor has been able to compete for power with business, but one result has been a pattern of consistent confrontation. The 1983 experience seems to point to a new pattern of cooperation.

One of Pennsylvania's more significant problems — a massive state debt to the federal government — was solved in 1983 because the state AFL-CIO and Chamber of Commerce, which usually are antagonistic, took the unusual step of working together to resolve differences instead of turning to the Legislature for help.

The leaders of those two groups — Julius Uehlein for the AFL-CIO and Cliff Jones for the Chamber — both have personalities geared more toward negotiating than toward old-style posturing. They led a group that drafted a compromise enabling the state to generate on its own the roughly $3 billion it had borrowed from the federal government to provide unemployment benefits. All the parties

involved — businesses, employees and benefit recipients — made financial sacrifices. The Legislature passed the plan, and, despite its sweeping impact, it has met little criticism.

Thornburgh's Icy Demeanor

Another important reason Pennsylvania gives the impression it can cope with its difficulties is the demeanor of its governor since 1979, Republican Richard L. Thornburgh. Calm and deliberate to the point of iciness, Thornburgh has managed the state budget well enough to need only one major tax increase in five years, even though Pennsylvania has been among the states hardest hit by the recession. He also has kept state government scandal-free, a contrast from the administration of his predecessor, Democrat Milton Shapp. The quintessential Thornburgh performance came during the 1979 Three Mile Island nuclear plant accident; his penchant for moving deliberately soothed fears during that crisis.

The qualities that help Thornburgh foster a positive impression about Pennsylvania's future, however, are the very ones that make it difficult for him to get along with the Legislature. The Legislature is almost everything Thornburgh is not — rambunctious, belligerent, colorful, given to passionate debate and rarely entirely free of the scent of corruption. Spending money to buy access and influence is a tradition in the Legislature.

Thornburgh remains aloof from person-to-person politicking, and is not close to the leadership. That represents a significant communications gap, since both chambers are dominated by strong leadership figures. Sparring between Thornburgh and the Legislature was considerable even in 1981-82, when Republicans controlled both chambers. It has intensified since the 1982 election, which gave Democrats control of the House.

In 1983, Thornburgh presented a no-frills budget calling for a tax increase to cover the deficit but containing no major new initiatives. House Democrats presented a dramatically different alternative. Their budget included a $1 billion program to expand human services programs, provide health care for the unemployed, establish food banks

STATE LEADERSHIP

Gov. Richard L. Thornburgh (R)

Born: July 16, 1932, Carnegie, Pa.
Home: Pittsburgh, Pa.
Education: Yale U., B.S. 1954; U. of Pittsburgh School of Law, LL.B. 1957.
Occupation: Lawyer.
Family: Wife, Virginia Judson; four children.
Religion: Protestant.
Political Career: Republican nominee for U.S. House, 1966; U.S. attorney for western Pennsylvania, 1969-75; assistant U.S. attorney general in charge of criminal division, 1975-77; elected governor 1978, 1982; term expires Jan. 1987.

GENERAL ASSEMBLY

SENATE
23D, 27R

Henry G. Hager (R)
President pro tem

HOUSE
103D, 100R

K. Leroy Irvis (D)
Speaker

and shelters for the needy and initiate job development and training programs.

The most important supporter of this ambitious new program was House Majority Leader James J. Manderino of Monessen, an industrial town south of Pittsburgh. Although Manderino nominally ranks below House Speaker K. Leroy Irvis, a black Democrat from Pittsburgh, Irvis employs his clout sparingly, and in practice Manderino dominates because he is an intense, almost tireless worker.

In the Senate, the dominant figure is Republican President Pro Tem Henry G. Hager of Williamsport, a small city in north central Pennsylvania. He gets along well with Manderino and at first expressed interest in the Democrat's spending plan, but later rejected it as too costly.

There is a strong coalition of fiscally conservative legislators that regularly exerts strong pressure to keep down the budget. The group consists mainly of Republicans — most of them from suburbia and from central Pennsylvania — along with some non-urban Democrats. Its members are wary of new programs because those programs usually include more money for Philadelphia, viewed by conservatives as an insatiable consumer of state funds.

Blocked by the conservatives, Manderino agreed to scale back his $1 billion program in order to get a budget that contained at least some of the new programs he wanted. The budget bill that finally passed contained tax increases not much less than those Manderino had originally requested. A hefty share of the new revenue will go not to fund new programs, however, but to erase a budget deficit that was larger than expected.

Legislative Reapportionment

The legislative reapportionment plan approved in 1981 was intended to be an incumbent protection map, and that goal was largely achieved in the 1982 election. Of the nearly 200 representatives and senators who sought re-election, all but a handful were successful. Few seats changed party control, although Democrats did gain a majority in the closely divided House with just a three-seat pickup there.

One consequence of reapportionment was Philadelphia's loss of four House seats, inevitable because of its population decline. The city, however, still has some strong voices speaking for it, such as House Appropriations Chairman Max Pievsky (a key Manderino ally) and Sen. Vincent J. Fumo, a South Philly Democrat whose aggressive lobbying has earned him influence in both the House and Senate. The city's Democratic delegation is smaller than it once was, but remains a sizable bloc in the party caucus.

The Pennsylvania GOP is remarkably strong in the Legislature, considering that it is far outnumbered among registered voters. Its formula for success is a moderate-to-liberal philosophy; its driving force is the progressive Montgomery County (suburban Philadelphia) organization, which provides considerable money and talent but has a reputation for consulting, not bullying, upstate Republicans. The current state party chairman, Robert B. Asher, is from the Montgomery organization.

Rifts and tension do exist, however. Some local Republican officials complain that Thornburgh concentrates power in an inaccessible group of aides, and there is an ongoing rivalry between Thornburgh and senior U.S. Sen. John Heinz for dominant status in the party. Democrats continue to widen their registration advantage, and they take encouragement from their unexpectedly strong gubernatorial showing in 1982. Thornburgh became a target for anti-Reagan sentiment and narrowly won re-election. ∎

A PROFILE OF

Pennsylvania

PEOPLE

Total Population: 11,863,895 (4th).
  White 90%, Black 9%, Asian and
  Pacific Islander 1%. Spanish origin 1%.

Urban:	69%
Rural:	31%
Born in state:	82%
Foreign-born:	3%

MAJOR CITIES

Philadelphia (1,688,210), Pittsburgh (423,938), Erie (119,123), Scranton (88,117), Reading (78,686)

LAND

Farm	31%
Forest	59%
Federally owned	2%

WORK

Occupations: 50% white-collar; 36% blue-collar; 13% service workers

Government workers:	129,284	federal
	147,466	state
	416,158	local

Unemployment rate: 13%

MONEY

Median family income (1980)	$19,995	(24th)
Tax burden per capita (1982)	$690	(21st)

EDUCATION

Spending per pupil through grade 12	$2,841	(10th)
Persons with college degrees	14%	(41st)

CRIME

Violent crime rate: 372 per 100,000 (30th)

POLITICS

1980 Presidential Vote: Reagan 50%, Carter 43%, Anderson 6%

Turnout rate in 1980:	55%
Turnout rate in 1982:	48%

U.S. House Delegation: 13D, 10R

RHODE ISLAND:

Dramatic Republican Gains Threaten Democratic Power

For years heavily ethnic Rhode Island has been one of the most Democratic states in the country. But after nearly a half century of virtually complete power, Democrats appear to be on the verge of losing their monopoly.

Dramatic and unexpected Republican gains in special state Senate elections in June 1983 stunned the Democrats. Long used to scrambling for the crumbs of state government, Republicans came close to capturing a Senate majority in the special election. They tripled their strength from seven to 21 seats in the 50-member upper chamber, and came within a combined total of 350 votes of winning the five additional seats that would have given them control. It marked the beginning of a political revolution in the state.

The special election became necessary when a federal court rejected a Democratic redistricting plan on the eve of the 1982 election. The court postponed the Senate election until 1983, and when the Senate failed to draft an acceptable new plan, the judges drew the lines on their own by combining recommendations from both parties.

While the Democrats approached the election "lazy, fat, dumb and happy," in the words of one legislator, the Republicans mounted a vigorous challenge. Together, the state and national GOP pumped about $50,000 into the Republican effort, while the normally abstentious business community poured in about $50,000 more.

Republicans focused their attacks on autocratic Senate Majority Leader Rocco Quattrocchi, who also served as chairman of the state Democratic Party. GOP advertising kept jabbing away at Democratic legislators as "Rocco's robots."

Quattrocchi himself was re-elected. But the GOP's efforts brought it striking success in the more liberal areas of the state, especially the fast-growing, politically marginal suburbs and small towns to the south of Providence. Most of the new GOP legislators are moderates in the mold of U.S. Sen. John H. Chafee and U.S. Rep. Claudine Schneider; about half are women.

Contrasts in Style

The Senate results came at a disastrous time for a Democratic Party that was polarized by the fight between four-term incumbent Gov. J. Joseph Garrahy and Warwick Mayor Joseph W. Walsh for its 1984 gubernatorial nomination. When Garrahy announced in September 1983 that he would not seek re-election, it was almost certain that Walsh would win the nomination.

The distinction between the two men is not ideological — both are in the mainstream of the state's labor-dominated Democratic Party. Their difference is mainly in style.

An affable former beer salesman, Garrahy fits traditional ethnic Rhode Island very well. But he has been harmed by a reputation as an inoffensive ribbon-cutter who lacks strong leadership traits. That reputation was exacerbated during the 1983 session, when the Legislature bucked his calls for a higher state sales tax and forced Garrahy to accept millions of dollars in spending cuts.

While Walsh is not widely regarded as a charismatic figure, he has gained a reputation as a more forceful leader than Garrahy during his years as mayor of Rhode Island's second-largest city. Walsh has flirted with races for higher office before, only to back away. But this time he seems intent on running.

Within the Legislature, Garrahy has drawn his major

STATE LEADERSHIP

Gov. J. Joseph Garrahy (D)

Born: Nov. 26, 1930, Providence, R.I.
Home: Narragansett, R.I.
Education: Attended U. of R.I., U. of Buffalo.
Military Career: Air Force, 1953-55.
Occupation: Brewery sales representative.
Family: Wife, Margherite DiPietro; five children.
Religion: Roman Catholic.
Political Career: R.I. Senate, 1963-69; lt. governor, 1969-77; state Democratic Party chairman, 1967-68; elected governor 1976, 1978, 1980, 1982; term expires Jan. 1985.

LEGISLATURE

SENATE
29D, 21R

William C. O'Neill (D)
President pro tem

HOUSE
85D, 15R

Matthew J. Smith (D)
Speaker

support from the allies of Quattrocchi — generally veteran blue-collar members from the party's traditional strongholds in Providence and the industrialized Blackstone Valley to the north. Walsh, 10 years younger than Garrahy, has attracted the support of younger, more reform-minded legislators from outside Providence. Some of them represent suburban professional constituencies with voters tied to Rhode Island's emerging high-technology industries.

Before the Senate election, the state legislative leadership was split between the two camps. Quattrocchi ran the Senate, while a longtime friend of Walsh, Matthew J. Smith, was House Speaker.

But the June election debacle cost Quattrocchi his leadership posts in the Senate and the state party. And with Quattrocchi's ouster, Garrahy lost his primary bases of support outside the executive branch. Quattrocchi was replaced as Senate majority leader by John C. Revens, the manager of Walsh's all-but-announced gubernatorial campaign. As part of the shuffle, nearly all of Quattrocchi's allies lost their Senate committee chairmanships.

Sen. Rocco Quattrocchi

The party chairmanship was not decided until mid-September 1983. With the House Speaker normally controlling most of the votes, the state committee elected Walsh's candidate, former Attorney General Julius C. Michaelson to head the state's Democratic Party.

But the lasting legacy of the Senate changes may be to pull the Legislature toward the center on economic and social issues. For years there has been almost total ideological conformity in the Legislature. It has been liberal on economic issues, conservative on social issues and decidedly pro-labor.

In the early 1980s, teachers comprised more than 20 percent of the Legislature and it was not unusual to see high-ranking labor officials holding major committee chairmanships. Unions usually got what they wanted. The state's generous labor laws, along with high taxes and high energy costs, have been cited as a major factor in the exodus of Rhode Island businesses to other states.

But on social issues, the Legislature has followed a different pattern. It killed a proposed state equal rights amendment in 1983. It has long had a reputation for being ardently anti-abortion.

Yet when the Senate convenes in 1984, Walsh reformers and moderate Republicans could form a majority capable of pushing the upper chamber to the left on social issues. And with fewer ties to the labor movement, the new breed would be likely to listen to the long-neglected business community.

Ironically, the dominant part of any new breed alliance in the Senate would be the Republicans. As recently as 1980, the GOP held no statewide offices, only one federal office and less than 20 percent of the seats in each chamber of the Legislature. Following the June special election, the energized Republican minority occupied the post of secretary of state, half the congressional delegation and 42 percent of the state Senate seats.

A PROFILE OF
Rhode Island

PEOPLE

Total Population: 947,154 (40th).
   White 95%, Black 3%, Asian and
   Pacific Islander 1%. Spanish origin 2%.

Urban:	87%
Rural:	13%
Born in state:	68%
Foreign-born:	9%

MAJOR CITIES

Providence (156,804), Warwick (87,123), Cranston (71,992), Pawtucket (71,204), East Providence (50,980)

LAND

Farm	12%
Forest	60%
Federally owned	1%

WORK

Occupations: 50% white-collar; 36% blue-collar; 14% service workers

Government workers: 9,123 federal
26,729 state
25,979 local

Unemployment rate: 8%

MONEY

Median family income (1980)	$19,448	(28th)
Tax burden per capita (1982)	$713	(20th)

EDUCATION

Spending per pupil through grade 12	$2,996	(8th)
Persons with college degrees	15%	(27th)

CRIME

Violent crime rate: 442 per 100,000 (25th)

POLITICS

1980 Presidential Vote: Carter 48%, Reagan 37%, Anderson 14%

Turnout rate in 1980:   65%
Turnout rate in 1982:   55%

U.S. House Delegation: 1D, 1R

SOUTH CAROLINA:

Rural Forces Control Senate, While Pluralism Rules House

As befits a growing New South state that still reveres its traditions, South Carolina has a government blending pluralism and gerontocracy.

The Legislature illustrates that dual personality. Its Senate is dominated by two small-town lawyers whose total  service adds to nearly a century, and whose first devotion is to rural concerns. The House, by contrast, is a blend of voices that speak for the "new" South Carolina politics — urban dwellers, blacks and Republicans. The Senate traditionally has dominated the Legislature and the state, but there are signs that the politics embodied by the House are taking over.

Some 59 years have passed since L. Marion Gressette won his first legislative election; at the age of 82, he is president pro tem of the Senate in a state where statute gives the Legislature a stronger hand than the governor. Force of personality, not bullying, is Gressette's strength. After watching Gressette persuade the Senate to reject the Equal Rights Amendment, a supporter of the amendment marveled at the charisma of his elderly adversary: "He didn't issue any threats. He didn't make any promises. He just imposed his will."

Gressette's "junior" partner is Rembert C. Dennis, 67, who has served since 1939. As chairman of the Senate Finance Committee, Dennis belongs to the five-person group that drafts the state's annual budget.

The philosophy guiding Gressette and Dennis is simple: spend as little state money as possible, keep rural areas dominant and maintain a tight relationship between government and business. This is the creed upheld by the predecessors of Gressette and Dennis, the famed "Barnwell Ring," a rural clique that controlled the Legislature from before World War II to the early 1970s.

In the past decade, the House has become the opposite of the Senate. In 1972, single-member House districts were adopted for the first time, a change that brought more diversity to the chamber and made it much less amenable to rural control. Solomon Blatt, the "Barnwell Ring's" Speaker for more than 30 years, gave up his post in 1973. Since then, several factions have competed for influence in an environment where power is decentralized. Finding a consensus is sometimes impossible — this year a majority of the House was willing to increase the sales tax, but the increase did not go through because educators, urbanites and other interests could not agree on how to distribute the new money.

One of the strongest factions among House Democrats is a group of younger centrists who came to the House in the mid-1970s. They include Rep. Robert L. Sheheen, 40, who is chairman of the Judiciary Committee, and Rep. Jean Hoefer Toal, also 40, who serves as chairman of the Rules Committee. This group often has the support of House Speaker Ramon Schwartz Jr., but the influence of the Speaker in today's House is nothing like what it was during Blatt's heyday.

Generally on good terms with the moderates are black legislators, who account for 20 of the 124 House members. While no single member is dominant in the black caucus, Rep. McKinley Washington Jr. and Rep. John W. Matthews Jr. are recognized as pragmatic legislative tacticians.

'Fat and Uglies'

As more white moderates and blacks came into the House during the latter half of the 1970s, younger Democratic conservatives began to coalesce. They and the older conservatives represent similar rural constituencies. But the populist rhetoric of the younger crowd is a shift from the segregationist politics their elders espoused.

The young conservatives call themselves the "Fat and Uglies," and originally their group was little more than an informal social club. It came to exercise influence in legisla-

---

STATE LEADERSHIP

Gov. Richard Riley (D)

Born: Jan. 2, 1933, Greenville, S.C.
Home: Greenville. S.C.
Education: Furman U., A.B. 1954; U. of S.C. Law School, LL.B. 1959.
Military Career: Navy, 1954-56.
Occupation: Lawyer.
Family: Wife, Ann Yarborough; four children.
Religion: Methodist.
Political Career: S.C. House, 1963-67; S.C. Senate, 1967-77; elected governor 1978, 1982; term expires Jan. 1987.

LEGISLATURE

SENATE

39D, 6R

1 vacancy

L. Marion Gressette (D)
President pro tem

HOUSE

103D, 20R

1 vacancy

Ramon Schwartz Jr. (D)
Speaker

tive affairs by joining with Republicans to form a conservative coalition holding about 40 votes. But the 1982 elections reduced the ranks of the "Fat and Uglies," eroding their bargaining strength.

The Republican House delegation is reliably conservative on fiscal issues, but frequently divides on social issues. There is an element in the GOP — sometimes called the "Bob Jones wing," after the fundamentalist university in Greenville — that argues passionately to protect the independence of private "Christian academies" when the Legislature discusses state accreditation of schools.

Although the clique of senior conservatives no longer rules the House, it still plays a key role. Committee chairmen such as Tom G. Mangum, Patrick B. Harris and B. L. Hendricks Jr. — all over 65 — retain power in their fiefdoms and can muster a majority in the House when in agreement with the GOP and younger conservative Democrats.

These days it is a constant struggle for Gressette and Dennis to preserve the Senate's dominant role. The Senate's power has been slipping since the 1970s, when reforms eliminated many tools senators had used to exercise power, including their near-total control of patronage and government spending in their home counties.

A key House-Senate power dispute came in 1982, when Gressette and Dennis tried but failed to force the House to go along with the Senate's plan for congressional redistricting. A federal court ended up approving a set of districts patterned on the House-passed plan.

The current House-Senate struggle involves adoption of a single-member districting plan for the Senate, to replace the existing multi-member district system. In a move that indicated Gressette may be losing control even in his own chamber, the Senate in February 1983 approved a single-member plan while he was in the hospital. But the House passed a different plan, and the matter went to a conference committee. Any single-member plan will produce some black senators (there have been none since Reconstruction) and begin to diversify the Senate.

Riley's Role

Democrat Richard Riley was elected governor in 1978 on a promise to "declare war on the Good Old Boy system," but most of his accomplishments have come through negotiation and compromise with the Legislature. Riley managed to win some changes in the appointment procedures for the Public Service Commission, which is becoming a more diverse body than it used to be. And though he is just one of five voices on the Budget and Control Board, Riley has managed to exercise personal influence over agencies' budget priorities.

Though Riley was re-elected overwhelmingly in 1982, his strong showing did not subdue the state's powerful business interests. They fiercely criticized the "Tax Equity" plan Riley proposed in 1983 and helped engineer its defeat in the Legislature. Riley's proposal called for reducing property taxes, increasing the sales tax and shifting the income tax burden to upper-income brackets. But both it and a watered-down version lost in the House, where it is still difficult to build a majority for tax increases.

Working against Riley were the state Chamber of Commerce and the South Carolina Textile Manufacturers Association. The Chamber has begun to assume a higher profile in politics. It has moved into a close alliance with the Textile Association, which represents the state's largest industry and has long been influential. ∎

A PROFILE OF

South Carolina

PEOPLE

Total Population: 3,121,820 (24th).
    White 69%, Black 30%. Spanish
    origin 1%.

Urban:	54%
Rural:	46%
Born in state:	73%
Foreign-born:	2%

MAJOR CITIES

Columbia (101,208), Charleston (69,510), North Charleston (65,630), Greenville (58,242), Spartanburg (43,968)

LAND

Farm	32%
Forest	63%
Federally owned	6%

WORK

Occupations: 45% white-collar; 41% blue-collar; 12% service workers

Government workers:	32,126	federal
	64,484	state
	113,375	local

Unemployment rate: 10%

MONEY

Median family income (1980)	$16,978	(41st)
Tax burden per capita (1982)	$628	(33rd)

EDUCATION

Spending per pupil through grade 12	$1,916	(42nd)
Persons with college degrees	13%	(42nd)

CRIME

Violent crime rate: 640 per 100,000 (8th)

POLITICS

1980 Presidential Vote: Reagan 49%, Carter 48%, Anderson 2%

Turnout rate in 1980:	51%
Turnout rate in 1982:	37%

U.S. House Delegation: 3D, 3R

SOUTH DAKOTA:

Legislature Follows the Lead Of Feisty, Powerful Janklow

South Dakota has retreated from its 1970s flirtation with populism, an affair that sent Democrats George McGovern and James Abourezk to the U.S. Senate and placed the governorship and the Legislature in Democratic hands for much of the decade. The state now seems comfortable

in the hands of a conservative GOP governor and a Legislature more than two-thirds Republican. The conservative mood of the 1980s has been reflected in votes on statewide initiatives as well — proposals to institute state and corporate income taxes in order to increase the level of state services have been soundly defeated in recent years.

South Dakota does not have the tradition of a strong Legislature, or a well-entrenched political system in the state Capitol. Pressure groups tend to coalesce around short-term legislative issues and then disband, rather than becoming part of a permanent governmental structure.

Combative, Controversial Janklow

The current Legislature is largely subservient to one of the nation's most combative and controversial governors, William J. Janklow. Because the Legislature meets for only two months each year, and because the state capital of Pierre is too isolated to draw much media attention, any governor has a good deal of independent authority. Janklow never hesitates to use it. He has reorganized state government by executive order, consolidating departments and revamping boards and commissions. He has acted unilaterally to sell Missouri River water to a coal pipeline

company in Wyoming and to have the state purchase bankrupt railroad lines and lease them to a private carrier for operation. Some of his moves are subject to disapproval by the Legislature, but rarely are they disapproved.

South Dakota has had chances to strengthen the hand of its Legislature against the executive, but has chosen not to do so. In the most recent round of constitutional revisions, in the early 1970s, voters approved new provisions giving the governor additional powers. But they rejected amendments designed to make the Legislature stronger and more efficient. Janklow is the current beneficiary of the constitutional situation.

Much of the publicity Janklow receives outside his state stems from angry personal confrontations. He sparked a feud with Minnesota's Gov. Rudy Perpich, for example, by offering inducements to Minnesota businesses to locate in South Dakota. When Perpich charged that South Dakota ranked last in the nation in virtually every category, Janklow retorted that his state has had three waves of immigrants — Scandinavians, Germans, and Minnesota businesses fleeing high taxes.

Meanwhile, the governor has become embroiled in two lawsuits over published allegations that he raped a 15-year-old Indian girl in 1967, while serving as a legal aid lawyer on an Indian reservation. Besides suing author Peter Mathiessen and *Newsweek*, Janklow is suing three South Dakota bookstores that stock Mathiessen's book, "In the Spirit of Crazy Horse," which contains the charges.

Within his state, however, Janklow is known as a tough and successful politician. Unlike some conservative governors, he plunges into debate on his own public policy initiatives. In an attempt to persuade banks to locate in his state, he lobbied vigorously and successfully during this year's session in favor of a measure allowing them to sell insurance. Janklow is not always polite or graceful in lobbying for what he wants, but he usually gets it. Even Democrats are hard pressed to think of a major piece of legislation in recent years that the governor sought but did not receive.

Republican Discipline

Janklow also benefits from the help of state House

STATE LEADERSHIP

Gov. William J. Janklow (R)

Born: Sept. 13, 1939, Chicago, Ill.
Home: Flandreau, S.D.
Education: U. of S.D., B.S. 1964, J.D.1966.
Military Career: Marine Corps, 1956-59.
Occupation: Lawyer.
Family: Wife, Mary Thom; three children.
Religion: Lutheran.
Political Career: S.D. attorney general, 1975-79; elected governor 1978, 1982; term expires Jan. 1987.

LEGISLATURE

SENATE

9D, 26R

Mary A. McClure (R)
President pro tem

HOUSE

16D, 54R

Jerome B. Lammers (R)
Speaker

Majority Leader Joseph H. "Papa Joe" Barnett, 51, who has served in the House for 16 years, and as majority leader since 1979. Bright and well-respected, he has a tight hold on the Republican caucus, which takes in 54 of the chamber's 70 members and meets every day before the Legislature's session. On an issue of importance to the governor, Barnett usually can keep his troops in line.

While Janklow is a policy activist, he is not considered a legislative craftsman, and he does not always think in strategic terms. He quickly loses patience with people who fail to see things his way. Barnett has the job of distilling the governor's proposals into concrete legislation that most Republicans can support. Republicans thrash out their differences in caucus, but usually emerge with a consensus resembling what Barnett wanted them to enact.

The state Senate, just as heavily Republican as the House, also shows a high degree of party discipline. But Senate Majority Leader G. Homer Harding is less influential than Barnett. Unlike the House Speaker, the Senate majority leader is unable to refer bills to committees. That power rests with the lieutenant governor, currently Lowell C. Hansen II.

Hansen has had his problems over the past year. He has seemed trapped between the legislative and executive branches. He has claimed that Janklow has ignored him while meeting daily with the legislative leadership. At times the dispute has sounded trivial: When Janklow brought a group of supporters to Sioux Falls for a rally after the 1982 election, he insulted the lieutenant governor, who owns a bus company, by hiring a firm other than the one Hansen operates. Hansen's firm complained that the rival bus company was not even properly licensed.

Within the Legislature, the eastern and western portions of the state, divided by the Missouri River, traditionally have pursued different interests. "East River" is part of the Midwest Corn Belt, symbolized by the Corn Palace in Mitchell, an auditorium with mosaics wrought into colored corn cobs on the exterior. "West River" is ranch country, and legislators who come from there sometimes speak contemptuously of the "silo-stuffers" on the other side of the Missouri. But because the west is sparsely populated, it has lost seats in the Legislature as a result of reapportionment, and its legislators now find themselves in a distinct minority.

Recently, the two parts of the state fought over efforts to establish a state-run rail system, which stood to benefit the eastern areas. Over West River's strong objections, the eastern interests won; the state now runs the system. ■

A PROFILE OF

South Dakota

PEOPLE

Total Population: 690,768 (45th).
   White 93%, Black 0.3%, American Indian, Eskimo and Aleut 7%. Spanish origin 1%.

Urban:	46%
Rural:	54%
Born in state:	71%
Foreign-born:	1%

MAJOR CITIES

Sioux Falls (81,343), Rapid City (46,492), Aberdeen (25,956), Watertown (15,649), Brookings (14,951)

LAND

Farm	93%
Forest	4%
Federally owned	7%

WORK

Occupations: 45% white-collar; 24% blue-collar; 15% service workers

Government workers: 9,927 federal
16,165 state
30,756 local

Unemployment rate: 5%

MONEY

Median family income (1980)	$15,993	(48th)
Tax burden per capita (1982)	$476	(47th)

EDUCATION

Spending per pupil through grade 12	$2,016	(36th)
Persons with college degrees	14%	(36th)

CRIME

Violent crime rate: 105 per 100,000 (49th)

POLITICS

1980 Presidential Vote: Reagan 61%, Carter 32%, Anderson 7%

Turnout rate in 1980:	75%
Turnout rate in 1982:	63%

U.S. House Delegation: 1D

TENNESSEE:

Regional Divisions Are Key In Two-Party Legislature

Tennessee has a stronger two-party tradition than any other Southern state, and that tradition has held up through the political turmoil of the past decade. While the GOP has been decimated at the legislative level in neighboring Kentucky and North Carolina, it has managed to  cling to respectability in Tennessee: Republicans not only have the governorship but a third of the Senate seats and nearly 40 percent of the seats in the House.

In general, the club-like Legislature has been relatively free of overt partisan tension. For years, Republican senators were allowed to hold committee leadership positions below the level of chairman. But the mood has been changing. The GOP lost its sub-chairmanship rights in 1981 after it had the temerity to run a candidate against Senate Speaker and Lt. Gov. John S. Wilder. In the aftermath of that election, which saw a general thrust against Democratic legislators by Republican Gov. Lamar Alexander, partisan voting lineups became more common as Wilder and House Speaker Ned R. McWherter began to show less willingness to accommodate the governor's wishes on appointments and other matters.

Still, the chief divisions within the Legislature have less to do with party than with ideology and constituency. Mountain Republicans from east Tennessee and rural Democrats from west Tennessee share a deep-seated suspicion of government spending to solve social problems; urbanites of both parties, although split over support of social programs, often unite in trying to win funds for construction or development projects in their cities. The sharpest conflicts have tended to come over spending on public works. With reapportionment augmenting their numbers, urban legislators have begun to challenge traditional rural control over distribution of state funds.

Urban-rural bickering has been complicated by the growth of the Memphis, Nashville and Knoxville suburbs, whose representatives have begun to play a swing role on tax and spending issues. When the state's gasoline tax was increased in 1981, suburbanites joined with urban legislators in an attempt to change the distribution formula for revenues from the tax, which had been drawn to favor the rural counties. Rural legislators barely beat the effort back. But the suburbs part company with the cities on mass transit spending; suburban commuters, who drive their own cars to work, are reluctant to spend funds on buses.

Urban-suburban tension has been especially strong in racially polarized Memphis and its Shelby County suburbs. In the city itself, blacks and whites have been fighting over political power for years, with the slim white majority still keeping tenuous control. Democrats running for the Legislature in heavily white districts around Memphis have had to shed their identification with national Democratic policies, and that does not always save them; the only major bloc of Republican state legislators other than the one from east Tennessee comes from the Memphis suburbs.

Dominant House Speaker

The dominant figure in the Legislature for the last decade has been McWherter. A beer distributor from rural west Tennessee, he presides over the House with a "good ol' boy" spirit that has kept outright strife between competing blocs to a minimum. McWherter has kept legislators with him in part by limiting his requests. When he does ask for something, or when he makes clear the limits beyond

---

STATE LEADERSHIP

Gov. Lamar Alexander (R)

Born: July 3, 1940, Blount County, Tenn.
Home: Nashville, Tenn.
Education: Vanderbilt U., B.A. 1962; N.Y.U. School of Law, J.D. 1965.
Occupation: Lawyer.
Family: Wife, Leslee "Honey" Buhler; four children.
Religion: Presbyterian.
Political Career: Campaign coordinator for Sen. Howard H. Baker Jr., 1966; legislative assistant to Baker, 1967-69; White House congressional relations staff member, 1969; Republican nominee for governor, 1974; elected governor 1978, 1982; term expires Jan. 1987.

GENERAL ASSEMBLY

SENATE
22D, 11R
Sen. John S. Wilder (D)
Speaker

HOUSE
60D, 37R, 1 Ind.
1 vacancy
Ned R. McWherter (D)
Speaker

Sen. John S. Wilder   **Rep. Ned R. McWherter**

which he will not go, he is usually accommodated.

McWherter's closest ties are to an informal caucus of rural west Tennessee Democrats who dominated the House until the mid-1970s, joining with east Tennessee Republicans to keep a lid on state spending for social programs. He has gradually moved beyond those alliances, becoming more receptive to urban pressures for greater state funding of social programs.

On other issues, however, he has guarded rural dominance of Democratic affairs. In 1983, McWherter and others tried to abolish Tennessee's presidential primary in favor of a party caucus, giving party leaders control over the state's choice of a presidential candidate. The move was opposed by Republicans and a group of younger urban Democrats, who failed to stop it in the House, but had the satisfaction of watching Alexander veto it.

Alexander has emerged as a strong political figure in Tennessee despite a first term that was light in major legislative proposals. Elected in 1978 on a wave of disgust at corruption in Democratic Gov. Ray Blanton's administration, he has maintained an image of calm integrity throughout his time in office. A master at public relations, he has traveled continuously around the state, keeping in close touch with voters.

Better Schools Program

The governor waited until the beginning of his second term to launch the chief policy initiative of his administration. His Better Schools Program, revamping the state's education system, drew national attention after it was unveiled in January 1983, especially its provisions for "master teacher" and incentive pay programs. Despite the publicity and Alexander's success at selling the idea to the state's voters, however, the measure failed in the Senate Education Committee, in large part due to the opposition of the Tennessee Education Association. Still, the idea's popularity around the state has made it all but certain to dominate Tennessee's attention in 1984.

Despite the collapse of the financial empire of Knoxville banker Jake Butcher, who was a leading economic and political power in the state, bankers will remain a pivotal influence on the Legislature. For years, big city banks have been pushing for legislation to allow them to take over smaller banks in other counties. In 1983, in the wake of the Butcher collapse, the Legislature passed inter-county banking to allow threatened small banks to be salvaged.

Liquor dealers are another important legislative force. This year they blocked a move to raise the drinking age to 21.

A PROFILE OF

Tennessee

PEOPLE

Total Population: 4,591,120 (17th). White 84%, Black 16%. Spanish origin 1%.

Urban:	60%
Rural:	40%
Born in state:	72%
Foreign-born:	1%

MAJOR CITIES

Memphis (646,356), Nashville-Davidson (455,651), Knoxville (175,030), Chattanooga (169,565), Clarksville (54,777)

LAND

Farm	51%
Forest	50%
Federally owned	8%

WORK

Occupations: 48% white-collar; 38% blue-collar; 12% service workers

Government workers: 36,655 federal 75,444 state 172,141 local

Unemployment rate: 11%

MONEY

Median family income (1980)	$16,564	(44th)
Tax burden per capita (1982)	$467	(49th)

EDUCATION

Spending per pupil through grade 12	$1,831	(47th)
Persons with college degrees	13%	(44th)

CRIME

Violent crime rate: 413 per 100,000 (29th)

POLITICS

1980 Presidential Vote: Reagan 49%, Carter 48%, Anderson 2%

Turnout rate in 1980: 57%
Turnout rate in 1982: 47%

U.S. House Delegation: 6D, 3R

TEXAS:

Liberals Have Electoral Clout But Lack Legislative Muscle

Long dominated by its conservative Democrats, Texas is witnessing a resurgence of the party's liberal wing. Blue-collar workers, minorities, urban liberals and rural populists alike flocked to the polls in 1982, helping the Democrats regain control of the Statehouse and boosting several  left-of-center candidates into statewide office. Democratic gubernatorial candidate Mark White, known for most of his career as a conservative, rode into office in 1982 on a platform loaded with populist themes.

But if liberals have become an increasingly significant force in the electoral arena, they have yet to demonstrate much muscle in the legislative sphere, where power is still in the hands of business-oriented conservatives. Liberals have shown they can control the Democratic Party's nominating process, at least in favorable years. It remains to be seen how that will affect state government in the long run.

Although Democrats maintain massive margins in both houses of the Texas Legislature, party labels have relatively little to do with the power structure there. Neither the House nor the Senate bothers to designate a majority or a minority leader, and Republicans have been appointed by the House Speaker and Senate president to chair key economic committees in both chambers. What bonds many of the Legislature's most powerful players is a shared suspicion toward activist state government — an outlook that meets with hearty approval among the bankers, lawyers and oil producers of the metropolitan Texas establishment.

The resulting environment traditionally has been one of fiscal restraint; Texas remains one of a handful of states in the country that has refused to establish a state income tax, and its annual per capita state government expenditure ranks near the bottom of the national scale. Burdened in 1983 with the state's gloomiest economic picture in nearly a quarter century, Texas legislators showed little tolerance for populist notions.

White tried to push through a tax increase to help finance a 24 percent increase in teachers' salaries, and he sought to make public utilities commissioners elected rather than appointed officials. He was defeated on both issues. The governor's critics scored him for not working more closely with the Legislature.

White's supporters point out that similar complaints haunted his predecessor, William Clements, when Clements took office in 1979, as the first Republican to occupy the Texas Statehouse since Reconstruction. Clements quickly learned how to play politics with the Legislature's Democratic majority, and many Democrats came to respect him as a political force. Clements, though, as a millionaire manufacturer of oil equipment, had much in common with the conservative Democrats and their outside allies — the oil industry, agribusiness and the highway lobby. White, whatever his pro-business sympathies, has to weigh them against the demands of the liberal electoral coalition.

Powerful Lieutenant Governor

There are limits to what even a popular and skillful governor can accomplish in Texas. State law restricts the chief executive's powers, and boards and commissions make many decisions that would be under the governor's jurisdiction in other states.

The lieutenant governor, by contrast, is vested with considerable power. Democrat William P. Hobby, who has held that post since 1973, has combined legislative skill with institutional clout to establish himself as the most influential figure in the Legislature, and probably the most politically significant lieutenant governor in the country. As presiding officer in the Senate, Hobby is empowered to

STATE LEADERSHIP

Gov. Mark White (D)

Born: March 17, 1940, Henderson, Texas.
Home: Austin, Texas.
Education: Baylor U., B.B.A. 1962, J.D. 1965.
Military: Texas National Guard, 1966-69.
Occupation: Lawyer.
Family: Wife, Linda Thompson; three children.
Religion: Baptist.
Political Career: Texas secretary of state, 1973-78; attorney general 1979-83; elected governor 1982; term expires Jan. 1987.

LEGISLATURE

SENATE
26D, 5R

Lloyd Doggett (D)
President pro tem

HOUSE
114D, 36R

Gibson D. Lewis (D)
Speaker

make committee assignments, appoint committee chairmen and schedule legislation. He also chairs the Legislative Budget Board, which sets spending targets traditionally used by the Legislature in making its final budget. Within the chamber, Hobby has a reputation as a quiet but effective leader. Outside, he has demonstrated notable political prowess. Hobby was instrumental in mounting an extensive voter mobilization drive in 1982.

In the state House, legislators are still adjusting to a change in leadership. Democrat Gibson D. Lewis replaced retiring seven-year veteran House Speaker Billy Clayton this year, and he has had some trouble filling his powerful predecessor's shoes.

Owner of a Fort Worth label company, Lewis benefited from business support in his drive for the speakership.

Lt. Gov. William P. Hobby

Those ties have proven a liability as well as an asset — he was hurt early in 1983 by disclosures that he had failed to detail business dealings with lobbyists for the liquor and horse racing industries. But the issue had largely blown over by the end of the session. Several close Lewis allies — including Bill Messer, D, chairman of the Calendars Committee, which schedules legislation for floor action, and Ways and Means Chairman Stan Schlueter, D — helped fill the power vacuum while Lewis was preoccupied with the disclosure issue. Lewis worked successfully to kill a trucking deregulation bill, and helped block tax increase legislation.

Nearly a third of the House was newly elected in 1982, a turnover spurred by redistricting following the 1980 census. That count showed a steady in-state migration to the state's metropolitan areas. Texas' urban legislators are chipping away at the traditional rural power base.

Tension between the rural and urban delegations was evident in 1983 during debate over legalizing parimutuel betting on horse racing. Members from Texas' northern and western plains helped block legalization, while most lawmakers from metropolitan areas supported it.

The shift in power toward urban Texas offers mixed clues about the state's political future. Conservatism is thriving in the comfortable neighborhoods of Houston, Dallas-Fort Worth and their surrounding suburbs. Most of the voters in those areas prefer the Republicans. But inner-city Houston, with its active core of blacks, Hispanics and labor sympathizers, is a crucible of Texas liberalism.

In 1982, the inner-city liberals in both Houston and Dallas joined forces successfully with the state's huge Hispanic population, which is concentrated in the lower Rio Grande Valley and in parts of West Texas. Texas is 21 percent Hispanic, and the group's vote has always been a potentially decisive force. But the potential has never been realized because of low turnout.

That situation began to change in 1982, as Hispanics throughout the state voted in unexpected numbers to nominate and elect not just White but the rest of the liberal statewide ticket. The San Antonio-based Southwest Voter Registration Education Project is involved in an ongoing effort to boost Hispanics' electoral strength. ∎

A PROFILE OF

Texas

PEOPLE

Total Population: 14,229,191 (3rd).
White 79%, Black 12%, Asian and Pacific Islander 1%. Spanish origin 21%.

Urban:	80%
Rural:	20%
Born in state:	68%
Foreign-born:	6%

MAJOR CITIES

Houston (1,595,138), Dallas (904,078), San Antonio (785,880), El Paso (425,259), Fort Worth (385,164)

LAND

Farm	83%
Forest	14%
Federally owned	2%

WORK

Occupations: 53% white-collar; 32% blue-collar; 12% service workers

Government workers:	152,115 federal
	199,483 state
	589,832 local

Unemployment rate: 9%

MONEY

Median family income (1980)	$19,618	(27th)
Tax burden per capita (1982)	$640	(32nd)

EDUCATION

Spending per pupil through grade 12	$2,012	(37th)
Persons with college degrees	17%	(23rd)

CRIME

Violent crime rate: 532 per 100,000 (16th)

POLITICS

1980 Presidential Vote: Reagan 55%, Carter 41%, Anderson 3%

Turnout rate in 1980:	51%
Turnout rate in 1982:	40%

U.S. House Delegation: 21D, 6R

UTAH:

Conservative Mormon Values Underlie Republican Control

Utah's Legislature, if not quite a monolith, is more uniform than almost any other in the country. Like the electorate by which it is chosen, it is overwhelmingly Republican, conservative and Mormon. The demographic and ideological differences that animate government in other states are not always easy to find in Salt Lake City — there is an underlying political consensus.

That consensus seems, if anything, to be growing stronger with the years. As recently as a decade ago, Democrats could count on respectable numbers in each legislative session, and in good national years for their party, they had a chance for control. Those days are over. Restricted to five of 29 seats in the Senate and 17 of 75 in the House, they are the equivalent of a Republican minority in the Deep South.

Remarkably, this evolution has occurred despite the presence of Democratic Gov. Scott M. Matheson, who is widely considered the most popular political figure in the state. Matheson has not acquired his popularity by impersonating a conservative Republican — his moderate politics are within the mainstream of his party nationwide. Nor has he won votes by being a conspicuously strict Mormon: Matheson once defined "integrity" by citing his own willingness to drink coffee (forbidden by church doctrine) in public as well as in private.

Matheson's personal popularity has brought him two gubernatorial terms, and offers the strong possibility of a third as well. But it does not guarantee any legislative power — the conservative majority in the Legislature rarely gives Matheson the autonomy he wants. Matheson is not shy about making proposals, but the Legislature accords itself the option of rejecting them. And because it is able to override any veto, Matheson is powerless to challenge it.

In 1983, Matheson wanted to raise money for flood control programs without a tax increase, largely by speeding up collection of revenue under existing law. The Legislature insisted he did not have the authority to do that. Matheson responded by calling a special session. The flood control money was found, but only through a one-year increase in the sales tax.

While the Republicans resist Matheson on policy issues, they recognize the governor's appeal to the state's voters, and seldom criticize him openly. One of the few who does is Senate Majority Leader K. S. Cornaby, of Salt Lake City, who is Matheson's likely opponent in the 1984 gubernatorial election. Cornaby has scored the governor on alleged mismanagement in state agencies, criticized some appointments and challenged his spending priorities.

The acknowledged leader in the Legislature is House Speaker Norman H. Bangerter. It was Bangerter's idea to raise the sales tax against Matheson's objections, and he sold it to the Legislature. Bangerter is popular with most members, and he is considered a skillful consensus builder. He has served as majority leader and Speaker for two terms each — unusual for Utah, where turnover in the leadership is high.

Bangerter's Senate counterpart, President Miles Ferry, is less influential, but still a formidable figure. "Cap" Ferry cultivates the image of a simple farmer, but has a reputation for being craftier than he likes to seem. Ferry currently is chairman of the Legislative Management Committee, which conducts legislative business between sessions. This panel is crucial in maintaining a legislative check on the governor, since the Legislature meets only 60 days during odd-numbered years, and 20 days during even-numbered years. The chairmanship of the panel alternates between the Senate president and House Speaker.

Regional differences sometimes intrude on the Legislature, with the urban majority from Salt Lake City, Ogden and Provo confronting the rural remainder of the state. But on most issues, the striking characteristic of the Utah Legislature is its homogeneity.

Dominant Mormon Influence

The Mormon Church has been the dominant influence

STATE LEADERSHIP

Gov. Scott M. Matheson (D)

Born: Jan. 8, 1929, Chicago, Ill.
Home: Salt Lake City, Utah.
Education: U. of Utah, B.S. 1950;
   Stanford U. Law School, LL.B. 1952.
Occupation: Lawyer.
Family: Wife, Norma Warenski; four
   children.
Religion: Mormon.
Political Career: Elected governor
   1976, 1980; term expires Jan. 1985.

LEGISLATURE

SENATE

5D, 24R

Miles Ferry (R)
President

HOUSE

17D, 58R

Norman H. Bangerter (R)
Speaker

in Utah since the first settlers arrived, and it remains the source of basic values for most politicians of both parties. Some 82 percent of the members of the Legislature belong to the Mormon Church (the Church of Jesus Christ of Latter-day Saints).

These values stress industry (the symbol of both church and state is the beehive) and individual liberties, and resent government intrusion into both. Believing that charity begins at home, the church has strongly opposed many social welfare programs. In 1971, Ezra Taft Benson, president of the LDS Church's Council of Twelve Apostles, said a liberal Democrat could not be a good Mormon. Some Utah Democrats complain that the qualifying word "liberal" has been erased from the proposition since then.

But Mormon doctrine also emphasizes some values not identified with conservatism. Mormons are strong advocates of public education, and the state has the fewest private and parochial schools, per capita, of any state in the country. Education lobbies are highly effective. The governor appointed a blue-ribbon commission in 1983 to study ways to improve state schooling.

The Church also helped lead the fight against placing MX missiles in Utah when the Carter administration proposed a "racetrack" basing system in Utah and Nevada. Together with liberals and environmentalists, Mormons put the state on record against the plan. The Reagan administration scrapped it.

The Mormon influence has affected the state's political agenda in subtler ways as well. Moral issues have a high priority in the Legislature. Utah has a unique capital punishment law — it is the only state to execute by firing squad — and that is a perennial subject of debate. Recently, cable television has become a big issue; some Mormon officials are concerned about questionable programming the state might be subjected to if it allows the new technology. Because of the controversy surrounding the cable television issue, the Legislature decided to place the question on the ballot in 1983.

On other issues, traditional economic interests remain important. The coal industry — centered in Carbon, Sanpete and Sevier counties — has traditionally been influential, although recently it has fallen on hard times. But it has succeeded in keeping the state's severance tax relatively modest. Utilities, another powerful interest in the state, have joined the coal industry in fighting to keep the severance tax low. ∎

A PROFILE OF
Utah

PEOPLE

Total Population: 1,461,037 (36th).
  White 95%, Black 1%, American Indian, Eskimo and Aleut 1%, Asian and Pacific Islander 1%. Spanish origin 4%.

Urban:	84%
Rural:	16%
Born in state:	66%
Foreign-born:	4%

MAJOR CITIES

Salt Lake City (163,033), Provo (74,108), Ogden (64,407), Orem (52,399), Sandy City (51,022)

LAND

Farm	23%
Forest	30%
Federally owned	61%

WORK

Occupations: 54% white-collar; 31% blue-collar; 12% service workers

Government workers:	36,510	federal
	30,566	state
	54,457	local

Unemployment rate: 9%

MONEY

Median family income (1980)	$20,024	(22nd)
Tax burden per capita (1982)	$651	(27th)

EDUCATION

Spending per pupil through grade 12	$1,842	(44th)
Persons with college degrees	20%	(7th)

CRIME

Violent crime rate: 299 per 100,000 (36th)

POLITICS

1980 Presidential Vote: Reagan 73%, Carter 21%, Anderson 5%

Turnout rate in 1980:	72%
Turnout rate in 1982:	61%

U.S. House Delegation: 3R

VERMONT:

Stubborn Yankee Traditions Still Survive in Legislature

Nowhere is Vermont's tradition of stubborn Yankee independence more striking than in its state Legislature. At times there seem to be as many possible coalitions as there are combinations of the 150 House members and 30 senators.

Party divisions mean little. In the late 1970s, a Republican House majority elected a Democratic Speaker, Timothy J. O'Connor Jr., who in turn appointed several Republicans to committee chairmanships. The current Republican Speaker, Stephan A. Morse, has been more partisan than O'Connor — he ousted a Democrat from the chairmanship of one important panel — but Democrats still control some of the committees.

Not only do members have a natural inclination to independence, but also the leadership lacks much institutional power to enforce a party line. Party apparatus is minimal; in the Senate, committee members are selected each session by a three-person panel which may include members of both parties. Party caucuses are held to exchange ideas and debate proposals, but rarely do they produce party positions.

Senate Democrats tend to be relatively united behind Minority Leader Peter Welch, but Republicans are less cohesive, and Republican defections produce some Democratic victories. President Pro Tem Robert A. Bloomer, the leading Republican figure, likes to think of himself as a Senate official rather than a party leader. The House is even more politically fractious than the Senate, with Democrats rarely achieving unity on any major issue.

The traditional alignment in the Vermont Legislature featured a rural, conservative, Republican majority and a small ethnic Democratic bloc, based in the Irish and Franco-American constituencies around Burlington, the state's largest city.

In the past decade, however, the alignment has changed. While rural Vermont still sends some of the old-fashioned fiscal curmudgeons to represent it in Montpelier, the statewide Republican Party has been moving in a moderate direction, influenced to a great extent by environmental issues. GOP Gov. Richard A. Snelling, considered a militant conservative when he first sought the governorship in the 1960s, emerged in 1981 as a leading national critic of the Reagan administration's budget cuts in social programs.

Democratic Influx

At the same time, the Democratic Party has been remolded by some of the new arrivals who helped swell the state's population by 15 percent in the 1970s. Liberal young professionals, moving in from New York and other Eastern states, have become active in Democratic politics and have turned the party leftward on most major issues. Three of the last four Democratic gubernatorial nominees were born outside the state.

The economic problems of the 1980s have produced some new ideological cleavages among legislators, but the divisions tend to cross party lines. As in many other states, an economic liberal in Vermont these days is one who wants to make up state deficits by increasing taxes; a conservative is one who emphasizes reduced spending. Snelling has been on the anti-tax side.

The Legislature had to meet in special session in 1983 to deal with the expected deficit. The House and Senate drew up different tax packages, with the House opting for an income tax increase and the Senate preferring to raise the tax rate on hotel rooms and restaurant meals.

STATE LEADERSHIP

Gov. Richard A. Snelling (R)

Born: Feb. 18, 1927, Allentown, Pa.
Home: Shelburne, Vt.
Education: Harvard U., A.B. 1948.
Military Career: Army, 1944-46.
Occupation: Founder, Shelburne Industries.
Family: Wife, Barbara Weil; four children.
Religion: Unitarian.
Political Career: Vt. House, 1959-61 and 1973-77, majority leader, 1975-77; Republican nominee for lieutenant governor, 1964; Republican nominee for governor, 1966; elected governor 1976, 1978, 1980, 1982; term expires Jan. 1985.

LEGISLATURE

SENATE
13D, 17R

Robert A. Bloomer (R)
President pro tem

HOUSE
65D, 83R
2 Vacancies

Stephan A. Morse (R)
Speaker

The Senate eventually backed down. Neither chamber was willing to follow the lead of the more liberal Democratic faction, which wanted to deal with the problem by making the income tax more steeply progressive. Snelling strongly opposed that idea, and it fell on a straight party-line vote in the Senate, 17-13.

Snelling has a solid bloc of supporters who hold the balance of power on many close votes. On some issues where the governor is involved, though, the Legislature makes a point of declaring its independence. Legislators openly running interference for the governor can run the risk of being labeled too pliant and hurting the cause they want to promote. In the 1983 special session, the House Agriculture Committee wanted to investigate the state's meat inspection program. Snelling did not want his program under scrutiny, so he persuaded an ally to offer a substitute redirecting the probe away from the executive branch. But when the governor's role was made clear, the substitute was defeated.

Strange Coalitions

On issues where ideology is muted, strange coalitions sometimes produce victories in the Legislature. In the 1970s, Vermont became the second state in the country to pass a bill requiring returnable bottles, largely through an unusual alliance between environmentalists and farmers, many of whom were concerned that cows were eating shards of glass. They won despite a rare influx of national lobbyists from bottle and can industries.

The state capital of Montpelier has few entrenched lobbies — utilities are the only corporate interests that send full-time lobbyists to the Capitol. This too is a symbol of legislative independence. Vermont legislators tend to be uncomfortable with outside pressure in a way that their counterparts in other states are not. They are as likely to resist a hard-sell approach from an economic interest as they are from the governor or a party leader.

In the 1983 special session, the Chamber of Commerce and the tourism industry launched a high-pressure lobbying effort against imposition of the new rooms-and-meals tax. They managed to hold the tax off, but at the cost of alienating some legislators who will be influential in future tax arguments, and who considered the tactics inappropriate for Vermont. ■

A PROFILE OF

Vermont

PEOPLE

Total Population: 511,456 (48th).
  White 99%, Black 0.2%. Spanish origin 1%.

Urban:	34%
Rural:	66%
Born in state:	62%
Foreign-born:	4%

MAJOR CITIES

Burlington (37,712), Rutland (18,436), South Burlington (10,679), Barre (9,824), Montpelier (8,241)

LAND

Farm	31%
Forest	76%
Federally owned	5%

WORK

Occupations: 51% white-collar; 31% blue-collar; 13% service workers

Government workers:	4,396 federal
	12,717 state
	17,554 local

Unemployment rate: 7%

MONEY

Median family income (1980)	$17,205	(40th)
Tax burden per capita (1982)	$650	(28th)

EDUCATION

Spending per pupil through grade 12	$2,365	(22nd)
Persons with college degrees	19%	(10th)

CRIME

Violent crime rate: 128 per 100,000 (48th)

POLITICS

1980 Presidential Vote: Reagan 44%, Carter 38%, Anderson 15%

Turnout rate in 1980:	61%
Turnout rate in 1982:	50%

U.S. House Delegation: 1R

VIRGINIA:

Rural, Conservative Alliances Still Hold Sway in Legislature

Virginia has a state government with one foot stepping tentatively into the future and the other anchored firmly in the past.

Democratic Gov. Charles S. Robb fits neatly into the new breed of Southern governors who emphasize economic

modernization and racial harmony. A resident of the fast-growing, cosmopolitan suburbs of northern Virginia, just outside Washington, D.C., he was elected with overwhelming black support and has made minority participation one of the hallmarks of his administration.

But Robb is pitted against a Democratic Legislature that is a monument to a bygone era of courthouse alliances and traditional business interests. The rural machine of Harry F. Byrd Sr. is dead, but the Senate and House of Delegates remain the preserves of the well-to-do. Rather than serving as an entry point for ambitious young people in state politics, as most state Legislatures do nowadays, the Virginia Legislature is a part-time, low-paying institution dominated by middle-aged lawyers. The legal profession is believed to occupy a higher share of the seats in Virginia than in any other state. Blacks are even more under-represented in Virginia than in most Southern states; they comprise nearly 20 percent of the state population and only 4 percent of the Legislature.

Although 1982 marked the first time in a dozen years that Democrats controlled both the executive and legislative branches in Virginia, many of the Legislature's veteran Democrats were more comfortable with Robb's conserva-

tive Republican predecessors. During the 12 years that Republicans sat in the governor's chair, not one veto was overridden.

Robb has not suffered any major legislative setbacks during his first two years in office, but he has yet to confront the Legislature with an ambitious agenda. That should come in 1984 when, for the first time, he presents a complete budget of his own. With Virginia's "one-term-and-out" law, this will be Robb's one chance to make a major impact on state government. He is expected to emphasize educational policy, including a push for increased teacher salaries, and an economic development program that would increase the state's attractiveness to high-technology firms.

Robb could have problems if the conservative "Old Guard" keeps its legislative control. Its personification is House Speaker A. L. Philpott, a 25-year legislative veteran from the small town of Bassett, near the North Carolina border. He runs a tight ship. Blunt and opinionated, he can wither his opponents with a scowl. Philpott controls committee assignments and bill referrals — a power that has enabled him to frustrate consumer and labor legislation for years.

But there is a large, restive minority in the House, headed by Majority Leader Thomas W. Moss Jr. of Norfolk. Moss has backed away from challenging Philpott directly, but the younger, more centrist Democrats loyal to Moss are poised to take control of House leadership positions as the "Old Guard" retires.

Partisan New Breed

Trained to function in Virginia's growing two-party system, the new breed legislators are more partisan than their elders, most of whom joined the Legislature in the days of one-party government and prefer to vote on the basis of conservative ideology rather than party label.

Many of the younger members are from Virginia's fast-growing suburbs, a portion of the state that is home for nearly half the voters but historically has lacked much legislative influence. It has been difficult for legislators representing competitive suburban districts to build the

---

STATE LEADERSHIP

Gov. Charles S. Robb (D)

Born: June 26, 1939, Phoenix, Ariz.
Home: Richmond, Va.
Education: Attended Cornell U. 1957-58; U. of Wis., B.B.A. 1961; U. of Va., J.D. 1973.
Military Career: Marine Corps, 1961-70.
Occupation: Lawyer.
Family: Wife, Lynda Bird Johnson; three children.
Religion: Episcopalian.
Political Career: Lieutenant governor, 1978-81; elected governor 1981; term expires Jan. 1986.

GENERAL ASSEMBLY

SENATE

32D, 8R

Edward E. Willey (D)
President pro tem

HOUSE

65D, 34R, 1 Ind.

A. L. Philpott (D)
Speaker

seniority needed to match rural and urban colleagues from one-party districts.

Partisanship in the Virginia House has intensified as the number of Republicans has risen. The GOP presently holds about one-third of the seats, a higher share than in any other Southern state except Tennessee. But Republicans had hoped to make deeper inroads in 1982. With the House forced to adopt single-member districts and reapportionment establishing more seats in the suburbs, the GOP had expected big gains. Instead they gained one seat. Still, the new lines do favor gradual increases in Republican strength as strong Democratic incumbents retire in the future.

With fewer Republicans in the Senate, there is less partisanship. Power is more diffuse in the upper chamber, but Senate Majority Leader Hunter B. Andrews of Hampton clearly is in charge. He has established a strong base by simultaneously holding several key positions, including the post of ranking Democratic member on the powerful Senate Finance Committee. Andrews essentially has run the committee himself in recent sessions because of the illness of its 73-year-old chairman, Edward E. Willey of Richmond.

An effective debater and a more moderate Democrat than Philpott, Andrews is viewed by many party officials as their most viable candidate against Republican U.S. Sen. John W. Warner in 1984. Andrews has remained non-committal about making the challenge while he weighs assurances of adequate financing.

Although the Senate reveres tradition and prides itself on displays of Southern gentility, its leadership is not adverse to jousting with the House and the governor. A classic case of legislative infighting came in 1983, when the Senate — tired of playing a secondary role in the budget process — sought to strengthen its position in the debate on the budget by drafting its own proposal.

Speaker A. L. Philpott

Robb has drawn criticism from the Senate leadership for not keeping its members better informed of his legislative plans. Some Senate critics are rankled that he deals more closely with House allies, such as Alan A. Diamonstein of Newport News and Alson H. Smith Jr. of Winchester. Diamonstein was Robb's choice to head the Democratic state committee; Smith is one of the chief fund-raisers for "Chuck PAC," the informal name for a gubernatorial kitty that finances Robb's travels and contributes to Democratic legislative candidates.

Factions are fairly fluid within the Legislature, but there is visible sectionalism when local interests are at stake. The northern Virginia suburbs, the Tidewater area and western Virginia all have regional caucuses, and legislators from the suburbs and the mountainous west have pooled their votes on several issues in recent years. Transportation has been one of them, with the west seeking funds to pave secondary roads and the northern suburbs wanting money for construction of the Metro subway system in the Washington, D.C. area. ∎

A PROFILE OF
Virginia

PEOPLE

Total Population: 5,346,818 (14th).
  White 79%, Black 19%, Asian and
  Pacific Islander 1%. Spanish origin 2%.

Urban:	66%
Rural:	34%
Born in state:	60%
Foreign-born:	3%

MAJOR CITIES

Norfolk (266,979), Virginia Beach (262,199), Richmond (219,214), Newport News (144,903), Hampton (122,617)

LAND

Farm	39%
Forest	65%
Federally owned	9%

WORK

Occupations: 55% white-collar; 31% blue-collar; 12% service workers

Government workers: 150,377 federal
  116,733 state
  201,050 local

Unemployment rate: 6%

MONEY

Median family income (1980)	$20,018	(23rd)
Tax burden per capita (1982)	$605	(36th)

EDUCATION

Spending per pupil through grade 12	$2,193	(31st)
Persons with college degrees	19%	(9th)

CRIME

Violent crime rate: 322 per 100,000 (33rd)

POLITICS

1980 Presidential Vote: Reagan 53%,
  Carter 40%, Anderson 5%

Turnout rate in 1980:	55%
Turnout rate in 1982:	46%

U.S. House Delegation: 4D, 6R

WASHINGTON:

New Democratic Generation Changes Political Landscape

Political debate in Washington has been abruptly altered by a young generation of Democrats who swept into the state House in 1982, bringing that chamber under Democratic control and supplanting the influence of staunchly conservative Republicans who ruled before them.

In this dramatically new House, 29 Democratic freshmen account for more than half of their party's caucus. Together with 14 freshman Republicans, they are nearly a majority in the entire 98-member body.

One particularly active group of Democratic newcomers has been described as "neo-liberals" or "pragmatic reformers" because their philosophy represents a new third force among state Democrats, who in recent years have been divided into two camps — labor and environmentalists.

To the dismay of some environmentalists, these neo-liberals are vigorous proponents of economic development, a cause long promoted by labor leaders who believe growth means jobs for the rank-and-file. But labor also is wary of the neo-liberals because their blueprint for development entails closer cooperation between government and business to promote high-technology "clean" industry. That sounds threatening to union leaders, who fear that technicians assembling computer circuits will not be as prone to unionize as workers in the lumber and maritime trades, the traditional cornerstones of Washington's economy.

The ambitious agenda of the House neo-liberals extends beyond economic development. The group provided key support for a proposal to establish a five-member commission to handle legislative reapportionment and congressional redistricting, a step intended to remove the Legislature from that intensely political process. They also lobbied for removal of the state sales tax on food as part of their larger goal of moving Washington away from heavy dependence on a sales tax and toward adoption of an income tax.

Several of the neo-liberal objectives were achieved in the first half of 1983. The redistricting commission plan cleared the Legislature and is expected to pass when it goes before the voters as a proposed constitutional amendment. The sales tax on food has been eliminated. But the dream of overhauling the state's revenue structure fell by the wayside because lawmakers occupied most of their time deciding what to do about Washington's pressing short-term budget difficulties.

Fiscal Problems

The recession severely hurt Washington's timber and aerospace industries, and during 1981 and 1982 state government lurched from one fiscal crisis to the next. Each new deficit projection released by GOP Gov. John Spellman showed matters worse than earlier predictions had forecast. The Legislature, then controlled by conservative Republicans more reluctant than Spellman to raise taxes, resorted to a series of special sessions that raised taxes and reduced spending to meet immediate needs. Those measures, however, did not dig the state out of debt. Adding to this picture of fiscal disarray was the downward slide of the Washington Public Power Supply System (WPPSS), which was watched closely by Wall Street investors.

The chore of lifting this pall of fiscal instability came to preoccupy Democrats after they took control in the House and the Senate in 1983. On straight party-line votes in both chambers, Democrats approved a sweeping increase in sales and other taxes, which generated nearly $2 billion in new revenue. The House's neo-liberals went along with the package, despite the sales tax increase.

STATE LEADERSHIP

Gov. John Spellman (R)

Born: Dec. 29, 1926, Seattle, Wash.
Home: Seattle, Wash.
Education: Seattle U., B.S.S. 1949; Georgetown U. Law School, J.D. 1953.
Military Career: Navy, World War II.
Occupation: Lawyer.
Family: Wife, Lois Murphy; six children.
Religion: Roman Catholic.
Political Career: Candidate for mayor of Seattle, 1965; King County commissioner, 1967-69; King County executive, 1969-80; Republican nominee for governor, 1976; elected governor 1980; term expires Jan. 1985.

LEGISLATURE

SENATE
26D, 23R

Barney Goltz (D)
President pro tem

HOUSE
54D, 44R

Wayne Ehlers (D)
Speaker

Pressing fiscal problems were not the only brake on the ambitious programs espoused by the House newcomers. A major drag on their progress was the Senate, which represents continuity in Washington politics as much as the House represents change. The Senate has an older, more experienced membership than the House and generally views House initiatives with skepticism.

Unlike the House, the Senate has not seen a dramatic influx of new members. In the 1982 elections, Democrats made a net gain of one seat, just enough to erase the GOP's single-seat pre-election majority. Of the seven freshman senators who were elected in 1982, six are former members of the House. Traditional Democratic constituencies such as labor have more influence in the Senate than in the House.

Decentralized Power

For the governor and for interest groups, dealing with the Legislature is a tricky task because power is so decentralized. Each party in effect has four chiefs — a leader and a caucus chairman in each chamber. Committee chairmen exercise power independently of the leadership, and even the most junior members expect to play a significant role in decision-making. This fluid structure might be less unwieldy if the Legislature were geared toward apolitical consensus-seeking. But partisanship in the Legislature has been fierce since 1978, when fiscally conservative Republicans won control of the House. After 1980, the GOP secured a Senate majority when a Democratic member crossed the aisle, a move that enraged Democrats.

In 1981, the GOP tried to turn its dominant position to full partisan advantage through legislative reapportionment, but their efforts were negated in 1982 by an electorate sullen about the economy and angry with the GOP.

During his first two years in office, Spellman was frequently portrayed as a "98-pound weakling" kicked around by the Legislature; the moderate governor's main obstacle then was the conservative GOP faction that preferred deeper budget cuts to higher taxes.

But the spokesman for that group, House Speaker Bill Polk, did not seek re-election in 1982, and a number of his allies lost. Since Democrats took the Legislature in 1983, Spellman has actually fared better; the final budget enacted was quite close to the one he proposed. Critics still say he is indecisive in dealing with the Legislature, but he has gained enough strength to restrain the once-widespread speculation that primary challengers would flock to oppose him in 1984.

The best-known and most powerful lobbying influence in the state capitol is the Boeing Company. The company's aircraft production business is so vital to the state's economy that it is scarcely an exaggeration to say that whatever is good for Boeing is good for Washington. The timber giants — Weyerhaeuser, Boise Cascade and others — are often pitted in their lobbying against the Washington Education Association, since taxes on timber are used to pay education costs.

A major outlet for interest groups is the state's thriving institution of direct democracy. Voters sometimes seem to use this mechanism to strike a moderating balance with their votes for elective office. In 1982, for example, as Democrats gained ground in the Legislature, voters rejected three initiatives widely supported by Democrats — proposals to cap interest rates, to charge a deposit fee on bottles and to impose a corporate income tax while phasing out some other taxes.

A PROFILE OF

Washington

PEOPLE

Total Population: 4,132,156 (20th). White 92%, Black 3%, American Indian, Eskimo and Aleut 2%, Asian and Pacific Islander 3%. Spanish origin 3%.

Urban:	74%
Rural:	26%
Born in state:	48%
Foreign-born:	6%

MAJOR CITIES

Seattle (493,846), Spokane (171,300), Tacoma (158,501), Bellevue (73,903), Everett (54,413)

LAND

Farm	39%
Forest	54%
Federally owned	28%

WORK

Occupations: 55% white-collar; 29% blue-collar; 13% service workers

Government workers: 62,360 federal / 90,887 state / 148,576 local

Unemployment rate: 11%

MONEY

Median family income (1980)	$21,696	(9th)
Tax burden per capita (1982)	$854	(11th)

EDUCATION

Spending per pupil through grade 12	$2,679	(17th)
Persons with college degrees	19%	(11th)

CRIME

Violent crime rate: 447 per 100,000 (23rd)

POLITICS

1980 Presidential Vote: Reagan 50%, Carter 37%, Anderson 11%

Turnout rate in 1980: 61%
Turnout rate in 1982: 50%

U.S. House Delegation: 5D, 3R

WEST VIRGINIA:

Dominant Democrats Split By Ideological Differences

Few states are as solidly Democratic as West Virginia; none has a Legislature that displays so vividly the contrasts in the party's umbrella coalition.

The state House is dominated by a conservative, pro-business "Old Guard." The Senate is ruled by a new breed

of pro-labor liberals. About the only thing the two chambers have in common, other than party, is ambitious leadership. Both House Speaker Clyde M. See Jr. and Senate President Warren R. McGraw hope to succeed Democratic Gov. John D. "Jay" Rockefeller IV, who by law must retire next year after two terms.

With Democrats controlling nearly 90 percent of the seats in the Legislature, ideology is more important than party affiliation. West Virginia's liberal Democratic legislators are of the New Deal variety, sympathetic to unions and quick to encourage state government regulation in economic policy. Conservative Democrats are frugal, business-oriented and not especially interested in social issues. In recent years, the liberals have successfully steered passage of the Equal Rights Amendment, repealed capital punishment and enacted consumer rights legislation.

Because liberals control the Senate and conservatives the House, governing can be difficult. In 1983 the two chambers stalemated on a pay increase for public employees and teachers, with the Senate favoring a hefty increase and the House backing a small one. Since the opposing sides were unable to reach a compromise, there was no pay raise.

The opposing camps have overlapping geographical bases. The West Virginia Manufacturers Association and the state AFL-CIO are both potent forces in the most industrialized areas, the populous Kanawha and Ohio river valleys. The United Mine Workers and the coal producers are important and sometimes colliding interests in the coal fields of southern West Virginia.

The legislative leadership reflects this situation. The chairmen of the House and Senate Finance committees, the second most powerful forces in each chamber, are both Democrats from the small Ohio River city of Huntington. The House chairman, Charles M. Polan Jr., is a businessman with close ties to West Virginia manufacturers. His Senate counterpart, Robert R. Nelson, is a one-time legislative director of the United Mine Workers.

Rather than go head-to-head against each other in the Legislature, the two powerful pairs of interest groups work in uneasy alliance. They often thrash out a common position on legislation and then present it to the Legislature.

Senate Revolution

An increasingly influential force in state politics is the West Virginia Education Association. With other elements of organized labor, it spearheaded the Senate revolution of 1980 that tilted the upper chamber to the left. In the forefront of the liberal electoral successes that year was Democrat Bob Wise (now in Congress), a young consumer champion from Charleston who upset conservative Senate President W. T. Brotherton in the Democratic primary. About a dozen new Senate members were elected in 1980, and nearly an equal number were elected in 1982. Enough were similar to Wise to make the West Virginia Senate one of the more liberal upper chambers in the country.

To replace Brotherton as its leader, the Senate chose McGraw, a former lawyer in the U.S. Justice Department's civil rights division. McGraw is the central figure in a group of liberal, pro-labor political figures known as the "Wyoming County Mafia."

In running the Senate, McGraw relies heavily on Finance Committee Chairman Nelson. On many issues, however, McGraw tends to make the key decisions himself. As

---

STATE LEADERSHIP

Gov. John D. "Jay" Rockefeller IV (D)

Born: June 18, 1937, New York, N.Y.
Home: Charleston, W.Va.
Education: Harvard U., A.B. 1961; attended International Christian U., Tokyo, Japan, 1957-60.
Occupation: Public official.
Family: Wife, Sharon Percy; four children.
Religion: Presbyterian.
Political Career: W.Va. House, 1967-69; W.Va. secretary of state, 1969-73; Democratic nominee for governor, 1972; elected governor, 1976, 1980; term expires Jan. 1985.

LEGISLATURE

SENATE
31D, 3R
Warren R. McGraw (D)
President

HOUSE
87D, 13R
Clyde M. See Jr. (D)
Speaker

Rules Committee chairman, for example, he often convenes brief meetings of the panel around the Senate podium to rubber-stamp his legislative agenda.

Although much more conservative, the House is run more democratically than the Senate. Speaker See, a lawyer from the small town of Moorefield in the rural eastern panhandle, is an easygoing legislator who likes to play Pac-Man in his spare time. He makes most of his decisions after consulting with his Rules Committee, an elite group that includes most of the House leadership.

With power more fragmented in the House, teachers and labor have found it difficult to take control. The House does seem to be gradually moving to the left — a huge freshman class in 1983 of about 40 members includes many that were elected with labor support. But the shift in the House appears to be a matter of evolution. The new breed is not likely to capture the leadership positions until the more conservative "Old Guard" gives them up.

Philosophically, Rockefeller is more in line with the liberal Senate than with the conservative House. But he has not been a strongly ideological chief executive. Critics claim he has left both camps confused by talking as a liberal and acting as a conservative. He has not, for example, strongly promoted one of labor's pet issues — collective bargaining for public employees. In 1983, he did not propose a salary increase for public employees or teachers.

Rockefeller enjoyed some major legislative successes during his first term, winning increased funding for reconstruction of the state's secondary roads and removing the sales tax on food. But his second term has been stymied by economic problems. It would be hard to find a state that has suffered more from the recession than West Virginia. Heavily dependent on the battered coal industry, it has been staggered by high unemployment and sinking revenues.

To Rockefeller's advantage, the West Virginia governorship is an institutionally strong position, especially when it comes to molding the budget. But to his disadvantage, that institutional power makes him the prime target of criticism when taxes are raised, salaries are frozen and state spending is cut.

Although Republicans are a mere corporal's guard in the Legislature, they seldom miss an opportunity to embarrass Rockefeller and the Democrats. GOP members in the House proposed a 5 percent pay raise in 1983 for teachers and public employees, forcing Democrats to defeat it and rebuff their traditional interest group allies. ∎

A PROFILE OF

West Virginia

PEOPLE

Total Population: 1,949,644 (34th).
White 96%, Black 3%. Spanish origin 1%.

Urban:	36%
Rural:	64%
Born in state:	79%
Foreign-born:	1%

MAJOR CITIES

Charleston (63,968), Huntington (63,684), Wheeling (43,070), Parkersburg (39,967), Morgantown (27,605)

LAND

Farm	28%
Forest	76%
Federally owned	7%

WORK

Occupations: 45% white-collar; 41% blue-collar; 13% service workers

Government workers: 15,280 federal
42,169 state
64,832 local

Unemployment rate: 18%

MONEY

Median family income (1980)	$17,308	(38th)
Tax burden per capita (1982)	$753	(17th)

EDUCATION

Spending per pupil through grade 12	$2,173	(33rd)
Persons with college degrees	10%	(50th)

CRIME

Violent crime rate: 175 per 100,000 (46th)

POLITICS

1980 Presidential Vote: Carter 50%, Reagan 45%, Anderson 4%

Turnout rate in 1980:	58%
Turnout rate in 1982:	47%

U.S. House Delegation: 4D

WISCONSIN:

As Labor Loyalties Weaken, 'New Breed' Democrats Rule

Democrats are the clear majority in Wisconsin's Legislature, but they are straining to make the transition from a party of ethnic labor loyalists based in Milwaukee to a statewide party with a broader range of ideologies and political concerns.

Like other medium-sized states, Wisconsin has gone to a virtually full-time Legislature over the past decade, and this is turning out to affect not only the internal politics of the Democratic Party but the balance between the parties. Within Democratic ranks, the blue-collar legislators who used to serve in office while keeping their regular jobs are yielding to a new breed of Democratic teachers, academics and former legislative aides who give up these careers and enter politics full time.

Meanwhile, as legislative work becomes more and more time-consuming, the successful farmers and small-town lawyers who used to populate Republican ranks are finding the work — at an annual salary of $22,000 — much less attractive. So the Democrats of the new breed, who are enthusiastic about campaigning and about government itself, are winning rural and small-town districts that used to vote Republican as a matter of course. Democrats actually lost seats in the Wisconsin Assembly in 1982, a partial consequence of reapportionment, but hidden in that result was the election of a significant number of new Democratic members from rural and small-town districts in northern Wisconsin.

The crucial decisions in the state Legislature today are being made by Democrats whose background is almost exclusively in universities and political staff work. The new Assembly Speaker in 1983 was 37-year-old Thomas A. Loftus of Sun Prairie, who began his career as an aide to a previous Speaker. He replaced Ed G. Jackamonis, who came to the state Legislature from the political science department of the University of Wisconsin in Waukesha. A decade ago, by contrast, lawyers made up the leadership of both chambers.

Organized Labor's Losses

The biggest loser in all this change has been organized labor. In the old days, a Democratic majority meant an AFL-CIO majority — Assembly veterans remember when few Democrats dared to stand up and oppose the labor position on any roll call deemed a test of AFL-CIO loyalty. Today, such displays of independence are routine. Earlier in 1983, for example, unions were outraged when Democratic legislative leaders and Gov. Anthony S. Earl agreed on a proposal to freeze unemployment benefits to keep the state's unemployment compensation system solvent. But there was little they could do, since most members of the Democratic majority were generally willing to go along with the idea.

Although the Democrats of the new breed are outspokenly liberal on many questions, especially social issues and those dealing with civil liberties, they have a tendency to question some of the bread-and-butter spending accepted as an article of faith by earlier Democratic generations. Some of the younger Democrats who represent Milwaukee made their reputations in the 1970s by fighting against freeway construction within the city, clashing head on with union leaders who saw freeways as a source of jobs

STATE LEADERSHIP

Gov. Anthony S. Earl (D)

Born: April 12, 1936, St. Ignace, Mich.
Home: Madison, Wis.
Education: Mich. State U., B.A. 1958; U. of Chicago, J.D. 1961.
Military Career: Navy, 1961-65.
Occupation: Lawyer.
Family: Wife, Sheila Coyle; four children.
Religion: Roman Catholic.
Political Career: Wausau city attorney 1966-69; Wis. House, 1969-74, majority leader 1971-74; sought Democratic nomination for Wis. attorney general, 1974; Wis. secretary of administration, 1974-75; secretary of natural resources, 1975-80; elected governor 1982; term expires Jan. 1987.

LEGISLATURE

SENATE
19D, 14R

Fred A. Risser (D)
President

ASSEMBLY
59D, 40R

Thomas A. Loftus (D)
Speaker

rather than an environmental issue.

Earl has proven adept at dealing with the new breed Democrats. He spent five years in the Assembly himself, three of them as majority leader, and he shares with them a skill at appealing to a broad array of constituencies.

The governor's 1982 campaign drew its crucial support from some of the traditional Democratic sources — especially teachers and public employees — but also built on liberal loyalties gained through his advocacy of a nuclear weapons freeze. In office, he has sought to reinforce his liberal support through his appointments — one aide comes from the gay community, and outspoken feminists hold key positions in his administration.

At the same time, Earl has been careful not to take a confrontational approach to business, using some of the economic development rhetoric that was another common theme of the 1982 campaign. Wisconsin has lost some of its major employers in the past several years, and officials of Kimberly-Clark, one of the largest remaining, have hinted at a possible move to Georgia. Republicans blame high-tax government under Democratic administrations for much of the state's economic problem; Earl has gone on the offensive to try to deflect that criticism.

On other issues, the governor has moved back and forth between strong partisanship and an apparent desire not to carry partisanship too far. He made no serious effort to attract Republican votes for his budget, which contained a 10 percent income tax surcharge, arguing that the price of Republican support would have been unacceptably high — massive spending cuts in social programs.

But when the Legislature included in the budget a redistricting plan for the Assembly and Senate that was designed to preserve Democratic strength, Earl used his item veto to strike it down on the grounds that it did not belong in a budget. In the end, the Legislature went back and passed separate redistricting legislation that made only modest changes from the original.

Partisan Assembly

Partisanship traditionally has been stronger in the Assembly than in the Senate, and that remains true. Assembly Republicans waged a filibuster against the Democratic redistricting bill in 1983, while GOP senators expressed their opposition more quietly.

But the distinction may not be as strong now as it was in the 1970s. For most of the past decade, Assembly Republicans were led by John Shabaz, an intense, strident and highly capable ideologue from suburban Milwaukee who tended to prefer conservative purity to negotiation and compromise. When Shabaz left the Legislature this year to accept appointment by the Reagan administration as a federal judge, he was replaced in his leadership role by the more pragmatic Tommy G. Thompson of rural Elroy. At the same time, several of Shabaz' ideological protégés have moved from the Assembly to the Senate, where they are bringing some of their mentor's confrontational style to a chamber more accustomed to collegiality.

The one hopeful sign for Republicans burdened with a shortage of candidate talent is the emergence of a new group of effective GOP legislators who are women. The Assembly has 22 female members, half of them Republican, and the only two women senators are Republicans. Party leaders hope the emergence of women candidates may be an answer to the recruitment problem that otherwise threatens to bury them in minority status for years to come. ∎

A PROFILE OF

Wisconsin

PEOPLE

Total Population: 4,705,767 (16th).
White 94%, Black 4%, American Indian, Eskimo and Aleut 1%. Spanish origin 1%.

Urban:	64%
Rural:	36%
Born in state:	77%
Foreign-born:	3%

MAJOR CITIES

Milwaukee (636,212), Madison (170,616), Green Bay (87,899), Racine (85,725), Kenosha (77,685)

LAND

Farm	53%
Forest	43%
Federally owned	5%

WORK

Occupations: 48% white-collar; 33% blue-collar; 14% service workers

Government workers:	26,546	federal
	80,749	state
	219,475	local

Unemployment rate: 10%

MONEY

Median family income (1980)	$20,915	(15th)
Tax burden per capita (1982)	$836	(13th)

EDUCATION

Spending per pupil through grade 12	$2,759	(11th)
Persons with college degrees	15%	(30th)

CRIME

Violent crime rate: 188 per 100,000 (44th)

POLITICS

1980 Presidential Vote: Reagan 48%, Carter 43%, Anderson 7%

Turnout rate in 1980:	75%
Turnout rate in 1982:	54%

U.S. House Delegation: 5D, 4R

WYOMING:

Growth of Energy Economy Aids Pro-Development GOP

The 1970s economic boom that caused Wyoming's population to explode and its revenues to grow has subsided, but the pro-development conservatism that accompanied it is still an important political force.

Wyoming has always been a conservative state, but

before the last decade its Legislature was dominated by wealthy farmers and ranchers, opposed to much change in their traditional way of life. Their view was symbolized by Gov. Milward Simpson (1955-59), who once suggested that the state build a fence around itself and keep everybody else out. The old power structure was not much disappointed when the 1970 census showed Wyoming to be the nation's slowest-growing state.

Soon after that, however, energy exploration began to change the climate of opinion. Between 1970 and 1980, Wyoming was America's fourth *fastest* growing state. Energy interests joined agribusiness as a powerful lobby in Cheyenne. Much of the political argument nowadays is between the development-minded Republican majority in the Legislature and the somewhat more restrained approach of Democratic Gov. Ed Herschler.

The oil and gas and mining industries have been active in recent sessions trying to temper environmental protection laws. The Wyoming Heritage Society, a Cody-based research group representing oil and gas companies, timber and livestock interests, has become a highly effective lobby. The group is visible throughout the state, publishing papers and news releases and presenting public service ads on television. The Heritage Society was active in 1983 in opposing a proposal to establish a trust fund to help preserve wildlife that might be threatened by development.

Development interests have been aided by the presence of an ally in Russ Donley, Speaker of the Wyoming House. Donley is regarded as a somewhat less dominating figure than his predecessor, Republican Warren A. Morton. But like Morton, Donley is a reliable friend of the energy industry. Donley helped block the wildlife trust proposal this year by referring it to an unfriendly committee.

While Wyoming has opted for development, though, it is not shy about taxing it. The state has the second-highest coal severance tax in the country, and in 1981, with Herschler's support, the Legislature raised the severance tax on oil and gas. To impose some controls on energy development, the state created an Industrial Siting Council to assess the environmental impact of new projects.

Conservative Democrats

Wyoming's Democrats, if somewhat more skeptical of untrammeled free enterprise than their Republican counterparts, still tend to be far more conservative than the national party position on most issues. When the Reagan administration unveiled its most recent siting proposal for the MX missile, which would place two-thirds of the weapons in Wyoming, Herschler agreed to support it without submitting it for review by the Industrial Siting Council. There were criticisms among the more liberal faction in the state Democratic Party, but the common view was that the party should remain unified behind Herschler.

Herschler has had his differences with the Republican Legislature on a variety of issues, but for the most part the conservative majority gets its way. The governor does not involve himself in too many issues. He has, however, vetoed more bills than most previous Wyoming governors, usually doing so at the end of the legislative sessions, when the Legislature cannot override them.

Herschler was beaten in a special session he called in 1983 to shore up the state's unemployment compensation

---

STATE LEADERSHIP

Gov. Ed Herschler (D)

Born: Oct. 27, 1918, Kemmerer, Wyo.
Home: Kemmerer, Wyo.
Education: U. of Colo., 1936-41; U. of Wyo., LL.B. 1949.
Military Career: Marine Corps, 1942-45.
Occupation: Lawyer.
Family: Wife, Kathleen Colter; two children.
Religion: Episcopalian.
Political Career: Lincoln County prosecutor, 1951-59; Wyo. House, 1959-69; sought Democratic nomination to U.S. House, 1970; elected governor 1974, 1978, 1982; term expires Jan. 1987.

LEGISLATURE

SENATE

11D, 19R

Edward D. Moore (R)
President

HOUSE

25D, 38R, 1 Ind.

Russ Donley (R)
Speaker

fund. Claiming that the fund would go broke in September, he recommended increasing the unemployment insurance tax rates and cutting benefits. The Legislature, unconvinced of Herschler's dire predictions, made stopgap changes to keep the system from going bankrupt, but put off major revisions in the system until the next legislative session.

Wyoming has a part-time Legislature, one that meets only 40 days in odd-numbered years and 20 days in even-numbered years. The House has a tradition of frequent changes in power — the most senior Republican usually is named Speaker for a two-year term, and then retires.

Casper's Power

There are regional differences among Republicans as well. Legislators from Casper, the state's largest city, have been feuding with those from the rest of the state over the distribution of state funds. Casper legislators wanted the state to establish a second four-year university there (the University of Wyoming is in Laramie), but lost. They have been successful, however, in maintaining a tax structure favorable to Casper's oil-based economy. Most of the sales tax revenue collected from the city's numerous energy equipment companies is retained in Natrona County, rather than being distributed to other localities around the state.

Casper can take advantage of the clout of its representatives. In the House, the Speaker, the Speaker pro tem and the majority leader all come from Natrona County. But Casper is also a beneficiary of the reapportionment that followed the population growth of recent years. Second to Cheyenne among Wyoming's cities in 1970, Casper overtook it by growing more than 30 percent in the following decade. Natrona County now has nearly a sixth of the state's population.

The traditional division in Wyoming politics is between the northern and southern parts of the state, with the southern area — the "Union Pacific Belt" — more Democratic and more labor-oriented than the northern ranch country. But the new energy-based economy is eroding that division, bringing the advantages and disadvantages of development and the accompanying issues to both parts of the state. ∎

A PROFILE OF
Wyoming

PEOPLE

Total Population: 469,557 (49th).
   White 95%, Black 1%, American Indian, Eskimo and Aleut 2%. Spanish origin 5%.

Urban:	63%
Rural:	37%
Born in state:	39%
Foreign-born:	2%

MAJOR CITIES

Casper (51,016), Cheyenne (47,283), Laramie (24,410), Rock Springs (19,458), Sheridan (15,146)

LAND

Farm	57%
Forest	16%
Federally owned	49%

WORK

Occupations: 47% white-collar; 36% blue-collar; 13% service workers

Government workers:	6,607 federal
	11,664 state
	28,036 local

Unemployment rate: 10%

MONEY

Median family income (1980)	$22,430	(7th)
Tax burden per capita (1982)	$1,622	(2nd)

EDUCATION

Spending per pupil through grade 12	$2,997	(7th)
Persons with college degrees	17%	(21st)

CRIME

Violent crime rate: 430 per 100,000 (27th)

POLITICS

1980 Presidential Vote: Reagan 63%, Carter 28%, Anderson 7%

Turnout rate in 1980:	59%
Turnout rate in 1982:	60%

U.S. House Delegation: 1R

ECONOMIC PROFILES

'Sun Belt' States Prosper, Others Face Economic Hardships

The different regions of the United States did not fare equally during the economic turbulence of the 1970s and early 1980s. For the "Sun Belt" states of the South and Southwest, those times brought unprecedented economic growth. But for other regions, most notably the Great Lakes states, Middle Atlantic states and parts of the Pacific Northwest, unemployment caused by the failing automobile, steel and timber industries painted a grim picture.

Other regions, struggling through major changes in the industrial capacities of their states, managed to maintain a relatively resilient economy. New England, for example, brought its sagging economy back to life by replacing its once-strong textile industries with more recession-proof high technology and electronics companies. And unemployment caused by the slowed-down timber business in the Pacific Northwest was offset in part by a rejuvenated aeronautics industry.

The South and West not only prospered economically but grew in population as people moved southward. The national census, which provides population and employment trend statistics every 10 years, in 1980 showed that for the first time in U.S. history there were more people living in the South and West than in the North and East. Between 1968 and 1978 two out of three new jobs gained by the country were created in the Sun Belt or Western states. The Rocky Mountain states experienced the nation's largest population growth. Throughout the South and West, population increased rapidly and the development of energy reserves, thriving tourism, booming light manufacturing and rising agricultural output attracted newcomers into the early 1980s.

In 1980 California continued to lead the nation in personal income even though high-technology competition from Japan and a decline in agricultural exports were beginning to plague the state's economy. The Plains states in 1980 continued to provide as much as one-half of America's corn and wheat production and close to one-third of the soybean production. But market prices for wheat, corn and other important grains had shrunk by one-third between 1981 and 1983. Farm income nationwide had nose-dived along with prices.

The region hardest hit by financial troubles was the Great Lakes states, where sharp declines in the automobile and steel industries sent unemployment soaring and revenues tumbling. The region's annual unemployment rate for 1982 was 12.0 percent, the highest rate of any census region and 3.7 percent higher than the national average of 8.3 percent, according to the U.S. Bureau of Labor Statistics. In 1981, 753,000 workers were employed by the automobile industry. By 1982 the annual average had slipped to 683,000. Michigan had the second highest unemployment rate in the country (17 percent) as of January 1983. By the end of 1981 Ohio, facing a rising deficit in its state budget, had enacted taxes on sales, tobacco, alcohol and utilities and laid off thousands of state employees in an effort to bolster depleted state revenues. Minnesota, in equally dire financial shape, was expected to face a $768 million budget deficit by June 1983. For the Middle Atlantic states, where industries were based on the manufacture of durable goods, the decade also brought high unemployment, low growth in population, employment and income, as well as low rates of capital investment.

As migration to the South and West continued in 1983, the political and economic makeup of the country was in a state of flux. But where regions continued to focus on one industry, rather than diversifying their economic interests, they remained vulnerable to recessions and high unemployment — regardless of their geographical location. As the U.S. economy became more dependent on international trade, competition forced regionally concentrated industries — such as automobile and steel — to look beyond U.S. borders to new markets. Each region's economic success depended on its adapting to worldwide competition and to ongoing technological changes.

Economic Gains in the Sun Belt

States generally included in the Sun Belt classification were California, Arizona, New Mexico, Texas, Oklahoma, Louisiana, Georgia, Mississippi, Alabama, South Carolina, North Carolina, Tennessee, Virginia, Arkansas and Florida. Population in this area increased by 22 percent from 1970 to 1980, nearly triple the rate in the rest of the country, according to the Census Bureau. The migration was due to the growth of new companies in the region — a growth encouraged by low wages, low taxes and, in some cases, special business tax incentives.

Per capita income increased most in the Southwest — 167 percent during the 1970s — compared with a 129 percent increase in the Middle Atlantic states and 134 percent in New England. According to figures compiled by the Northeast-Midwest Institute and published in John Naisbitt's 1982 book *Megatrends,* investment in capital equipment increased 74 percent in the South and the West, compared with 23 percent in the Northeast and Midwest.

The Southwest also was blessed with an abundance of energy resources. Oil and gas drilling, especially in Texas and Oklahoma, continued to increase in 1982. Military installations in Texas, Oklahoma, New Mexico and Arizona helped insulate the region from cuts in federal spending. Factories in the region generally were new and efficient, and steady population growth was driving up the value of commercial and residential real estate — promising a boom in the construction industry as interest rates fell in 1983. The diversity of the economy shielded it from failures in any one industry. For example, according to an article published in the Jan. 19, 1982, *Washington Post,* the shutdown of a General Motors plant in Oklahoma City was offset by a boom in oil and gas exploration to the west of the city where twice as many rigs were working in January 1982 as were a year earlier.

But the Sun Belt was beginning to inherit a full measure of social problems that accompanied its economic upsurge. Crime, congestion, pollution and physical decay — problems that long had haunted Northern industrial cities — were beginning to infest the Sun Belt cities. And despite the economic growth, the Sun Belt as of summer 1982 had yet to catch up with the nation as a whole in per capita wealth. A greater percentage of its people continued to live in poverty than in the nation at large. Experts also pointed out that finite natural resources, particularly water in the Southwest, were threatening to limit growth.

The most vulnerable of those states, according to the census, were those located in the Southeast. Manufacturing employment, in every Southeastern state except Virginia, accounted for at least 22 percent of the total. In North and South Carolina, the percentage was 28 percent — a higher figure than the percentage in Michigan. In no Sun Belt state outside the Southeast did the percentage go as high as the national average of 20.6 percent. The higher the percentage of manufacturing — the sector of the economy most likely to suffer from a recession — the more likelihood of unemployment in that region.

Sun Belt, Snow Belt Controversy

Success stories in the Snow Belt areas — such as New England — helped dispel the theory that the economic gains of the Sun Belt states were made at the expense of the beleaguered Northern states. According to the theory, industries that deserted the industrial North — especially New York, Pennsylvania and New Jersey — were enticed by the South's favorable economic climate, which included low taxes on businesses, a preponderance of "right to work" laws and the overall weakness of organized labor. In short, the Sun Belt region was thought to be "booming in great part because it's pro-business and the Northern cities, by and large, aren't," wrote Gurney Breckenfeld in the June 1977 issue of *Fortune.*

Business Week magazine in 1976 had characterized the situation as a "civil war between the states," with the economic arena as the battlefield in a "struggle for income, jobs, people and capital." That "war," as perceived by a number of business writers and even sociologists, continued throughout the 1970s. There was an outpouring of articles, studies and reports, and at least two books, *Power Shift* by Kirkpatrick Sale (1975) and *The North Will Rise Again* by Jeremy Rifkin and Randy Barber (1978), chronicling a shift of economic power from North to South. Lobbying groups such as the Northeast-Midwest Congressional Coalition and the Council for Northeast Economic Action were set up to advance the economic interests of the North.

By some accounts, the North's economic slippage had been going on for decades and — except for New England — had worsened after the 1974-75 recession. But not everyone accepted the thesis that the Sun Belt's success had come at the expense of the Northern states. James Lothian,

a senior consultant with the Fantus Co., an industrial location consulting firm, called it "a myth" that "all the industries in the North are relocating in the South." Although many Northern plants had expanded their capacity in the South, "there have been very few instances where a plant in the North packs up totally and moves to the South."

A U.S. Department of Commerce study reinforced Lothian's view. The study, issued in 1976, found that during a previous three-year period only 1.5 percent of job losses in the North were caused by companies moving; more than half the losses occurred because companies went out of business. According to John Naisbitt in *Megatrends,* the shift from an industrial society to an information society had led inevitably to new industries springing up in the Sun Belt. Manufacturing industries in the North were replaced by new high-technology companies that found the South's "frontierlike" climate attractive.

In addition, the increasing worldwide competition among manufacturers of automobiles and steel encouraged investors to move toward high-technology industries. Outdated factories and businesses, located mostly in the Northeast and Great Lakes states, were abandoned and new companies opened elsewhere. The migration, Naisbitt agreed, was not merely a relocation of manufacturing industries from the North to the South, but a change in the types of industries expected to prevail in the future.

Energy: Regional Weapon of the Future

Politicians from energy-poor states complained that a massive transfer of wealth from their states to energy-producing states would occur in the late 1980s. Rather than a North-South migration of population and capital, future shifts would be from East to West, based upon the availability of energy resources.

In 1982 Eastern states already were complaining about the large revenues generated for Western states by severance taxes levied on exports of oil, gas, coal and other minerals. (Severance taxes are taxes on depletable minerals that are "severed" from the ground.) The energy-rich Western states expected to earn more than $200 billion from severance taxes during the 1980s. In 1980, for example, the 33 states with severance taxes collected $4.2 billion, which amounted to 3 percent of all state tax revenues. In 1981 state revenue from severance taxes grew by 52 percent, to $6.4 billion — 4.3 percent of all tax revenue they collected. Although 33 states had taxes, the bonanza from higher energy prices went to the dozen or so states whose severance taxes were based on energy. *(Severance tax, box, p. 109)*

Eastern states complained that the energy-producing states' increased wealth enabled them to attract industry by favorable tax policies, while their states were losing industries and tax revenues needed to support government services. The Western states maintained the taxes were adequate compensation for the economic and environmental costs of producing the energy.

One visible regional battle erupted over congressional attempts to limit the severance taxes that Montana and Wyoming levied on coal production. Montana levied a 30 percent tax, and Wyoming a 17 percent tax. In July 1981 the Supreme Court upheld the Montana tax, rejecting a suit brought by the coal utilities and supported by the Northeast-Midwest Coalition. However, the court said Congress could set limits on such taxes if it chose, but Congress had passed no legislation as of April 1983.

Regions of the Country

The eight sections that follow examine the American economic mosaic by focusing on the separate regions or, in the case of California, separate pieces of regions, that over the years assumed an importance or uniqueness of their own. Aside from New England, no agreement has existed even among experts as to precisely what constituted each region in the 48 contiguous states. Map makers looked to political affiliations, religious preferences and ethnic origins of the people in an attempt to determine the distinguishing characteristics of the various geographic regions.

Faced with this lack of accord, Congressional Quarterly divided the country as follows: New England, the South, the Rocky Mountain states, the Great Lakes states, the Middle Atlantic states, the Pacific Northwest, California and the Plains states. Many of this chapter's statistics were derived from the 1980 census, yet the regional divisions did not always conform to the standard U.S. Census Bureau divisions. For example, the Census Bureau separated the South into three groupings: the South Atlantic, East South and West South. Where Census Bureau regional data used is for states that differ from regions used in this book, that has been so indicated.

While general trends from North to South, manufacturing to high technology and energy-depleted states to energy-rich states dominated the overall employment picture in the United States, each region continued to maintain its own distinct economic picture. The following portraits are merely thumbnail sketches, with an emphasis on each region's economic picture as a whole.

New England

(Maine, New Hampshire, Vermont, Massachusetts, Connecticut, Rhode Island)

The end of World War I marked the end of a boom for New England's manufacturing and mercantile industries and the beginning of a long period of economic decline. Textile and shoe manufacturers increasingly relocated in the South, and by 1929 over half the textile spindles in the nation were in the South. Employment in the textile and shoe industries dropped from well over 500,000 in the early years of this century to less than 150,000 by the early 1970s.

World War II, like World War I, gave New England's economy a badly needed boost. From the days of the American Revolution, New England had been a major supplier of precision equipment in time of war. Samuel Colt, together with Eli Whitney, did pioneering work in developing mass production techniques at a gun factory they began in Hartford. The Winchester Arms rifle company was started in New Haven during the Revolution. And the Springfield Armory, later turned into a museum, first produced guns for the U.S. military services in 1795. Shipbuilding, above all the submarine construction and repair facilities at Groton, Conn., and Kittery, Maine-Portsmouth, N.H., became a mainstay of the region's economy.

New England's universities also did highly important research and development work for the military, notably on radar. From the end of the war to the present the region's industries built a wide variety of military equipment — jet engines, electronic components, and missile and space systems.

In the 1970s, however, U.S. defense budget reductions hurt New England more than any other part of the country. The loss of research and procurement work, together with the closing of many military bases, posed a threat to the regional economy. When energy prices began to rise sharply in late 1973, the long-term outlook for the economy seemed bleak indeed. Exceptionally dependent on energy, and more reliant on fuel oil than any other region of the country, New England seemed to many a place whose day had passed. Both the 1969-70 and 1973-75 recessions hit exceptionally hard. In May 1975, for example, New England's unemployment rate was 11.6 percent, compared with 9.2 percent nationwide; in Rhode Island it stood at 16.2 percent.

Signs of Recovery Since the Middle 1970s. Much to the surprise of the doomsayers, however, New

---

Handful of States Get Most of Revenues

Although 33 states imposed severance taxes on depletable resources in 1981, five energy-rich states collected the bulk — 80 percent — of the $6.4 billion in state severance tax revenues.

Eight energy-producing states got at least one-fifth of all their tax money from severance taxes in 1981. In 1975 only one state got that much of its revenue from severance taxes. The top five states in order of money raised were Texas, Alaska, Louisiana, Oklahoma and New Mexico. Together they took in $5.1 billion in 1981 severance taxes, according to the U.S. Census Bureau. At the bottom end of the scale, Nevada collected just $11,000 on its mining operations.

It is that 30 percent rate that brought the coal-consuming states' wrath down on Montana, as well as Wyoming, which had a coal severance tax rate of about 17 percent, including local taxes. Actually, Wyoming ranked eighth in 1981 in severance tax revenues, collecting $138 million on coal, oil and gas. Montana was 10th, garnering $99 million, mostly on coal.

Texas had much lower severance tax rates but collected far more money than Wyoming, Montana or any other state. It took in $1.1 billion in 1981, almost all of it from a 4.6 percent tax on oil and a 7.5 percent tax on natural gas.

Alaska, flush with oil produced on its North Slope, had the highest tax on oil — 15 percent, although the rate varied with the age of a particular well. The $1.2 billion Alaska got from severance taxes in 1981 came on top of several billion dollars the state received in oil royalty payments. Almost all of Alaska's oil production was on state-owned land.

Only two Eastern states were in the top 10 states in severance tax revenue in 1981. Kentucky ranked sixth, getting $194 million, mostly on coal. Florida was seventh, getting $169 million from its taxes on oil, natural gas and phosphate production.

In addition to energy sources, some states had severance taxes on minerals such as potash, iron ore and uranium. Some, such as Oregon, taxed timber, and — partly in retaliation for the taxes they said their citizens had to pay to energy-producing states — several midwestern states were considering imposing severance taxes on their agricultural products.

England's economy showed signs of making quite·a comeback. After 1975 manufacturing employment in the region kept abreast of the nation as a whole, and signs of vitality appeared in many areas. High-technology industries, many of which had located in abandoned mills around Boston, along the Merrimack into southern New Hampshire, and in Connecticut, continued to prosper. New England also prospered from rapid expansion in business services, health services, finance, insurance and wholesale and retail trade. According to the Bureau of Labor Statistics, the annual unemployment rate for 1981 was 7.2 percent, the lowest of any census region in the country. By September 1982, according to an article in the Nov. 30, 1982, *Washington Post,* Boston's unemployment rate was 6.4 percent — lower than Phoenix's (8.4 percent), Los Angeles' (9.4 percent) and Houston's (8.2 percent).

The fishing industry also revived in the late 1970s after years of suffering from foreign competition in New England's offshore waters. Congress in 1976 declared that national economic interests extended for 200 miles out to sea, giving U.S. fishermen priority in this economic zone. After that, many of New England's coastal towns refurbished their waterfronts, not just as tourist attractions but as commercial centers.

According to Lynn E. Browne, economist for the Federal Reserve Bank of Boston, New Hampshire led the way among the New England states in staying in the same league as the fast-growth Sun Belt states. New Hampshire — with low taxes, low wages and pro-business governmental zest for luring out-of-state businesses — was New England's most evident economic success story. The state gained 381 new firms between 1975 and 1980, most of them involved in making machinery of one type or another. But even in New Hampshire, the rural areas, especially those north of the state's capital of Concord, had not shared fully in the new prosperity.

Rural areas and small towns still were beset by economic stagnation, but the problem also extended to urban workers who lacked job skills that could be used in the new computer and telecommunications fields. High-technology companies were growing and expanding beyond the Boston area, but they nevertheless had not reached the stage where they employed thousands on a mass-production basis.

Job Creation Through Technology and Taxes. New England had prospered once before on technology-based industry. Textiles and shoes, in their New England beginnings, were considered high-technology industries. But the memory of what happened before did not take the edge off of the region's modest economic gains in the late 1970s. New England bankers, who had been downcast, became upbeat. This optimism translated into loans for new business ventures and tended to have a snowball effect. While the region shared the entire country's concerns over economic instability, experts at the Boston Federal Reserve Bank in 1980 pointed out that New England was likely to suffer less than the rest of the country from drops in the automobile manufacturing and housing construction industries.

The High Technology Council, representing 89 fast-growing computer and electronics companies in Massachusetts, complained in the late 1970s that the state's reputation for high taxes ("Taxachusetts") repelled many out-of-state engineers and managers they sought to attract. The council in 1980 entered into a so-called "social contract" with Gov. Edward J. King, promising to create

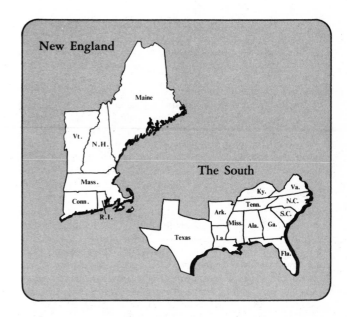

150,000 new jobs in the state by 1982 if he brought down state taxes to the average for 17 other industrial states. In a move attributed to lobbying by the Associated Industries of Massachusetts, the state Legislature in 1979 cut the state's capital gains tax by 60 percent. And King limited local government spending to a 4 percent yearly increase, bringing about property tax reductions in more than half of the 351 cities and towns.

Most economists agreed that New England would continue to benefit from the same assets that had always enabled it to stay afloat: its early adjustment to problems such as high energy costs, problems that the rest of the country had not fully confronted; its university-based research establishment; its sizable skilled labor force; its experience in precision manufacturing; its possession of numerous cultural assets (including attractive scenery and historic sites) that made New England a pleasant place to live and work; the ready accessibility of capital, both in the Boston banking business and the Connecticut insurance industry; and, not least, its disproportionate political influence at the national level.

The South

(Virginia, North Carolina, South Carolina, Kentucky, Tennessee, Georgia, Florida, Alabama, Mississippi, Arkansas, Louisiana, Texas)

In 1938 President Franklin D. Roosevelt took a long, appraising look at the South and declared the region "the nation's No. 1 economic problem." Although various New Deal agencies had pumped large amounts of money into the area during the 1930s, the South, and especially the Deep South, remained mired in poverty. The region's average annual income was only about half that of the country as a whole. The rest of the United States also was suffering from the effects of the Depression, but the South was so much worse off, Roosevelt said, that its poverty produced an "economic unbalance in the nation as a whole."

The South's economic problems antedated the national economic crisis of the 1930s. They originated with the destruction of the Southern economy by the Civil War. A report by the President's National Emergency

Council in 1938 attributed the perpetuation of the section's poverty to a high degree of absentee ownership of its resources, high interest rates, disadvantageous freight rates and a protective tariff policy, which, by holding down imports, made it harder to sell abroad agricultural commodities the South had for export. Noting, however, that the region was rich in population and natural resources, the council called it "the nation's greatest untapped market and the market in which American business can expand most easily."

By the early 1980s, the South had come a long way toward fulfilling its economic potential. *Business Week* magazine in 1972 compared the South to a developing country that had reached the "take off" stage of its economic development. From 1972 to 1977, according to John Naisbitt in *Megatrends,* capital investments in manufacturing increased nearly 300 percent in Texas alone. The state replaced Michigan in 1977 as No. 1 in new capital investments in manufacturing. *Business Week* in September 1972 acknowledged some unaddressed and unsolved problems in the region — pollution and congestion and urban sprawl — but on the whole it sketched a glowing profile."The South today means economic growth . . . a still pleasing environment and rich new markets for all sorts of goods and services." The influx of people and industries into the region, it said, was producing social as well as economic benefits.

Businesses Relocate to the South. Southern industrial growth remained strong throughout the 1970s. Non-agricultural employment grew by 27.4 percent in the period 1970-77, compared with a 15.8 percent increase nationwide. As in the rest of the nation, the biggest job gains were in state and local governments and in service industries such as banking, real estate and retail trade. The Southern states were better able than their Northern neighbors to absorb workers leaving the agricultural sector, to provide jobs for the large number of young people entering the work force and to accommodate workers migrating from other regions. The South's annual average unemployment rate remained below the U.S. average throughout the 1970s, although the gap gradually narrowed during the latter part of the decade.

According to a report published in 1976 by *U.S. News & World Report,* between 1970 and 1976 corporate or regional headquarters of 55 domestic and foreign companies moved to Georgia, most of them to Atlanta. About 450 companies shifted headquarters or major divisions to Tennessee during the same period, while 180 corporation headquarters, subsidiaries or major divisions relocated in the Houston area.

The South's prosperity in the 1970s was in sharp contrast to the economic decline that plagued many states in the industrial Snow Belt. Accusations surfaced in the mid-1970s that of the billions in public funds that were transferred annually from the federal to state and local governments, a disproportionate amount was going to the Sun Belt states. Others charged that the Southern states were unfairly offering a wide variety of incentives to attract industries from other sections.

Although income growth in the South outpaced the national average in the 1970s, it still remained below national levels. According to the South Growth Policies Board, regional per capita income for the South in 1977 was 89.6 percent of the national average. One reason was that the South remained the least unionized region in the United States. About 29 percent of the nation's workers

Texas the Superstate

For many people Texas always would be the quintessential American state — perhaps because the state was too big, too diverse, "too much of a world of its own," as John Gunther wrote in *Inside U.S.A.* in 1947, to be categorized along with any other state.

Texas lies in the center of the "Sun Belt," the southern rim of states running from Virginia to southern California. Like the other Sun Belt states, Texas has experienced an unprecedented influx of people and industry in recent years. Between 1960 and 1980 the state's population grew by approximately 36 percent, to more than 13 million.

Houston, the ultimate boom town, was the fifth largest city in the nation in 1980, with a population in excess of 1.5 million. Of the 500 largest corporations in the United States, as listed by *Fortune* magazine, 18 had headquarters in Houston or Dallas in 1980. Oil and associated service industries contributed greatly to urban growth in the state. Equally important, however, were high-technology industries such as electronics, semiconductors and aerospace.

Even with its large cities and thriving industries, in 1980 Texas still somehow seemed a rural state, with many small farming towns with names like Muleshoe, Kerrville, Sweetwater, Ozona and Levelland.

Texas remained by far the biggest livestock-producing state in the nation. But the character of the beef industry had changed, especially in the Panhandle region.

Since the early 1960s, traditional cow-calf ranches had given way to stocker operations that import yearling calves from other regions — East Texas, Louisiana, Alabama, Florida, Georgia — where more rain falls and grasses grow lusher. Stocker ranches keep the calves through the winter, fattening them by 200 pounds or so, then selling them to feedlots clustered around Amarillo. There they are prepared for market on grain sorghums grown on the High Plains.

The residents of Texas did not share equally in the state's new wealth. About one-sixth of the population lived below the poverty line in 1980. Poverty was especially prevalent among the state's Mexican-Americans, who accounted for at least 18 percent of the population.

were members of unions or employee associations, according to the Department of Labor. But in the 12 Southern states the percentages were much lower. They ranged from a high of 29 percent in Kentucky to just 10 percent in North and South Carolina. Between 1963 and 1974 union membership declined in all the Southern states except Georgia, Alabama and South Carolina.

The notion that the Sun Belt prospered mainly by stealing from its neighbors was disputed by a study released in November 1976 by the Commerce Department's Economic Development Administration. During a three-year period of study (1969 to 1972), the report said, only 1.5 percent of the job losses in the North were caused by companies moving, while more than half the losses occurred because companies went out of business. During that same period more than 2.6 million new jobs appeared in the 13 Southern states (The Confederacy, plus Kentucky and West Virginia). Of that number, 35 percent were created by the founding of new companies, 64 percent by the expansion of existing companies and a mere 1 percent by in-migration.

Yet the migration of people and industries to the South appeared to be slowing, according to an economic survey published in *The New York Times* Jan. 6, 1980. "Many states of the Northeast are providing tax benefits and other incentives for companies and their jobs to stay put, and, to a great extent, these incentives have been effective," said Wendell Rawls Jr., author of the survey. As a result, Southern governors had begun courting foreign investors and had been having "considerable success." In Atlanta alone there were nine full-time foreign consulates, four foreign trade and government offices, and honorary consulates representing 23 countries in 1980. Miami, Fla., was a magnet for Latin American trade and investment. About half a million Latin Americans visited Miami in 1978 and spent an average of more than $1,000 each. The city's economy also had been bolstered by the thousands of Cubans who had settled there since Fidel Castro came to power in 1959.

Northern states in the early 1980s had stepped up their efforts to match the South's industrial drawing power. The cost of living in the South was growing in 1983, and wages were expected to follow suit. Freight rates, a primary factor in the location of new plants, were catching up to rates in other parts of the country. Decreased federal funding, spurred by the Reagan administration's "new federalism," drained state and local coffers of needed funds for social welfare programs subsidized by the federal government since the New Deal.

In 1982 many employers in the South were shrinking the size of their industries. According to an article published in *The New York Times* on July 6, 1982, five out of nine Southern states had unemployment rates higher than the national average of 9.5 percent in May of that year and three had unemployment of 10 percent or more. In July 1982 jobs in the textile industry — the top employer in both North and South Carolina — had fallen 11 percent since the summer of 1981.

But unionization remained low in 1983 and relatively low taxes — with special business tax incentives — continued to cushion the region from insurmountable recession. In February 1983 *The New York Times* reported that major cities in the South still appeared to be doing significantly better than large cities in the North in income, employment and racial patterns.

Lingering Poverty in Rural, Black Areas. Amidst the towering office buildings, shiny new factories and other signs of the South's economic boom, many pockets of poverty remained, especially in the black rural sections of the Deep South and the isolated hollows of Appalachia. In 1975 almost 10 million people in 14 Southern states (Oklahoma and West Virginia in addition to Kentucky and The Confederacy) — nearly 16 percent of their total — lived below the officially defined poverty line, according to the Census Bureau. In 1975 the federally defined poverty threshold was $5,500 for a non-farm family of four and $4,695 for a farm family of four. According to the National Commission for Employment and Unemployment Statistics, 60 percent of the nation's rural poor lived in the South in 1977. Another study, published by the Institute for Policy Analysis in 1978, found that 22 percent of the counties in the South had 25 percent or more of their families living below the poverty line. Of the 295 counties, 284 were in rural areas in 1978.

The incidence of poverty among Southern blacks in 1980 was three times as high as that among Southern whites — although in absolute numbers there were more poor whites than poor blacks. In 1978 the median income for black families was just over half (57 percent) as much as for white median families, according to the National Urban League. Some of the South's poorest blacks were found in the unpainted shacks that dotted the Mississippi Delta — the crescent-shaped area of fertile land stretching along the Mississippi River southward from Memphis.

In 1980 about 60 percent of the Delta's population was black and, according to Mississippi's State Department of Public Welfare, 43.5 percent of the area's inhabitants were on some form of welfare. "When the plantation aristocracy decided to mechanize their farms, it wreaked spectacular havoc throughout the whole system," Tony Dunbar wrote in *Our Land Too* published in 1971. "The black tenant farmer and sharecroppers had nothing of their own to fall back on, no alternate sources of employment, no land, no history of diverse occupation." The result, Dunbar said, was "a poverty unparalleled in this country today."

Large pockets of poverty also remained in Appalachia. Congress in 1965 approved an aid and development program for this mountainous region stretching across 13 states, most of them Southern. Some 2.7 million of the 19 million inhabitants lived in poverty, according to the Appalachian Regional Commission. In only six of the region's 397 counties was average per capita income above the national average in 1978. By 1980 evidence suggested, however, that Appalachia was slowly turning itself around. In the late 1970s its poverty population had decreased to about 14 percent, down from 31 percent in 1960. Between 1965 and 1976 per capita income climbed from 78 percent to 85 percent of the national average. Perhaps the most telling indication of an economic turnaround was the reversal of out-migration. In the 1970s there was a net increase of people going — or going back — to the Appalachian region.

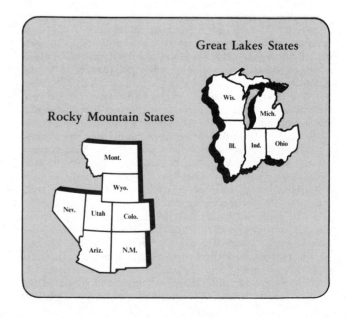

Rocky Mountain States

*(Montana, Wyoming, Utah, Colorado,
New Mexico, Arizona, Nevada)*

In 1980 not only was the West growing rapidly, but in Colorado, Arizona, Utah and Nevada three-fourths of the people were concentrated in metropolitan areas. Between 1950 and 1980, more than 1,250,000 had moved into Colorado's Front Range area stretching south from the Wyoming border through Denver to Colorado Springs and Pueblo. Eighty-one percent of the state's population in 1980 lived in this corridor, roughly 50 miles wide and 200 miles long. Another 1,250,000 were expected to arrive in the next 20 years.

Denver had emerged as the regional center for transportation, communications, trade and high-technology industries. By 1980 more than 2,000 energy-related companies had made the Front Range their headquarters for developing oil, gas, uranium, coal and oil shale resources throughout the Rocky Mountain region. Phoenix had experienced similar growth, mushrooming from a city of 80,000 at the end of World War II into a metropolitan area of more than 1.2 million. In 1980 Tucson, whose population stood at 40,000 in 1945, was the center of an area approaching 500,000. Albuquerque in 35 years had grown from 50,000 to nearly 400,000. And in Utah more than three-quarters of the state's 1.2 million residents lived within 45 miles of Salt Lake City's Mormon Temple Square in a urbanized strip extending from Ogden south to Provo between the Wasatch Mountains and the Great Salt Lake.

Energy-Related Jobs. The development of Western energy reserves was accelerating the growth of Rocky Mountain cities, especially Denver. Gulf, Texaco and Standard Oil Co. of California, among other energy-producing companies, had set up offices in Denver as they prepared to tap oil and gas from Utah and Wyoming's Overthrust Belt, coal from New Mexico's Four Corners area and Wyoming's Powder Basin, oil shale from the Piceance Creek Basin of northwestern Colorado, and uranium from the Four Corners and Wyoming's Red Desert. A Colorado Energy Research Institute study in 1979 calculated that there were 28,000 energy-related jobs in the Denver area, including 11,000 that had been created since 1970.

Important though they were, energy companies in the Denver area provided less than a third of the new employment in 1970-78. Tourism also was important to the local economy, while federal and state government offices, light manufacturing and the region's traditional trade and agricultural businesses together contributed substantially to a growing economic base. Companies such as IBM, Hewlett-Packard, Eastman Kodak, Sunbeam, Frito-Lay, Johns Manville and AMAX opened Denver-area plants and offices, and the Front Range began to rival the San Francisco Bay area's "Silicon Valley" and Boston's Route 128 as a center for high-technology companies. "The technology companies are here probably because of the amenities and general market growth," observed Denver economist David Bramhall in a March 1979 article in *Business Week.* "They're also here for the skilled labor, and because executives and their wives like to live out here."

In Wyoming, weekly wages in the energy industry in the summer of 1982 averaged $447. Towns in the oil and coal zones were booming and a steady incoming stream of workers continued. The expansion was accompanied by growing strains on public services needed to accommodate the burgeoning population. Growth in the region by the early 1980s was outstripping the ability of state and local governments to keep pace with increasing demands on water, sewage, school and public safety services.

In Arizona and New Mexico, service industries and clean, light manufacturing were replacing mining and agriculture as economic mainstays. Arizona drew 15 million tourists a year, six times the state's permanent population, and the Phoenix area was swollen by about 100,000 people who lived there only part of the year. Affluent older people flocked to Arizona to live in posh retirement communities and travel trailer campgrounds. Yet more migrants to Arizona were young, well educated and well paid.

Ranching's Old Values, New Uncertainty. No occupation was more emblematic of the West than that of ranching. The huge 19th-century cattle spreads were long ago broken up, and livestock raising in the late 1970s often was identified with tax shelters for oilmen and other absentee owners. But throughout the Rocky Mountain states, cattle and sheep ranching remained a family occupation, with fathers and sons sharing the work of branding, round-ups and wool shearing.

But traditional Western ranching was a risky venture. Beef, lamb and wool markets were volatile, while the cost of labor, vaccines, supplemental feed and equipment had climbed upward. By the late 1970s a rancher who ran 150 cows and their calves could clear $20,000 one year and less than half that two years later. In *The Last Cowboy,* a study of Texas Panhandle ranching first published in the *New Yorker* in 1977, Jane Kramer noted that "Ranching lately had less to do with an individual's adventure with a herd of cattle than with that global network of dependencies and contingencies that people had taken to calling 'agribusiness.'"

Rocky Mountain ranchers depended heavily on obtaining grazing rights on national forest and Bureau of Land Management (BLM) public range lands. Much of those lands, overgrazed in the past, had been declining in forage production. But when the BLM tried to reduce grazing, the agency encountered resistance from ranchers. Montana and Wyoming ranchers felt threatened by the strip mining of coal from beneath the grazing lands. Some sold their ranches and left, but others resisted and even formed Sierra Club chapters in the fight to preserve the land. In the long run, however, traditional ranching seemed destined to vanish gradually as older people retired and died.

Western farmers also faced an uncertain future mainly because water was so critical in a region where rainfall was minimal. Western agriculture generally was limited to a relatively few areas where rivers, federally financed reservoirs and underground water aquifers provided a dependable water source for irrigation. In the late 1970s President Jimmy Carter's water policies made it clear to Rocky Mountain farmers that the era of expensive federal dam-building projects to store water for irrigation was coming to an end. In the meantime, ground-water irrigation was ebbing as underground water tables dropped, pumping costs rose and cities expanded onto surrounding farm land.

In central Arizona, where irrigated agriculture accounted for 89 percent of water consumption, the growth of Phoenix and Tucson was increasing competition for limited surface and ground-water supplies. Farther north, "Colorado is rapidly approaching an agricultural crossroads," a Colorado Department of Agriculture study declared in 1979. According to the report, ground-water reserves were declining on the state's eastern plains, and energy projects competed for water on the West Slope, as the western side of the Rocky Mountain range was called.

The Rocky Mountain West states were bracing for continued rapid change in the last two decades of the 20th century. With the spread of big cities, the miseries of boom towns and a troubled outlook for Western agriculture, the region had shifted away from its traditional faith that all-out growth would fulfill its destiny.

Great Lakes States

(Michigan, Ohio, Indiana, Illinois, Wisconsin)

On Dec. 2, 1942, on the University of Chicago campus, the first self-sustaining nuclear reaction took place under the direction of Enrico Fermi. The atomic age had begun. One side effect would be the birth of a technology that took root outside of the auto-and-steel-centered Industrial Belt.

The great factories that soon were built for the production of atomic bombs were located not in the old industrial heartland but rather in Tennessee, New Mexico, Washington state and South Carolina. As for the planes that would carry these bombs, they were built primarily in the Southwest and Southeast. Once guided missiles were developed, they were produced mainly in the West, while nuclear submarines and carriers naturally had to be built along the nation's seacoasts.

The high-technology precision instrumentation that was increasingly essential to the operation of advanced weaponry tended, like the planes and the missiles and the ships, to be made mainly in the Southeast, the Southwest and New England. The man who presided over a major shift from reliance on conventional weapons to weapons for mass destruction was, ironically, a former president of General Motors, Charles E. Wilson. Wilson was famous for remarking, as President Dwight D. Eisenhower's secretary of defense, "What's good for the country is good for General Motors and vice versa." What Wilson actually did as defense secretary was not especially good for General Motors or for the industrial Midwest generally.

With the nation's most advanced high-technology industries leading the way in a movement out of the industrial heartland, other industries found plenty of reasons to follow suit. Whereas in the North businesses contended with high taxes, more unionization and a decaying infrastructure, in many sections of the South and West they were able to build from scratch under favorable tax incentives and draw on pools of lower-paid labor. Especially after energy prices began to soar in 1973, businesses had a strong motive to locate in the sunnier regions of the country.

Not only did the Great Lakes states see businesses move funds earned in the industrial heartland into other regions of the country, but they had to put up with the indignity of subsidizing the out-migration. Largely because three-fourths of all federal expenditures for procurement go to the defense industries, and because in a typical year the Great Lakes region receives only about 10 percent of the prime contract awards, it suffers the nation's largest net loss of tax dollars each year. In 1976, according to the congressional Northeast-Midwest Coalition, the Great Lakes States sent the federal government about $20 billion more than they got back, while the South showed a net gain of more than $20 billion and the West of $12 billion.

According to a report entitled "The Pentagon Tilt: Regional Biases in Defense Spending and Strategy," prepared by the Northeast-Midwest Institute and partially published in the *Christian Science Monitor* in January 1983, the Northeast-Midwest regional share of defense spending had dropped from 20 to 15.3 percent between 1981 and 1983, even though the military construction budget had increased 43.4 percent. The region's share of the population at large was 45 percent. The Northeast-Midwest regional share of prime weapons contracts also dropped from 72 percent in 1951 to 39 percent in 1981.

National Policy Effects and Fiscal Strains. After World War II the economic growth of the Great Lakes states was well below the national average. From 1950 to 1975, manufacturing employment in the region grew 4.3 percent, compared with 76 percent in the Southeast, and 141 percent in the Southwest. The national average stood at 20 percent. Although the Great Lakes states were thought to be exceptionally sensitive to recessions, because of their dependence on durable goods industries that were the first to suffer in times of economic downturn, the region — apart from Michigan — generally had not suffered higher-than-average joblessness.

It was no secret that in the late 1970s serious problems afflicted the steel and auto industries, the two industries on which the Great Lakes states depended most heavily. U.S. steel production peaked at 111.4 million net tons in 1973, and by 1978 it had dropped to 97.9 million tons. In 1981 imports accounted for close to 20 percent of steel sold in the United States. By January 1982 imports accounted for 26.3 percent of the U.S. steel market.

American steelworkers were among the best paid of any manufacturing workers. But the United States had lost more than 100,000 steel-making jobs between 1960 and 1980, and it was quite likely that many more would be lost in the years ahead. In 1980 U.S. Steel closed 15 manufacturing facilities, laid off 10 percent of its work force — some 13,000 steelworkers — and recorded the biggest quarterly loss in American corporate history. According to an April 24, 1983, article in *The Washington Post*, employment in the domestic steel industry fell 36 percent from an annual average of 454,000 workers in 1976 to 289,0900 in 1982. Bethlehem Steel, the nation's second-largest steel producer, decreased its employment roles from 105,000 employees in 1976 to 67,000 employees in 1982.

The auto industry, which purchased about a quarter of the nation's steel production yearly, appeared to be in little better shape. In 1982 imports accounted for 27.9 percent of all cars sold in the United States. The Chrysler Corp.'s 1980 $1.1 billion loss was the largest ever by an American company, sending its management to Congress to plead for aid in an attempt to avert bankruptcy. In January 1981 Congress provided Chrysler with $1.5 billion in loan guarantees

Federal Intervention vs. Belt-Tightening. In May 1979 the United Auto Workers, the United Steelworkers and the International Association of Machinists joined in publishing a study based on an "intensive study of policies and practices to cope with economic dislocation in three highly industrialized countries, Sweden, West Germany, and the U.K. [Britain]." On the basis of these findings, the three industrial unions recommended the adoption of national planning to ensure full employment, advance notice of industrial layoffs, federal procurement and credit allocations to prevent job dislocations. To stop the flight of capital south and west and the migration of poverty north, they also recommended federalized unemployment insurance and workers' compensation, repeal of right-to-work legislation and abolition of state and local tax abatements to lure industry from one region to another.

In contrast to that position, there were those who argued that regions such as the Great Lakes could solve their problems by tightening their belts and making themselves more attractive to business. That had been Cleveland's goal since its populist mayor, Dennis Kucinich, was defeated in 1979 and replaced by George V. Voinovich. Soon after, the city ran the following ad in several major newspapers: "There's a new frame of mind in Cleveland. This new frame of mind recognizes ... that the financial community must have confidence and understanding before they can extend the credit necessary for a smoothly running city; and that businessmen, large and small, must have the hope of making a profit before they will venture the money and effort which creates new jobs, wealth and needed tax revenues." Under Voinovich, Cleveland as of April 1983 had paid off its debts, balanced its budget, developed its downtown and won a 1982 "All-American City" award from the National Municipal League.

Jane Byrne, as mayor of Chicago from the late 1970s until April 1983, also appeared eager to restore her city's attractiveness to business. Her efforts to curb the power of the city unions, however, led to bitter confrontations with transit workers, teachers and firefighters. At the same time, the city's poor blacks — for whom the Irish-run city never worked very well — had been increasingly outspoken in demanding more, rather than fewer, services. At a time when urban tax bases were shrinking, while many inner-city neighborhoods remained impoverished ghettos, belt-tightening was a difficult and risky business.

Even though growth trends favored other regions of the country, average per capita income still was higher in most Great Lakes states than in the Southeast and Southwest in 1980. While some areas in the industrial Midwest had experienced serious economic difficulties, and while many neighborhoods had become miserable places to live, many people nonetheless had managed to make a lot of money. These people typically moved to the affluent suburbs. Chicago's suburbs, for example, in 1980 included three of the five richest congressional districts in the United States. The irony was that for those who were working, the average income in Michigan at least was among the highest in the nation.

Middle Atlantic States

(New York, Pennsylvania, District of Columbia, New Jersey, Delaware, Maryland, West Virginia)

In the early 1980s the economic concerns of the Middle Atlantic states were real, although sometimes overstated. In this region — New York, New Jersey, Pennsylvania, Maryland, Delaware, West Virginia and the District of Columbia — unemployment between the 1974-75 recession and 1980 had averaged about one percentage point above the national average. The Middle Atlantic had lost more manufacturing jobs than any other section of the country as of 1980.

In this region where heavy manufacturing — along with mining — had been dominant since the 19th century, the stagnation was all the more obvious. One problem, possibly the main one, was that many of the industrial facilities were old and could not function efficiently. Competitors using the latest equipment — whether they were in Germany, Japan or the South — had a built-in advantage.

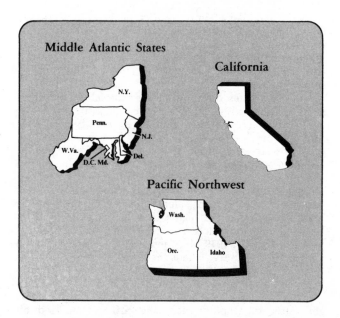

"The best way to appreciate this is to take an Amtrak ride through the once great workshop cities of Pennsylvania, New York, Ohio or Illinois," columnist Nicholas von Hoffman wrote in *The New York Review of Books* in 1980. "... [W]hen you see Reading, or Altoona, or Youngstown, or Schenectady you'll think you are touring a museum showing the Birth of the Industrial Revolution. These places look like the English Midlands and the factories are often as old." In western Pennsylvania are "sudsy, sooty montages of the Edwardian era, iron work barns where the old ways of forge and open hearth are passed down from father to son."

Instances of Success in City Revitalization. The overall picture, however, was not one of unrelieved gloom. New York City, for example, despite fiscal ills, remained the nation's banking, cultural and communications center. Tourism continued to boom, attracting more visitors (16.9 million) in 1982 than any other U.S. city, according to the city's Convention and Visitors Bureau. In 1981 personal income in New York state grew at a rate above the national average.

While the city's losses of corporation headquarters and manufacturing jobs were well documented, across the Hudson River in New Jersey, especially in semi-rural Morris County, new offices, hotels and convention facilities were springing up. Farther south, Atlantic City was in the midst of a mini-boom, brought on by legalized gambling. State officials were predicting multimillion-dollar annual tax receipts from casinos in Atlantic City, which had been economically depressed.

Despite the economic problems that New Jersey shared with most Northern states, its per capita personal income was one of the nation's highest and was the highest among the Middle Atlantic states in 1980. Only two of these states, Pennsylvania and West Virginia, were below the national average ($7,810) in 1978.

Pennsylvania, the nation's second most populous state for more than a century, in 1980 was fourth in per capita personal income, behind California, New York and Texas. But its two biggest cities, Philadelphia and Pittsburgh, both experienced some degree of revitalization in the late 1970s. Pittsburgh, the "Steel City," advertised itself as the

"City of Champions," in recognition of the national attention devoted to its professional baseball and football teams, the Pirates and the Steelers. They played in Three Rivers Stadium at the edge of Pittsburgh's gleaming downtown area, the site of one of the nation's most acclaimed urban renewal areas.

In many cities, downtown urban renewal did not bring new life. But Baltimore, like Pittsburgh, appeared to be one of the success stories. Baltimore's vitality was measured not only by the visual appeal of its new architecture and the restoration of old residential sections but also in reams of statistics on trade and commerce. In nearby Washington, D.C., where federal employment cushioned the shock of recession, a building and restoration boom was also under way. Personal annual income for residents of Washington, D.C., was higher than in any state in 1978. Delaware and Maryland both projected budget surpluses for fiscal 1983. In 1979 Maryland posted a surplus of $300 million. In Delaware, where there was no sales tax, the General Assembly enacted an income tax cut in 1979, only two years after overcoming a budget deficit.

West Virginia's economic future brightened considerably after the rapidly increasing cost of imported oil prompted greater reliance on coal — the state's primary natural resource. The U.S. Geological Survey estimated that at least 1.7 trillion tons of coal lay beneath American soil in 1980. A significant portion was in western Pennsylvania and West Virginia. Bituminous coal, the soft coal used in making steel and other industrial products, long was the economic cornerstone of the two areas. Northeastern Pennsylvania, moreover, was the site of large deposits of anthracite, the hard coal used for home heating.

But coal's heralded comeback had, as of 1980, been disappointing in the Eastern United States. There was fear in the industry that coal remained "the fuel of last resort" because of the soaring costs of mining and shipping it and abiding by anti-pollution rules in burning it. The future of coal was not in the East, analysts also said. According to the brokerage firm of Dean Witter Reynolds, the Eastern states would supply the nation's utilities with 50 percent of their coal in 1985, compared with 78 percent in 1975. The gap would be filled by coal mined, especially strip-mined, in the West where the coal-mining companies were owned primarily by the nation's large oil corporations.

Fiscal Ills of New York and Other Cities. Economic problems were not confined to private enterprise in the Middle Atlantic region. New York City repeatedly faced the specter of municipal bankruptcy in the 1970s. When the city was unable to borrow money to meet and pay debts in 1975, it was bailed out by loan guarantees from New York state and later from the federal government. Moreover, the city was forced to give much of its control over fiscal affairs to a state-created Municipal Assistance Corporation (MAC) as a condition for receiving aid from Albany and Washington.

New York's fiscal problems were not unique. Observers said symptoms of fiscal insolvency — increasing costs of social services, education and city salaries that were unmatched by revenues — were evident in a number of large cities in the nation, including Philadelphia and Washington. In 1980 the city government in the nation's capital faced a budget deficit estimated at some $172 million. In Philadelphia, the city's municipal and school system budgets were expected to run a deficit of $93 million by mid-1981.

Many of the older cities of the industrial North were suffering from wear and tear by the early 1980s. Buildings, streets, sewer and water lines typically were aged and overused. These cities also tended to be the ones that had been hurt most by the departure of the white middle class, leaving behind a lower tax base and a heavier welfare load.

Thus the financial resources to mend physical deterioration and care for the social ills had shrunk as the needs had increased. While there had been success stories here and there, most of the cities continued to be haunted by the same litany of problems they had faced for two decades or more: racial crime, declining revenues and municipal service.

The Pacific Northwest
(Washington, Oregon, Idaho)

There was a time not long ago when the Pacific Northwest might have qualified as one of the country's best-kept secrets. Life in this far corner of the United States was an unpublicized pleasure that residents jealously guarded and people elsewhere usually associated with endless rain. But as of the early 1980s the weather was one of the few things that remained the same. Change in the late 1970s came to the coastal states of Washington, Oregon and neighboring Idaho, and it was not entirely welcome.

Attracted by the Pacific Northwest's spreading reputation for "livability," outsiders migrated there in growing numbers in the late 1970s. The sharp influx of newcomers and the problems they inevitably brought with them left many natives wondering if the region's best qualities — the unspoiled beauty of its forests and shores, the peace and quiet of its urban areas — could survive its new popularity.

Fluctuating Job Market Destabilizes Economy. In Oregon, where the population rose by 18 percent during the 1960s and 21 percent from 1970 to 1979, coping with the strain of more people became a problem considered by many to be greater than economic concerns. Once considered one of the most liberal states in the nation — in 1971 it decriminalized marijuana and banned throw-away clear containers — Oregon in 1980 began moving gradually toward the right, as a post-Proposition 13 climate began to take hold there. In June 1978 California voters had approved Proposition 13, a ballot initiative that effectively cut the state's property tax revenues in half.

In Washington during the 1970s the main concern was jobs. The economy suffered a severe jolt in the early 1970s when the Boeing Co. began laying off aircraft workers. But the company by 1980 was back on its feet and Washingtonians were turning their attention to what some called "the hazards of good fortune" — finding work for new arrivals and supplying the state with enough energy to meet the demands of a growing population.

Washington also had problems coping with its rapidly increasing population. In a 1981 special session, the Washington Legislature cut spending by $284.6 million, raised sales taxes by 1 percent, and still had to borrow $400 million from New York banks to pay its bills.

Idaho, principally a rural state, escaped many of the woes that accompanied rapid growth. Its largest city, Boise, had tripled in size since 1960 but still had not reached the 100,000-mark by 1980. However, it was beginning to show signs of urbanization, brought on by "platoons of young executives, drawn from the Stanford and Harvard business schools by such corporations as Boise Cascade, Morrison-Knudsen and Hewlett-Packard," according to Wallace and Page Stegner in the April 1978 issue of *The Atlantic.*

Idahoans were troubled less by outside pressure than by internal differences. In a sense the state was split between the growing social and political influence of Mormons in the agricultural southeast, the home of Idaho's much-advertised potatoes, and the "live-and-let-live" outlook in the northern panhandle, where mining and lumbering were the economic mainstays and prostitution, although illegal, was openly tolerated in a number of towns. One indication of Idaho's conservative temper was passage of a Proposition 13-style tax cut in 1979. Unlike similar ballot measures elsewhere, no significant opposition existed in Idaho.

The problems faced by Washington, Oregon and Idaho differed only in degree. Each saw itself threatened by social change and resource shortages. And in each the 1980s were seen as a test, one that could determine whether the region would remain livable and whether it would have enough to live on.

One of the major barriers facing the Northwestern states during the early 1980s was the unprecedented financial disaster caused by an inadequately financed and poorly managed nuclear building program. The Washington Public Power System, responsible for building five huge nuclear plants, as of December 1982 had no money left to pay its creditors. Further construction of two of the plants, which were partially completed at that time, had been canceled. Eighty-eight utilities in three states still owed $7 billion in principal and interest on the defunct plants, even though they would never go into operation. The five unfinished nuclear power plants carried the greatest long-term, tax-exempt bond debt in American history.

Postwar Upsurge in Aircraft and Timber. The Northwestern economy was enhanced during World War II when the aircraft industry began to flourish in western Washington. Boeing, which produced bombers for the war effort, became a prime factor in the upsurge of Washington's economy during the 1950s and 1960s. But building airplanes proved to be anything but a steady business. Prior to 1970, Boeing employed as many as 101,000 people — nearly 8 percent of the state's work force. In 1970, however, its employment rolls dropped to 38,000. One year later, 55,000 people left the state to search for work elsewhere. As a result, the bottom fell out of the real estate markets in Everett, Tacoma and Seattle. Washington's economy took a nose dive.

New military and civilian contracts, including work on the cruise missile, brought Boeing's employment level back near the pre-1970 mark, and Washington's economy improved accordingly in the late 1970s.

Around the time Boeing began building World War II bombers, the Weyerhaeuser Co. started planting the first U.S. tree farm in Grays Harbor County, Wash. Like Boeing, Weyerhaeuser and other big timber companies — such as Boise Cascade, Georgia-Pacific, Crown-Zellerbach and St. Regis — flourished in the years after the war. The postwar demand for housing created a boom business. Timber prices shot up and the Northwest, where most of the nation's prime housing and construction wood grew, prospered.

As the lumber market expanded, Congress in 1960 enacted the Multiple Use-Sustained Yield Act, declaring that the national forests should be "utilized in the combination [of ways] that will best meet the needs of the American people." The industry in the Northwest benefited, but many environmentalists argued that the legislation was a blanket "license to log." The law, they argued, was too vague. For years, the Sierra Club and other environmental groups petitioned the federal government to tighten restrictions on the timber companies. In 1971 Congress responded by passing the National Forest Management Act. This measure directed the Forest Service to curb timber-cutting abuses on federally owned land. To make up for these curbs, however, companies stepped up harvesting by other methods.

Generally, the states had little to complain about since they received taxes and payments for timber cut on county, state and federal land. The Washington state public school system, for example, received more than $40 million by this means in 1978. But in 1980 the slump in the building and construction industry created the possibility of a serious recession. Oregon officials estimated that 7,000 of the state's 76,000 lumber industry jobs had vanished between November 1979 and June 1980. Authorities in Washington said the state had lost 7 percent of the 52,000 lumber and wood products jobs it had early in 1979.

It appeared likely that many jobs never would reappear. As more Northwestern forests were stripped by logging or declared off-limits by the government, lumber companies were moving their operations to the Southeastern states. Even Weyerhaeuser, the Northwest's biggest private landowner, with 2.8 million acres, had built up its timber holdings in the South to 3.1 million acres.

California

If California were an independent country, its gross national product — estimated at close to $300 billion in 1980 — would be greater than those of all nations save six — the United States, the Soviet Union, West Germany, Japan, France and China. Agriculturally, it would be among the leading nations; it already ranked first in the United States in 1980. California farm goods brought more than $12 billion into the state's economy in 1979. California in 1980 ranked behind Alaska and Texas as the third largest oil-producing state. Its 40,000 wells produced approximately 918,000 barrels of oil a day. According to John Naisbitt in *Megatrends,* capital investments in manufacturing in the state increased 110 percent from 1972 to 1977. In 1981 California created 212,000 new jobs, 27 percent of the U.S. total.

Is was difficult to characterize in a phrase a state with more than a thousand miles of coastline, a variety of landscapes and more than 22 million people. Nevertheless, it often was said that California was not just a state but a state of mind. For some, it represented the final embodiment of America's frontier spirit; for others, it was a version of El Dorado, a place to find fortunes or spend fortunes made elsewhere. California led the nation in fads, fashion and self-indulgence. New religions, new living arrangements, new forms of entertainment, new attitudes toward work, family and education, all were nurtured by California's tolerant social climate.

California's major physiographic regions were the narrow coastal area between the mountains and the sea; the Central Valley walled by the coastal ranges to the west and the Sierra Nevada Mountains to the east; the desert basins of the southern interior; and the rugged mountainous regions to the north. The Tehachapi Range — a short connecting link between the coastal ranges and the Sierra Nevada situated approximately 335 miles south of San Francisco and 115 miles north of Los Angeles — unofficially divided northern and southern California.

The contrasts between northern and southern California extended beyond geographic differences. The Gold Rush, so important to early California history, hardly touched the southern part of the state. It was not until the 1880s that the first significant migration to the southland occurred. As late as 1906, more than a third of the state's population lived within 75 miles of San Francisco. In 1980 more than 60 percent of California's residents lived in the southern third of the state. As the southern section's population grew, so did its political power. "It is becoming increasingly difficult for anyone outside Los Angeles to win a statewide race," California political analyst Ed Salzman wrote in 1979.

Southern California, the third of the state below the Tehachapi Range, had a character and a mood quite different from the northern two-thirds. "This is the California of petroleum, crazy religious cults, the citrus industry, towns based on rich *rentiers* like Santa Barbara and Pasadena, the movies, the weirdest architecture in the United States, refugees from Iowa, a steeply growing Negro population, and devotees of funny money," John Gunther wrote in *Inside U.S.A.* "It is, above all, the world where climate is worshipped as a god." Gunther made his observations in 1947, but, for the most part, they still held true in the 1980s.

The sprawling south, centered in the 6,600-square-mile Los Angeles Basin, was the economic center of the state. The tax revenues from its citizens and companies provided California with much of its income. The Los Angeles area ranked behind New York as the second-largest commercial center in the United States. Southern California's economy was diversified, but four areas dominated: the entertainment business, including films, television and recording studios; aerospace and defense industries; the oil industry, including both production and refining; real estate development and sales.

History of Film, Aerospace and Oil Industries. At first, Angelenos, as citizens of Los Angeles were called, showed a pronounced dislike for members of "the movie colony" — signs on apartment buildings often read "No Dogs or Actors Allowed." But by 1915 the residents had undergone a change of heart. People made a lot of money from the movies, and Hollywood and Los Angeles reaped the benefits. Real estate values soared as actors, producers and movie moguls built residential monuments to their success. Businesses grew up around the industry — fine restaurants, hotels and shops. And there was all that free publicity. Because its name was linked to the world's most publicized industry, Hollywood became one of the best-known cities in the world.

Despite the growing popularity of location shooting, southern California still retained much of the glitter — if not all the gold — of the movies. In 1980 almost 150 films a year were made in the Hollywood-Los Angeles area. Although 60 percent of the 20,000 members of the Screen Actors Guild were unemployed at any given time, the entertainment industry — films, television and records — brought in $13 billion in 1979.

Southern California's aerospace-defense industry dated from World War II, when massive government involvement in the aircraft industry brought thousands of workers and jobs to the southland. In 1980 the list of leading aerospace and defense industries headquartered in southern California included General Dynamics, Hughes Aircraft, Lockheed Missiles and Space Co., McDonnell Douglas and Rockwell International.

In 1892 Edward Doheny, a metals prospector, discovered oil in the form of tar inside the city limits of Los Angeles. Three years later, according to a contemporary account, oil wells in Los Angeles were "as thick as the holes in a pepper box." The new fuel was substituted for coal, and California suddenly found itself with an enviable supply of energy. In the 1920s huge deposits of oil were discovered in Huntington Beach, Long Beach and Whittier. Los Angeles became the oil capital of the world. The dollar value of oil produced in California in the 1920s exceeded the value of gold mined in the state.

One of the byproducts of the oil boom became more associated with southern California than did the huge deposits themselves. Gasoline, initially an unwanted byproduct of petroleum, was found to be the perfect fuel for the horseless carriage. As early as 1925, Los Angeles was heralded as the unabashed leader of the car culture, with one automobile for every three residents.

One outgrowth of Los Angeles' car mania was that it had one of the lowest population densities of any major American city. Scores of small towns developed because of the presence of highways, and access to the city led to the characterization of Los Angeles as "one hundred suburbs in search of a metropolis." In the early 1980s, with one of the best intra- and inter-city road systems in the country, the Los Angeles area remained built around the car. It was one of the few major cities in the world without an extensive mass transit system.

California's High-Tech Leads Nation. California benefited from a burgeoning high technology industry, centered around the Silicon Valley area just south of San Francisco. According to an article in the April 15, 1982, *Christian Science Monitor,* California had posted the largest job growth in the nation during the 1970s — 15.4 percent. The number of jobs in high-technology industries in California grew by 71.6 percent, from 261,000 to 448,900.

"High-tech jobs will account for nearly 50 percent of the growth in basic industry jobs in the 1980s. Computer services is projected to have the highest rate of growth among individual high-technology industries. Jobs will nearly triple to 128,300 in 1990 from 43,300 in 1980," wrote Stephen Levy, senior economist at the Center for Continuing Study of the California Economy in a 1982 report entitled "The California Economy: 1970-1990."

California's electronics industry, however, was in an ambivalent state, mainly due to increasing competition from Japan. In 1983 California was the acknowledged center of the development of low-capacity computer chips, but the higher capacity market — considered to be the more progressive edge of the technology — had been lost to the Japanese who claimed 70 percent of the market. Motorola

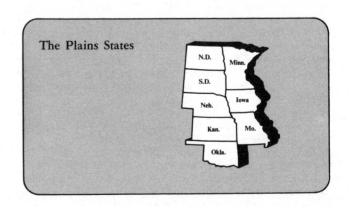

The Plains States

(in Arizona) and Texas Instruments (in Texas) accounted for the remaining 30 percent.

The Plains States

(North Dakota, South Dakota, Nebraska, Kansas, Oklahoma, Minnesota, Iowa, Missouri)

Although the Plains states lay in America's "Farm Belt," most of the people who lived in this region were not engaged in agriculture by the early 1980s. Mines and factories accounted for much of the employment. In petroleum production, Oklahoma ranked fifth and Kansas eighth among the 50 states in 1980. A large part of the country's known uranium deposits was in South Dakota, much of it on lands claimed by Indians, and huge lignite coal deposits in North Dakota provided a center for synfuels production. Numerous corporations — Minnesota Mining and Manufacturing ("3M"), Honeywell, and Control Data in Minnesota; Maytag and Winnebago in Iowa; General Dynamics, McDonnell Douglas, Emerson Electric, and Chromalloy American in Missouri; and Boeing, Cessna and Beech aircraft in Kansas — were engaged in activities that had little or nothing to do with farming. Only Michigan manufactured more automobiles than Missouri.

St. Louis, historically a gateway city to the Western plains, in the early 1980s suffered many of the same problems that afflicted most large cities: suburban migration, shrinking tax revenues, a stagnant inner-city economy, and — most recently — loss of automobile industry jobs. From 1970 to 1977, the inner-city population dropped nearly 17 percent, and St. Louis in 1980 had the highest murder rate of any major city in the United States — more than double New York's.

Wichita, Kan., on the other hand, resembled a Southwestern boom town. It was the nation's leading producer of small aircraft in 1980; Boeing, Beech and Cessna aircraft companies all had installations there. According to a journalist who visited the city in 1980, the aircraft manufacturers "can't begin to fill the positions they have available."

For every St. Louis or Wichita, however, there were five or 10 medium-sized cities, prosperous but unspectacular, that functioned as banking, insurance, food processing and farm machinery centers for the surrounding agricultural communities. Companies such as John Deere had manufacturing plants and retail outlets throughout the region. And in the larger cities as well, big industries depended heavily on the agrarian hinterland.

In 1980 Kansas City, its downtown rejuvenated by the Hallmark Center and convention site, presented to the world a more cosmopolitan air than in past years when its vast (and now vanished) stockyards filled the nostrils. But agriculture still accounted for much of the city's prosperity. It ranked first in farm equipment and frozen food distribution, and second in grain elevator capacity and wheat flour production in 1980. In Minneapolis, General Mills and Pillsbury vied for leadership in commercial bakery products.

Agribusiness With Wheat, Corn and Hogs. The economy of the Plains states continued to depend heavily on agriculture in the early 1980s, and the monetary value of farm products failed to represent their importance to the country and indeed the world. These states accounted for nearly one-half of America's corn and wheat production, and about one-third of the soybean production in 1980. The United States, in turn, provided about three-quarters of the world's corn exports, nearly half of the wheat exports, and almost nine-tenths of the soybean exports. Kansas and Nebraska, the country's leading wheat states, produced about one-quarter of the total U.S. crop. Iowa and neighboring Illinois harvested roughly two-thirds of the country's corn and one-third of its soybeans. Corn-fattened hogs were another staple of the economy; the two states raised more than a third of the nation's hogs in a typical year.

Midwestern farms, although shrinking in number, had climbed steadily in size throughout the 1970s. As farm operations became larger, costlier, more complex and in some ways riskier, the successful farmer had to be a person of many talents — the master of diverse manual skills, knowledgeable in agricultural science and economics, and an accountant to boot. Many families hedged their bets with "marginal farming," the standard term for an arrangement in which one or more members of the family work at paying jobs away from the farm.

As farming came to resemble other business operations, standard forms of business ownership became prevalent. Many farms were organized as partnerships, and a partnership was sometimes a steppingstone toward a corporate structure. The Census Bureau found in its 1974 survey of agriculture that the "1,421 farm partnerships which planned to incorporate had average sales of $172,347, or more than two times the average sales of all partnerships reporting...." Incorporation often led in turn to a takeover by an absentee agribusiness company; in many cases the original farm family stayed on the property to act as employee-overseer for the company.

Closely related to anxiety about the familiy farm was concern about loss of crop land to urban and industrial development, foreign purchases of U.S. farm land and the agribusiness shipping scandals that afflicted the Mississippi River transportation system in the late 1970s.

Pushing Land's Productivity to Its Limits. One important concern in 1980 was the falling level of water in the Ogallala Formation, a vast underground reserve that stretches from South Dakota to Texas. Farmers in the western parts of Kansas and Nebraska, southwestern South Dakota and the Oklahoma Panhandle, along with the Texas Panhandle, depended heavily on this geologic formation for water. It was brought to the surface by heavy pumps fueled with natural gas. With water supplies dropping and natural gas prices rising, more and more farmers were shutting off their wells and putting fields back into dryland cultivation.

Like water, the number of plant varieties also was decreasing, and this too worried some environmentalists. Farmers naturally concentrated production in the crop varieties that gave the highest yields, but if a blight were to hit, uniform varieties might mean uniform disaster. With the country and much of the world dependent on Midwestern agriculture, a crop failure would be disastrous indeed. ∎